The Entertaining Survival Guide

THE
ENTERTAINING
SURVIVAL
GUIDE

A Handbook for the Hesitant Host

LORA BRODY

William Morrow and Company, Inc. / New York

Mangospacho, page 212, reprinted with permission from *Miami Spice*
by Steven Raichlen.
EEK AND MEEK cartoon, page xii, reprinted with permission.
Copyright © 1985 by Howie Schneider.

It is the policy of William Morrow and Company, Inc., and its im-
prints and affiliates, recognizing the importance of preserving what
has been written, to print the books we publish on acid-free paper,
and we exert our best efforts to that end.

Library of Congress Cataloging-in-Publication Data

Brody, Lora, 1945–
    The entertaining survival guide : a handbook for hesitant hosts
/ Lora Brody.
        p.   cm.
    Includes bibliographical references and index.
    ISBN 0-688-12295-7
    1. Entertaining.   I. Title.
TX731.B75   1994
642'.4—dc20   94-7761
                                                               CIP

Printed in the United States of America

First Edition

1 2 3 4 5 6 7 8 9 10

BOOK DESIGN BY RICHARD ORIOLO

To my *beloved New Orleans Family*—

Ella, Dottie, Dick, Ralph, Susan, Cindy, Eddie, Lally, Ti, Dickie,
Jamie, Emeril, Chuck, Gigi, Claire, Derby, and Gerard.
A Sazerac, a bowl of gumbo, a scoop of bread pudding soufflé,
and y'all—

That's
entertainment!

Chafing dishes brimming with gratitude and champagne flutes overflowing with love to Harriet Bell, Susan Ginsburg, Bill Johnson-Gonzalez, Kathy Antrim, Skip Dye, Wendy Maidman, Richard Oriolo, P. J. Hamel, and Lynne Bail.

And a very special thank-you to Mary Goodbody, who was a bright light at the end of a dark tunnel.

Contents

CHAPTER SIX

Suggested Menus

131

CHAPTER SEVEN

Recipes

183

Index

395

The Entertaining Survival Guide

The Premise
and the Promise

If the Joneses have invited you over so many times that it's getting
downright embarrassing to Rollerblade past their house but you are
not quite sure how to keep up with them in the social arena, then this
book is for you. If you have more than a few untested kitchen skills
but have a hankering to gather some folks around the table for good
food and good conversation, then you have come to the right place. If
you just got your own apartment and long to show it off by giving a
party but haven't a clue where to begin, you are in good hands. With
this book, you can relax—help is on the way. I promise to show you
how to entertain guests and survive so that when the last one leaves,
you will happily realize that you actually had a good time at your own
party. Or was that a great time?

When I was growing up, a warm welcome, a clean house, an ironed tablecloth, and plenty of food were symbols of hospitality. I still believe this is true—and relying on this premise, I entertain frequently and happily. Remember, when you decide to throw a party, there's no reason to dazzle your friends with your (perhaps nonexistent) culinary genius. Plain, good food does just fine. Don't worry that the ingredients in the salad are not trendy or that you have neglected to pour the perfect wine with every course. If you serve well-cooked, tasty food and provide a warm, pleasant atmosphere, I guarantee the party will be a success. The trick is to get past the performance anxiety and feel confident as a host.

And that's easier than you may think because I am with you every step of the way. I promise to give you ideas for choosing a menu; to explain how to issue invitations by phone or mail; to provide shopping lists so you don't run out of cocktail napkins just as Great-aunt Sophie reaches for the Swedish meatballs; and to show you how to do a quick cleanup around the house (I even point out places you missed!). Perhaps best of all, I give you foolproof recipes that will wow your guests without requiring that you first enroll in the Cordon Bleu. And there's more: I teach you how to set the table, how to clear the table, when to serve cocktails, and when and how to hire a caterer. I explain how to cope with unexpected guests and very young children, as well as with mundane catastrophies such as spilled wine or broken dessert plates. Most important, I explain how to make people feel at home in your home. And please, don't hesitate to invite me over to dinner. I'm looking forward to it.

The Rules of Entertaining

I will expound upon, elaborate on, and otherwise elucidate the following twenty-two "rules" for entertaining, but to begin, I will list them to give you an idea of the wealth of information to come. When you need a refresher course, run your eyes down this list—you'll feel better.

1. This is not rocket science. You're just making dinner.
2. Plan ahead.
3. Work ahead.

4. Make notes and refer to them (you have my permission to write in the margins of this book! Unless you got it from the library or borrowed it, of course).
5. Always shop with a list.
6. Write your menu and time line down and tape it on the refrigerator door.
7. Always prepare more than you think you will need.
8. Don't try out a new menu without making the difficult dishes at least once beforehand.
9. Don't serve weird stuff.
10. Don't comment on the eating habits of your guests: "Why haven't you finished? Don't you like it?"
11. Carry a timer in your pocket or on a string around your neck to remind you when you need to stir the soup, check the cake, or turn the chicken in the marinade (put the timer away when your guests arrive).
12. Don't apologize if something doesn't work out exactly as you wanted it to—pretend it's just the way you planned.
13. Remember, mix and match is in (but don't go overboard).
14. Always taste before adding salt, and always add the salt last.
15. Don't do the dishes until the company has left.
16. Don't serve the same ingredient in more than one course.
17. Don't make foods that are all the same color and texture.
18. Keep the music low enough to hear conversation, and the lights bright enough to see what you're eating.
19. Graciousness, good manners, and a sense of humor will help you through any crisis.
20. Even take-out food looks great in a nice serving dish.
21. Remember that someday this will get easier.
22. Have fun!

Entertaining 101: The Overview

Entertaining is the act of showing someone a good time through goodwill, good manners, good planning, and more often than not, good food. The key is to make this activity seem natural and to have as good a time as your guests have. The first step, whether you're a novice or a more seasoned host, is to read this book. In these pages you will find practical tips and time-tested advice. Although some of the advice may seem elementary it is meant to reassure the confident as much as to soothe the nervous. After years of party giving, raising three sons, and professionally, being part of the "food world," I have conquered all fear, put out numerous fires, and learned that the best way to entertain successfully is to *want* to please your guests. And, hey! I like to have a good time.

How to Use This Book

The book is divided into seven parts, and the last two are menus and recipes. The first four parts are chock-full of the sort of advice your mother would have given you if your mother were a combination of Emily Post and Dear Abby. In other words, etiquette is important (manners, a well-set table, polite conversation, etc.), but so is a sense of humor and a distinctly practical approach to party giving. Inviting friends, family, or colleagues to your house, to a picnic, to a sporting event, or to a restaurant is supposed to be fun, and if something goes wrong . . . well, fix it! But don't panic. I will show you how to remain calm despite a fallen cake or still-frozen-in-the-center chicken.

The best way to use this book is to sit down and read the first five chapters straight through. They are organized sequentially as you might plan a party, beginning with stocking your house with the china, cutlery, pots, pans, and staples you need for entertaining. I continue with deciding on the type of party and number of guests, preparing for the party, and finally seeing that everything comes together during the party. In Chapters 4 and 5, I deal with general miscellaneous advice about subjects as diverse as kitchen disasters, hiring caterers, and dealing with overnight guests.

The last two sections of the book—the menus and the recipes—are self-explanatory, but ultimately necessary. I cannot emphasize enough how important it is to plan the menu well in advance, whether you are giving a dinner party, a cocktail party, a backyard barbecue, or a picnic at the beach or ballpark.

The Kinds of Entertaining

I see entertaining as falling into two categories: social and business. The lines blur with random regularity, but they are definitive enough to have clear distinctions between the two. While all entertaining involves being social and has the same standards of appropriately hospitable behavior, always keep clearly in mind why you have planned a certain event. Don't invite your lawyer to an intimate gathering of friends with the idea that she will help you write your will after dessert and coffee. Conversely, don't take your supervisor to lunch and regale her with stories of your toddlers's toilet training before turning the conversation to your much-deserved promotion.

I guess you have figured out by now that advance planning is all-important, but there is more to planning than writing a shopping list and figuring when to put the roast in the oven. Because the first rule of entertaining is to make your guests feel welcome, it's imperative to let them know, implicitly, that you have their best interests at heart. Therefore, consider your budget, space, energy level, and available time and then make realistic choices. A cocktail party for fifty may seem like a terrific idea, but not in your studio apartment. Aunt Mabel may be thrilled to be invited to dinner, but given her recent skiing mishap, can she make it up to your fifth-floor walk-up? Cousin Barry is allergic to dogs, so be sure to send Rover to the kennel before Barry arrives for brunch. This kind of consideration is demanded whether you are planning a social or business party.

⤸ **SOCIAL ENTERTAINING:** Social entertaining is when you create an occasion to show your friends a good time and is the sort of entertaining we are most likely to be involved in. It is meant to be a relief from the world of business and the day-to-day cares and responsibilities that go along with the workplace. It can be as informal as inviting a neighbor over for a cup of coffee, as spontaneous as a last-minute picnic of leftovers, or as involved as a wedding reception. It can be casual, informal, or formal.

Casual is the most relaxed form of entertaining. A picnic, potluck supper, backyard cookout, or Super Bowl, pool, or post-marathon party are all examples of casual entertaining. Casual usually means the invitation is given by telephone and can be delivered as close to the event as a day or two before. Specify the kind of party and be sure to say whether children are invited. Casual means people can come in jeans and sneakers (unless you tell them not to), and the atmosphere is definitely relaxed.

Informal events include birthday parties, family holiday dinners, brunches, theme parties, and open houses. Informal can mean either a written or telephoned invitation, but one given with plenty of notice—I suggest no less than two weeks and if your guests lead busy lives, give them three weeks' notice. Children are included only if specified, although most of us would not dream of excluding children from holiday, birthday, and anniversary celebrations. Informal means that no one wears running shoes. Men wear nice sweaters or sports jackets, but leave the ties at home. Women are dressed equally nicely but teetering high heels are not expected. The table or buffet is set with real dishes and cutlery or the very best quality paper goods. Unlike casual, the "informal" label does not mean the host or hostess can wait until that morning to start planning.

Formal, to me, does not mean a black-tie affair (although it might). It means dinner parties with several courses, where guests arrive dressed in nice clothes and leave the kids at home with a sitter. It may also be a wedding reception in your backyard or living room (yes! you can do this), or a dessert and champagne party on New Year's Eve. Or it may be you and your lover sharing a candlelight dinner with the phone turned off. Get the picture? Formal entertaining may sometimes mean hiring help to cook and serve, or it may mean cooking ahead and freezing months before the event. It means learning to tackle a serious undertaking with a sense of humor, firm planning, and a long list.

↪ BUSINESS ENTERTAINING: This is a situation in which people get together in a pleasant and more relaxed manner than the office affords, with the goal of getting work done or getting to know co-workers better. The work can be as serious as plotting a corporate takeover, as light-hearted as planning the office Christmas party (more entertaining!), or as simple as having lunch with a new assistant to summarize your overall expectations. Business entertaining can also be more social, such as a party to bid a colleague farewell or to celebrate someone's promotion.

While in-office functions are rarely as social as those that take place outside the office, if you are in charge, pay attention to the niceties that make things a little more pleasant. For example, make sure you serve real, not instant, coffee. Wash both the coffee carafe and filter basket with hot water and detergent to remove buildup that makes for bitter coffee. See if you can get an electric kettle for tea water, or at least bring in a thermos of boiling hot water and a good selection of tea bags. Make sure there are clean and ample cups or mugs, or have high-quality, heat-resistant paper cups on hand. Offer real milk or half-and-half instead of the powdered substitute and real sugar as well as sugar substitute. If you are serving muffins or pastries, arrange them on a ceramic plate or in a basket and be sure there are enough napkins. Position a wastebasket nearby for used napkins and cups if they're paper.

In her book *Emily Post's Etiquette* (HarperCollins, 15th ed., 1992), Elizabeth Post lists the following occasions when people can do business in a more relaxed manner: to thank someone for a service rendered, to celebrate a newly closed deal, to woo a prospective client, to hash out common problems in a neutral place, to get to know someone better, to ask a favor, to propose or discuss ideas, to introduce people. I'd like to add the following: to offer advice (career or personal) in a private setting, to review performance, to celebrate a promotion or retirement. If you plan to do a lot of business entertaining I suggest you invest in a copy of *Emily Post's Etiquette*. There is an exhaustive chapter on this very subject. I will deal here with the basic logistics.

Most often daytime business entertaining is done over lunch (although sometimes breakfast as well) in a restaurant, club, function room (in a hotel, for instance), or in a corporate dining room. If you are the one issuing the invitation(s) or organizing the luncheon, it is up to you to choose an appropriate setting. A bustling restaurant where people go to "see and be seen" is probably not the best atmosphere to stage a delicate negotiation, while on the other hand I wouldn't take a client with a hearty laugh and booming voice who tends to "drink his lunch" to an uptight conservative dining room. It's up to you, as host, to make (and confirm) the reservation. The last thing you want is to have to hang around in a crowded restaurant bar waiting for a table.

Punctuality is important, especially if you have a large party. Show the restaurant the courtesy of appearing on time. If you don't want to be distracted with a lot of hustle and bustle, ask for a quiet table when you make the reservation. Some restaurants and many hotels have private dining rooms where you can hold luncheon or dinner meetings.

If you invite a guest or guests to a business lunch it is understood that you will pick up the check. When several people or a crowd go out together, how the check will be handled should be agreed upon beforehand. *It's not done to ask a restaurant for separate checks.* If one person can quickly and quietly divide the total by the number of people, then he or she should do so, letting everyone know how much he or she owes, including the tip. If not, one person should pay the check and collect from the others later. Try at all costs to avoid the pitiful scene of asking, "Whoever had the pasta primavera and the glass of Chablis, please raise your hand . . ." etc.

Business dinners outside the home (in clubs, restaurants, function rooms) tend to be somewhat more social than business luncheons. The pace of dinners is usually more leisurely since people are not under pressure to rush back to the office. At dinner people are more likely to consume alcohol, which gives a more relaxed air to the meal, and sometimes spouses are included, which makes for conversations that are not always centered on the office.

The same care should be taken in restaurant selection and reservations. If you have organized a dinner at which people do not know each other, it is important for you, as host or hostess, to arrive first and to introduce everyone. If you know that certain people have the wish to "do business" during dinner, you should arrange a seating plan beforehand. It might make sense, if you are having the dinner in a private room, to have place cards. See Entertaining in Restaurants, page 39, for additional information.

If you are called upon to organize a large catered function for your firm, a Christmas party, or a summer outing, for example, read the section about hiring a caterer (page 96). Before you accept this job, understand that it's a big one that will take a lot of time, energy, patience, diplomacy, and planning. It is a major responsibility. Talk to the person who did the job before you to get as much information as you can—what worked, what didn't. If the firm has done this kind of thing before and had good results from the caterer, hotel, or function facility, get the name and contact them. They will welcome the repeat business and will be able to use their previous experience to make your event successful.

Get a clear description of your firm's budget and your superiors' and/or co-workers' expectations of the event in writing. Your idea of a swell Christmas party may be a few cookies and a glass of eggnog, while they may be thinking a hot buffet and full bar. It's far easier to meet concrete goals than amorphous ideas. Sit down periodically with the other people in your office to give them updates ("Here's a tape of a band that I thought would be great for the dinner dance, what do you think?"). Don't worry about getting raves from 100 percent of the staff; be happy with a consensus. To avoid misunderstandings later, get your superior's approval for the budget, the place, the menu, the music, and the flowers. Keep careful, well-organized notes of your conversations and negotiations with caterers, musicians, florists, etc. Ask for contracts from the providers spelling out their services (menus included) and costs. Go over the contracts very carefully and ask questions. Find out about gratuities and deposits. If your responsibility includes a seating plan, make sure that you have people respond to the invitation in plenty of time for you to organize the seating—you cannot knock it off an hour ahead of time. This job is probably best done with a committee, for the more input the better. Finally, keep careful notes for the next time you are asked to perform this job. Or, if once is enough, they will be a big help for your successor.

Business entertaining can spill into social entertaining when you invite colleagues into your home simply to socialize. Try to be clear in your mind what your goals are when you plan this sort of entertaining. Do you want to get to know these people better to improve working relations, or do you want to build friendships? Think of the significant others in these situations (most likely they will be included in the party). They share no common ground with anyone except that they are attached to someone who works with you. Several hours of office gossip, even accompanied by good food, probably is not their idea of a great evening. Instead, it might be a better idea to pick one or two people from the office and invite them with their mates or dates along with one or two couples who you know from someplace else. This mix will keep the conversation more general and the evening more social than business-oriented.

If you invite your boss home for dinner, make sure you are the model of efficiency. No matter how well you two get on in the office, this is a stressful situation. Superefficiency is even more important if you have to entertain *and* cook the meal. The key to success is planning. Try to remember that "nothing exceeds like excess"— so keep it simple. If you go overboard into areas where you don't feel comfortable (very formal entertaining, for example), you will only end up looking silly, and, boy, will your face be red come Monday morning! The best bet is a small dinner party for three or four couples with simple yet elegant food served with care and attention to detail. It's especially important to choose a reasonable menu, such as the ones on pages 142 to 145, where most courses can be completed well ahead of time and all last-minute things are extremely straightforward.

It will ease the stress to invite one or two people, perhaps from work but not necessarily, who are good at making lively conversation. If you are determined to make something you know your boss loves (such as cheesecake or a fanciful chocolate dessert), practice the recipe ahead of time so that you don't hold your breath as she takes her first bite. If your superior is a wine lover, visit a reputable wine store, menu in hand, and consult with a knowledgeable salesperson about the selection. If your boss compliments you on the wine, admit you had help—otherwise you might find yourself engaged in "winespeak" with an expert, and you will be in yet another position for looking silly.

Both social and business entertaining can take forms other than traditional parties and dinners, but because most occasions require the traditional, I have concentrated on that. In Chapter Four, I address "other" types of entertaining, such as overnight guests, visits to sick friends, and condolence calls.

Props
and
Equipment

Before you dash to the mall to buy a full set of plates and a giant-sized serving platter, assess how your entertaining will fit into your lifestyle. Are you happy with casual get-togethers or do you aspire to more formal dinner parties? Do you have the time and inclination to wash delicate wineglasses and fragile china and polish silver, or do you like the idea of stacking everything in the dishwasher? Is it important that everything be coordinated, or are you into "mix and match"? Does the idea of renting or borrowing china and glassware when you entertain more than eight people appeal to you or leave you feeling overwhelmed?

Obviously, you won't be able to answer every one of these questions now, and as you grow more proficient at the entertaining game, your style and aspirations may change and you may decide to acquire more equipment. Because of this, it's a good idea not only to decide if you have enough dishes, flatware, glassware, and serving pieces for the kind of entertaining you want to do now, but when shopping for these essentials, to think about the kind of entertaining you plan to do in the future.

Dishes

You don't have to own twelve place settings of fine china and monogrammed sterling flatware to be a successful party giver. You don't even need to own one place setting. You do, however, need some plates so that your guests can eat, and unless you are having a picnic, barbecue, or very informal get-together, paper and plastic will not do.

While mix and match is acceptable, my preference is for matching dishes, which means color and shape. For example, if you are having ten people for dinner but have only six white dinner plates, borrow four white plates from a friend. It doesn't matter if they are not identical. You can pull the whole thing together with napkins. But if you have three yellow dinner plates left over from Mom and one red plate from the garage sale that sort of goes with the green Christmas plate from your secretary, then you need to give some serious thought to outfitting yourself with dishes to use for entertaining. If you're the creative type, you can put together a stunning table with mismatched plates and colorful napkins, but be sure there is a method to your madness. It does not always work.

I recommend buying service for eight. When you do this, visit a restaurant supply store or keep your eyes open for sales. When you shop, don't buy wafer-thin plates: The edges chip easily in the dishwasher. Make sure the store has lots of the dishes you like in stock. Avoid buying a discontinued pattern—you will be out of luck when you want to buy more. If you discover that the china you bought last year is discontinued this year, try matching it with solid-colored plates of approximately the same shape and size.

You might be really lucky and hit a major sale where acceptable plates cost only one or two dollars. In this case, stock up with as many as you can lug home. Years ago, I bought twenty-four thick, white, rustic dinner and salad plates at a restaurant supply store and still use them for everything but the most formal dinners—I save my wedding china for those. I'm hard on my dishes (which is why I have used the wedding china only a dozen times in twenty-five years), yet I have never managed to break one of these heavy-duty dishes. When I want to dress up the table, I use linen napkins and a pretty tablecloth or place mats to offset the white dishes.

If you can't live without patterned or colored china, make doubly sure the store where you bought them has stock. Decide whether the color you choose cohabits peacefully with your other color schemes—especially with any existing linens you might own.

The standard size for a dinner plate is ten inches. I suggest you buy plates that are this size. While oversized plates and bowls are fine for restaurants, chances are they will be too big for your dishwasher. Do not buy dishes that won't go in the dishwasher or microwave (those with gold or silver rims, for instance). You may not own either appliance right now, but you most likely will someday, and probably long before all the dishes break. Both over- and undersized plates present problems when it comes to serving food. You are either tempted to serve too much or, on the other hand, cannot fit reasonable portions on the plate without having the food fall off the edges.

The standard size for salad and dessert plates is eight inches. If you buy eight-piece sets of ten-inch and eight-inch plates, you will not need any others—although you may have to wash the salad plates between courses so you can use them as dessert plates. However, if you just can't live without bread and butter plates, these should be six inches across. Remember that you can always rent or borrow china for those times you invite more than eight people for a meal.

Soup bowls are ideal for salad, soup, stew, and any dessert that requires a spoon. If you really want to be fancy, set the salad plate under the bowl. While soup bowls do not have to match the plates, it does make sense to buy bowls that complement the dishes and that hold at least two cups of liquid so that they can serve many purposes. Soup bowls have an actual bowl, while soup plates are very shallow and are, quite frankly, pretty useless.

Even if you have only one dented saucepan and two chipped dinner plates in your cupboard, chances are you have half a dozen ceramic coffee mugs, most with silly slogans or cartoon characters on them. These are great for the morning brew, but when you serve coffee and tea at a party, matching cups and saucers or small, tasteful mugs are in order. Leave the breakfast mugs in the cupboard.

High-quality, sturdy paper plates have their place. They're fine for children's birthday parties, cookouts, picnics, and the like. They are also acceptable for informal occasions when the food is neither drippy nor needs vigorous cutting with a knife. Sandwiches fall into this tidy-to-serve category. My general feeling is that as long as you are a grown-up doing grown-up entertaining, save the paper plates for the Super Bowl party or for when the electricity goes out. The environment will thank you and so will your guests.

Serving Dishes

Unless you are dishing out the food in the kitchen from the cooking pot, you will need bowls, platters, and casserole-type dishes for serving. The exception to this rule is an attractive oven-to-table casserole dish. While it is safe to buy white serving dishes that go with your china, it is not necessary. Here is where a little whimsy comes into play. Buy serving dishes with pretty patterns and bright colors, or scour antique shops and tag sales for useful sizes and interesting designs. Check them for chips and cracks and never pay a king's ransom. If a serving platter or bowl breaks and you don't have to match it with a set, you can buy a replacement in a completely different pattern or color.

There is a fine line between dishes that are large enough to hold food for everyone at the table yet light enough to be passed from guest to guest. I have a set of enamel-covered cast-iron casseroles that are very handsome and keep food warm (another important consideration), however, a guest would have to have arms like Arnold Schwarzenegger to pass them. When I use one of these for serving a stew or similar dish, I stack the plates next to my place or ask guests to pass their dishes to me. The casserole is placed on a trivet or hot pad near me.

Don't use heirlooms or fragile dishes for serving. If they get chipped or broken while being passed not only will your guests be embarrassed, but you may find yourself delaying dinner while you search for the missing pieces of china buried in the spinach soufflé.

When choosing a large platter for passing, buy one with raised edges or a rim so the roast potatoes won't slide onto Mary Jane's lap as she spears a slice of roast beef. When you're serving a large amount of food—a holiday turkey, for instance—it's fine to slice the meat onto two smaller serving dishes: white meat on one, dark meat on the other. This way, guests will not have to flip through to find their favorite parts and you can pass the dishes in two different directions to serve everyone more expeditiously. Use a bowl to serve sauce or gravy. It does not have to be a regulation gravy boat but should be sitting on a saucer to catch drips and hold the ladle at rest. Bowls for vegetables, rice, and dishes such as pasta and grain salads do not need to be gigantic but should be large enough to hold at least one serving for everyone. If you don't care about colors, I recommend sturdy, white, one-and-a-half- to two-quart-capacity soufflé dishes for all-purpose serving bowls; they handily go from oven to freezer. Salad bowls can be wood or ceramic. If you do use a wooden salad bowl, wipe it with a damp paper towel. Don't use soap.

Other items you need are a pretty sugar bowl with a one-and-a-half- to two-cup capacity and an accompanying spoon. This can be the sugar spoon that comes with your flatware (not all services include one) or a regular teaspoon. You will also need a pitcher for serving cream or milk. I despise those miniature pitchers that hold barely enough milk for two or three people. Try to find one that holds at least two cups. You don't have to fill it to the brim, just enough so that there is at least two to three tablespoons for everyone who would like some (for eight people, that comes to a cup or cup and a half). Here's a good trick: If you find the milk does not pour out evenly or drips as it pours, smear a little butter under the pitcher's spout.

You will need salt and pepper shakers that look attractive sitting on the table. If you live in a humid area, put a teaspoon of rice in the salt shaker to keep the salt from clumping and your guests from thumping. A pepper grinder is a nice (and fairly inexpensive) addition to the table and once you taste freshly ground pepper, you'll never buy the nasty, stale kind in the metal tin again.

Unless you are having Chinese takeout during a snowstorm or hosting an outdoor barbecue, milk cartons, soda cans, cereal boxes, and pickle jars do not belong on the table when you are entertaining guests. Take a few extra minutes to pour the maple syrup into a pitcher instead of putting the container on the table (I don't care if it is shaped like a log cabin!), spoon the mustard into a small bowl and add a teaspoon for serving, and take the butter out of the wrapper and off the refrigerator storage tray and set it on a saucer-size plate. Small efforts make big differences.

Flatware

This used to be called silverware before the Hunt brothers manipulated the market and the price of silver went through the roof. Now most people use stainless steel, but if you have silver or silver plate (a thin coating of silver on steel), it will need to be polished before you use it. Using tarnished silver is akin to serving water or wine in glasses covered with spots and smudges.

The usual players in the flatware game are dinner and salad forks, teaspoons and soup spoons, and dinner and butter knives. Dinner forks are the big ones used for the main part of the meal. Slightly smaller forks, sometimes with fewer tines (prongs) and often shaped slightly differently, are used for appetizers and salad (if these are served as separate courses) and dessert.

Teaspoons are used when coffee and tea are served and for eating desserts that require a spoon, such as ice cream and pudding. Soup spoons are used for soup but should also be offered when you are serving pasta or stews such as chili.

Most knives that come with standard place settings are sharp enough to cut fish and chicken but not beef, lamb, or pork. It is pretty frustrating for a guest to saw away at his dinner while the host watches, worrying that the meat is too tough. Only the very most expensive cuts of meat can be cut with a dull knife, so if meat appears frequently on your menus, invest in a set of steak knives with sharp or serrated edges. If you use bread and butter plates, you will want small butter knives, although neither these nor utensils such as pickle forks are vital for entertaining.

Serving Utensils

You will need large spoons, forks, ladles, and tongs (grabbers) so that you can transfer food to plates either at the table or in the kitchen, or so that guests can help themselves from platters and bowls. Make sure the utensils are long enough so that they won't get lost in the food, and large enough to hold a decent serving. I suggest sticking to stainless steel or another metal for utensils. Wood eventually splinters and picks up odors that you may not want imparted to the food (garlic and lemon mousse are not a great mix), and plastic, except for some Lucite items and unless you are serving potato salad on the deck, is really pretty tacky. At all costs, avoid china and glass serving tools. They may look pretty but one wrong move and you will be fishing glass chips from the soup—and your guests will be rightfully wary of eating it.

Carving knives—and other sharp kitchen knives—are personal objects. I keep mine very sharp and am very particular about who can use them. You may have a carving set (a common and welcome wedding gift) that includes a sharp-pronged fork as well as a knife. The knife, if it's a good one, will hold its edge as well as any knife, but because some are not as well honed as those knives relegated to the kitchen, it's perfectly acceptable to bring the kitchen blade to the table to carve the roast.

A good set of kitchen knives is a valuable investment. Take good care of them. This means storing them in a knife rack away from other cutlery so that they don't jostle against it and lose their edges. For this same reason it's advisable to wash your knives by hand rather than in the dishwasher. Sharpen them regularly with a good manual or electric knife sharpener.

Glasses

If you plan to entertain more than once or twice a year and want to feed more than four people at a time, call the nearest restaurant supply store (look in the yellow pages) and tell the salesperson you want sturdy, all-purpose wineglasses that can go in the dishwasher. Mention your price range and then plan to buy two dozen. If you pick a glass that is reasonably priced and sturdy enough, you won't have to worry about buying another wineglass for many years. Keep six or eight glasses on a shelf and store the rest in the box in a safe, out-of-the-way place. I would suggest doing the same with water glasses, and if you're into them, glasses for mixed drinks. It's not a bad idea to keep a stash of good-quality plastic glasses on hand, either.

I use twelve-ounce wineglasses for red wine and let them double for water glasses. (Water can also be served in glass tumblers.) Red wine traditionally is served in a large glass with a wide opening so that the wine can "breathe," which enhances the flavor. White wine is served in a more closed glass to keep it cold. Champagne is poured into flutes (tall skinny glasses with very narrow openings) to keep the bubbles in—not those shallow, wide-mouthed glasses supposedly molded from Marie-Antoinette's breast!

I am not suggesting that you run out and buy all these different kinds of glasses. If you need champagne glasses for a special party, rent them. This goes for red and white wineglasses too. For most entertaining needs, feel free to serve both red and white in any kind of wineglass—as long as it's clean.

It's as easy to go cross-eyed trying to figure if you have enough dinnerware, serving utensils, and glasses as it is trying to select something to wear from a disorganized closet. To make the former task easier (I couldn't begin to help you with the latter!), I have devised the following lists for basic items that are very helpful to have on hand. I recommend service for eight.

DISHES, GLASSES, AND UTENSILS

Dinner plates, 10 to 12 inches in diameter

Salad/dessert plates, 8 inches in diameter

Rimmed soup bowls for soup, pasta, salad, cereal, and some desserts

Coffee cups and saucers

Wineglasses, 12-ounce standard, all-purpose

Water glasses

Dinner forks

Salad/dessert forks

Knives

Teaspoons

Soup spoons

SERVING PIECES AND ACCESSORIES

Serving spoons, regular and slotted

Serving forks

Carving knife

Ladles, large for soup and small for sauces

Pie server

Serrated bread knife

Flat (unrimmed) cake plate, 12 inches in diameter

2 rimmed serving platters

Casseroles, 8- and 12-cup capacity (freezer-to-oven and microwavable are recommended)

Serving bowls

Salad bowl

Tray for serving and clearing dishes

2-cup pitcher for cream or milk

Sugar bowl

Water pitcher

Salt and pepper shakers

Corkscrew

Hot plates or trivets

Tablecloth or place mats

Cloth napkins

OPTIONAL

Candlesticks and candles

Vase for flowers

Extra set of wineglasses

Teapot

Bread and butter plates, 6 inches in diameter

Pretty china, glass, or wooden bowl for fruit

Steak knives

Wooden board for bread

Bread basket

Extra set of teaspoons

Ice bucket

Tongs

Pepper mill

Chopsticks

Place Mats,
Tablecloths, and Napkins

If your table is attractive, then place mats and napkins can set the mood for the most informal to the fanciest dinner. I use brightly colored, cotton place mats and napkins for informal entertaining and throw them in the washing machine after the meal. If I remember to put some fabric softener in the dryer and to take the place mats and napkins out as soon as they are done, I don't have to iron them if I lay them flat or fold them immediately. What a relief!

For those dinner parties I put in the formal category, I use simple white linen place mats and matching linen napkins. White? you say. I don't worry. I had the foresight to take my linens to the backyard and apply Scotchgard to the entire set. Trust me: The napkins and place mats have been stained with everything from red wine to chocolate sauce, but these come right out. If the linens have not been treated with a protective spray, rinse the stain immediately with seltzer (sparkling water) and then cover it with a generous amount of salt. Leave the salt in place for several hours before washing or dry cleaning the linens. (There's lots more on stains on page 65.)

I love the way linen place mats look on a polished table. Nothing compares in terms of elegance and a sense of fine living. But the effect requires effort. The linens need to be ironed after they are washed (all the fabric softener in Marge Simpson's laundry room won't rid just-washed linen of wrinkles). If you don't use linen very often, you might justify the expense of dry cleaning.

If your table needs to be covered for cosmetic reasons or because you want to protect the finish with table pads, use a tablecloth. Ideally, a tablecloth should hang a minimum of twelve inches—but no more than fifteen inches—down from the edges of the table. In other words, it should cover comfortably without dragging on the floor and getting in the way of knees and shins and shiny shoes.

It's amazing how quickly something as elementary as the dimensions of your dining table can fly from your head the instant you enter the housewares department of a store. Therefore, keep the measurements tucked into your wallet when you go tablecloth shopping.

Many tablecloths and matching napkins are made from polyester. Wonderful stuff if you're setting a table aboard a NASA space shuttle, but for home use I urge you to buy cotton, linen, or a high-quality cotton/polyester blend. Straight polyester feels slimy and flimsy and stains take to it like a magnet to due North. It slides around on the table and the napkins make you think you are wiping your chin with a plastic bag. Get the point? And while you are at it, get your iron, too, because tablecloth wrinkles cannot be fought with a box full of fabric softener. Spreading a wrinkled tablecloth on the table even a full two days before the party will not make the wrinkles disappear. There's no way around it. You have to iron or rely on the dry cleaners.

When we have informal family dinners that involve messy foods like lobster or messy eaters like three-year-olds, I use a homemade plastic-coated tablecloth. I bought plasticized fabric at Liberty of London and hemmed the edges on my sewing machine. The pattern is much prettier than those of the old-fashioned vinyl-coated tablecloths and it is just as easy for cleanup: A damp sponge and a little elbow grease do the trick. Try your local fabric store or sewing shop for a good selection of handsome plasticized fabrics.

Napkins are supposed to stay on your lap while you eat. Who the heck expects some guy to balance a silly doll-sized square of cloth on one knee while he eats? (Probably the same person who puts those embroidered, paper-thin hand towels in the bathroom.) How do you expect him to be able to wipe tomato sauce off a man-sized chin (not to mention mustache and full beard) with one of those useless little napkins? When you go shopping for napkins, buy generous squares that cover the lap of your largest friend without being so large that your guest will feel like he or she is wearing a small tablecloth. A good size is twenty-four by twenty-four inches.

If you want an easy, inexpensive way to dress up your table, a set of colorful cotton napkins is great. You can toss them in the washing machine and the dryer and, as with place mats, avoid ironing if you use fabric softener and remove and fold them as soon as they are dry. Linen or damask napkins are beautiful and certainly have their place, but they need ironing. They are the height of elegance on a formal table—one usually set with sterling silver flatware—so if you've inherited a set or receive some as a gift, save them for very special occasions.

Don't get uptight about everything matching when it comes to napkins. The napkins and the tablecloth don't have to be a set. They can be coordinated by color or design, and they can be different fabrics. The napkins can be a selection of different colors as well, just as long as it doesn't look as if you've set the table using napkins you've lifted from a dozen different restaurants.

Paper napkins have come a long way in design and quality. They are fine for informal buffets and really informal suppers, especially those featuring messy food such as shellfish, pizza, ribs, and pasta with drippy sauce. For these meals it's a good idea to have an extra stack of napkins nearby, or even on the table, so guests can help themselves. Avoid those flimsy one-wipe paper napkins that are virtually useless.

Essentials in the Kitchen

A successful host thinks through every facet of the event, regardless of its size. Every piece that is in place before your guests arrive represents one less thing you have to worry about later. I have years of entertaining experience under my belt and I am happily ungirdling that belt to share the following lists with you. Consider them a checklist and you will be organized before you know it.

Think how you will feel if halfway through a delightful meal a light goes off in your head: no extra trash bags! Help! Or, no dishwasher detergent! Yikes! Relax. With the following lists you will have not only plenty of trash bags on hand, you'll also have toothpicks, decaffeinated coffee, paper towels, sugar substitute, clean dish towels, birthday candles, and lots more.

ENTERTAINING SURVIVAL BASICS

Trash bags

Dish detergent

Dishwasher detergent (if you have a dishwasher)

Abrasive cleanser

Food storage bags (I like heavy-duty plastic freezer bags)

Sponge

Steel wool pad

Nonabrasive scrub pad for Teflon-coated pans and utensils

Spot remover

Clean dish towels

Pot holders

Dish drainer

Stopper for the sink

Paper towels

Plastic wrap

Aluminum foil

Cheesecloth

Pad for keeping lists

Coffee (ground, not instant)

Decaffeinated coffee (ground, not instant)

Tea bags

Herbal tea

Lemons for tea and garnishing nonalcoholic drinks

Sugar

Sugar substitute

Milk or half-and-half for coffee and tea

High-quality paper napkins, cocktail size and dinner size

Plastic glasses

Toothpicks

Birthday candles

Ice cubes

Nonalcoholic beverages and mixers

Parsley for garnishing food

KITCHEN GEAR, COOKWARE, APPLIANCES, AND
HELPFUL GADGETS

Coffeepot, preferably the electric drip kind with a 10-cup capacity

Coffee measure

Kitchen timer with a loud ring

Aprons, presentable enough to wear to the table

Pot holders, presentable enough to bring to the table

Extra dish towels

Plastic containers with snap-on lids

Large colander

Instant-read thermometer

Knife sharpener

OPTIONAL

Teapot

Salad spinner

Electric frying pan or wok

Slow cooker

Double boiler

Electric warming tray

Let's Have
a Party

You have the china and the wineglasses. Your utility cupboard is stocked with extra garbage bags and dish detergent. The tablecloth is ironed. Now, what about the party?

A party can be as elementary as having your in-laws to dinner or as complicated as a buffet supper for fifty. It can be held in your living room, backyard, or even a restaurant. It usually lasts several hours, although preparation requires far more time than that. I'm not talking about the kind of party we all remember (fondly?) from our college days when friends started arriving sometime around four P.M. with six-packs, by seven you'd called the local pizza joint for delivery, and by eleven the music was cranked to neighbor-annoying levels. In those days no one cared if the towels in the bathroom were freshly laundered or if the glasses matched (who used a glass anyway?). But those days are long gone and the parties you give now require far more planning—and less cleanup the next day!

The first thing you have to decide is what kind of party to give. In this section I talk about dinner parties, buffets, open houses, outdoor get-togethers, and restaurant entertaining. Certainly there are more kinds of parties, but all fall roughly into these categories. After defining the party, I lead you through the nitty-gritty of preparing for it, beginning with the guest list and ending with saying good-bye to the last guest.

Dinner Parties

Sit-down dinner parties run the gamut from you and your best friend sharing takeout around the kitchen table to a drop-dead six-course megafeast for eight. Since the first example is a no-brainer, I will concentrate on the high-end party: the informal or formal dinner party. If conversation, tight organization, and being in control are important to you, a sit-down dinner party is much easier to predict than a buffet. In your novice state, I suggest starting small with one or two couples. When you have pulled that off, you're on your way. The exception to this "keep it small" rule is a holiday dinner where you have lots of help from cousins, sisters, uncles, and the blueprint of Grandma's traditions to follow.

Plan about forty-five minutes to one hour at the beginning of the evening for the guests to arrive, get introduced, have a drink and some hors d'oeuvres. A drink can be white or red wine (or a choice), a glass of champagne, or an aperitif such as dry sherry. I suggest waiting until you are an experienced host or hostess before offering your guests mixed drinks—although scotch on the rocks shouldn't be too much of a stretch. Make sure to have ginger ale and club soda available, as well as lots of ice.

When it is time to come to the table, light the candles, open the dinner wine and adjust the lights in the dining room. A cold first course such as a cold soup or salad could already be on the table when the guests are seated. You can also fill the water glasses, if you choose to use them, and don't forget the ice. Wine should be poured after you sit down. If you are serving the same wine at dinner that you had with the hors d'oeuvres, it's fine to ask people to bring their glasses in with them.

When asking your guests to sit down, you don't have to sound stuffy ("Dinner is served"). Instead say something pleasant, such as "Dinner is ready, would you all like to come and sit down?" "Please come and eat" or "I'd like to invite everyone to the table." Out of politeness, your guests will ignore you (unless they are overeager boors, in which case they will stampede past you in an attempt to be the first ones at the grub). If they don't come right away, don't run for the dinner gong or pull the rug out from under their feet. Simply walk into the room and offer your arm to someone and jokingly say, "May I escort you to the table?" As soon as you are able to move one body, the others will follow like lemmings.

At this point—if you haven't used place cards for designated, no-fuss seating—you want to tell people either to seat themselves (saving a chair for yourself so that you can get into the kitchen easily to serve and clear) or where you would like them to sit. "Joe, why don't you sit at the end next to Marie" or "Phil, please sit here between Jane and Phoebe so they can hear all about your raft trip down the Ganges." It is not necessary or even customary to seat husbands and wives or other meaningful relationships next to each other. A dinner party is a chance for your friends to get to know each other.

If wine needs to be poured, walk around the table pouring it into each glass from the right side. Alternatively, you can ask one of your guests to pour the wine, and if you are serving a large number of people you can pour one bottle while a guest pours another. In a very informal setting (if there are more than six people) it's fine to have a bottle on each end of the table and indicate that everyone should help himself. As soon as your guests are settled and have had time to place their napkins on their laps, you can either begin to serve at the table or bring the filled plates out from the kitchen. If you are serving "family style," begin to pass the serving dishes around the table. You, as host or hostess, serve yourself last. Picking up your spoon or fork signals your guests to do the same, so you should be mindful that your more polite guests are watching your every move.

When *everyone* is finished with the food on his or her plate, collect the plates. Remove both the plate and the fork or spoon that was used. For very informal dinners you may tell people to hold on to their forks for the next course. Don't allow more than fifteen minutes to elapse between the first course and the main course, which is why most of the entrées in the menu section of this book can be prepared ahead and held until serving time. If you are serving the main course from the table (as opposed to putting the food on individual plates in the kitchen), guests are expected to wait until everyone is served before they begin eating. If you are serving in the kitchen, guests should wait until everyone receives a plate. When everyone is served, pass around bread or sauce or other side dishes so people can help themselves. If you are serving family style, it's a good idea to start one dish in each direction around the table. Be sure to have hot plates, mats, or trivets on which to set the dishes to protect the table.

Let your guests relax for a while between the main course and dessert. You may choose to serve a salad in this interval. If so, make it light so that people have room for a sweet ending to the meal. You can opt to serve the salad from the bowl right at the table or pass the bowl around for people to help themselves.

After the salad plates are removed you may have to wash and dry the forks and plates for dessert. This will give the company a breather. Assemble these plates and forks and either place them at your place setting so that you can serve the dessert, or if you are serving family style, pass the plates and forks around first before the dessert.

I think it is fine to ask another guest to pour the coffee while you serve dessert. Place the coffee cups and carafe or pot of coffee at his or her place, and the sugar bowl, sugar spoon, and pitcher of milk or half-and-half in the center of the table. Things get more complicated when you deal with tea and decaffeinated coffee. Nowadays many people simply serve decaf and if you use good, freshly ground beans, that's fine. A pot of tea is pretty straightforward to brew.

After dessert you have several choices. You can clear the dishes, leaving the coffee cups in case your guests want a second cup (in which case you'll have to be prepared to make another pot of coffee). Your guests can remain at the table and continue their conversation, or you can invite them back into the living room or den, which has the benefit of giving everyone a chance to stretch his legs. The trick here is to have cleared the living room or den of the glasses and food you used before dinner. The time to do this is just before you invite everyone back into the room. You can excuse yourself by saying, "I'd love for us to sit in the living room where it's cozy and warm. Just give me a minute to straighten up."

If you wish to offer your guests a cordial or brandy, this is the time to do it. You don't have to have a bar with a hundred different varieties but good things to have on hand are sherry (cream or dry or both), cordials such as Grand Marnier or Drambuie, cognac, or other brandies. Usually after-dinner drinks are served in small cordial glasses or brandy snifters; however, you can do very well with small 6-ounce wineglasses.

Buffets

A buffet is an easy way to serve dinner or another meal to a large number of people. If you have room at your dining table for only eight but want to invite twelve or more, consider a buffet. At a buffet, the food is placed on a sideboard or large table (usually the dining table) where guests help themselves or are served by the host or designated server. Usually this is done in two stages: dinner and then dessert. The dinner is often preceded by passed hors d'oeuvres and a glass of wine or champagne.

There are several types of buffet dinners, including the seated buffet, where tables are set with napkins and flatwear and the dishes are stucked at one end of the buffet for the guests to pick up before they make their way down the line. You'll often find this kind of setup at weddings or other functions where large numbers of people need to be served. If you are entertaining in your home, chances are you won't have room for a seated buffet. This situation calls for an informal buffet, where after your guests have picked up their food they roam around your living room, dining room or den looking for some place to sit and eat. I would strongly discourage them from hanging around the dining room, as this makes it difficult for the other guests to move through the buffet line. Couches, armchairs, kitchen chairs, stools, and ottomans all do for seating. At really informal buffet suppers, a cushion on the floor is perfectly appropriate. Some people are adept at standing and eating or manuvering the food to their mouths while they hold their plates on their laps, but that leaves the problem of what to do with the wine or water glass. Others have trouble unless they have something solid to eat on. Try to place a coffee table and small tables in strategic places.

You can cover the buffet table with a pretty cloth, a row of place mats or hot plates, or a runner—a twelve- to eighteen-inch wide strip of cloth you place down the middle of the table lengthwise. Even if your table is impervious to food spills, it looks nicer to have something under the dishes. And don't forget a centerpiece or candles to make the table look pretty. For an informal buffet to be successful, don't expect your guests to wield more than a fork—knives or any food that needs to be cut with one have no place on a buffet table. An easy trick is to wrap each fork in a napkin. Tying pretty bows of ribbon around them makes them look especially pretty and festive. Place them in a shallow basket right next to the dinner plates at the beginning of the buffet line. Next comes the food. Use the biggest serving dishes you have so you won't have to go back and forth to the kitchen for refills. The order of the food is usually main course, vegetable, grain or potato, and then bread. This is not written in stone. Be sure to place serving utensils next to each dish and make sure they are large enough not to get lost if invertently dropped into the chicken paprikas.

You can have drinks set up at the other end of the buffet table or on another smaller table either nearby or in another room. Your job is to wander through the crowd offering refills. Put extra glasses on this bar—you can use plastic as a backup. Don't forget a bowl or bucket of ice, as well as something to serve the ice with such as tongs, a ladle, or large spoon. A stack of napkins is a good thing to place here, too. Be sure to keep an eye on the bar throughout the evening, replenishing wine, soda, ice, and glasses, as well as an eye on the buffet table in case things need neatening or replenishing.

For buffet food, my rule of thumb for new cooks or those new to entertaining is to offer one (nonthreatening) entrée (such as a chicken dish), one large vegetable dish with no meat in it, one grain or potato dish, and some bread that comes buttered, such as herbed garlic bread. This way if people don't eat chicken they can load up on veggies, rice, and bread. (See the sample buffet menus in Chapter Six.) If you are planning to let people help themselves, then it's a good idea to make extra food; I make one extra serving for every six people. But if you are serving or have hired servers, you can more easily control the amounts you dish out.

Allow approximately thirty to forty minutes for people to eat before you begin collecting dirty dishes, first asking people if they would like more. It's a nice gesture for you to bring the food to them, but if you're a one-person show, it's fine to suggest they help themselves. Once all the dishes have been collected and all the serving plates and utensils removed from the buffet table, check to make sure the cloth or other table covering is still fairly clean; brush off any crumbs and hide any stains with a place mat or a strategically placed pile of dishes. Set out dessert forks (dinner forks can be recycled for this purpose once you have have washed and dried them), and a stack of extra napkins (guests always seem to lose them and even if you have used cloth napkins for dinner you can use nice paper napkins for dessert), teaspoons for tea and coffee, dessert plates, coffee cups and saucers, a pitcher of half-and-half or milk, a sugar bowl, and sugar spoon. If you have sugar substitute in small packages or a small dispenser you should put that out too since someone will invariably ask you for it.

If you are serving a dessert that needs to be served in the kitchen, position the filled plates on the buffet table and place a fork on each one. If you are serving the dessert at the table, stack the dishes nearby so that you can serve it or people can help themselves.

After everyone has finished dessert you can offer more coffee and then clear the dishes, quickly putting away any leftover food. This is not the time to start doing the dishes. I recommend turning off the lights in the dining room at this point—the table is often a bit of a shambles and not the most attractive focal point and this encourages people to congregate away from the kitchen and dining room area.

There are variations to the traditional buffet dinner, such as cocktail buffets and dessert buffets. The former is what fifties- and sixties-generation adults called cocktail parties, and the latter is a super excuse to bake as many chocolate cakes as you want without feeling guilty. A cocktail buffet usually includes passed hors d'oeuvres as well as plenty of finger foods (dips, spreads, even a sliced ham or turkey) on the buffet table. There is also usually a bar set up in the dining room or living room where guests can pour their own drinks or be served by a hired bartender. It is perfectly acceptable to serve only wine, beer, and soft drinks at the "cocktail" party of the nineties. (For more information on setting up the bar, see page 77.)

A dessert buffet is a great party for a Sunday afternoon or other quiet day when you want to gather friends and family for something special. I think the cold-weather months are the best time to plan this sort of party, as folks seem more eager to eat sweets in cool weather.

Dessert buffets are great ways to entertain a crowd and have all the food prepared in advance. Actually, unless you choose to serve chocolate fondue (not if you have white rugs, of course), the only last-minute thing will be plugging in the coffee and reheating desserts such as bread pudding.

If you follow the menu on page 166, you can start cooking several weeks ahead and freeze most of the desserts you'll be serving. Other things can be done early in the day; fresh fruit can be sliced up to eight hours ahead of time, and strawberries dipped in chocolate can be made and refrigerated about four hours ahead of time.

A very informal version of a dessert buffet is a potluck party where you invite your friends to bring a dessert. A classic example is the cookie exchange our neighborhood holds every Christmas season. We send out (or hand-deliver) Xeroxed sheets inviting families to come from eleven to one (usually it's held on the morning of Christmas Eve) and bring two dozen cookies, bars, or other pickup desserts. Everyone puts the dessert on the table, has a glass of punch or cup of coffee (while the kids run around like lunatics), and then leaves with a dozen cookies or bars to take home. It's a lovely way for a neighborhood get-together without a lot of work for the host.

Another way to do this is to invite friends to bring their favorite dessert. You as host supply a large platter of fruit (to cleanse the palate and provide a break from the procession of richness), punch, wine, and coffee and tea as well as plates, cups, forks, spoons, and napkins. At a really informal gathering high-quality paper products are perfectly acceptable—and make for a speedy cleanup.

The secret to a successful buffet, regardless of its menu, is timing. Typically, the evening begins very much like a sit-down dinner, with the guests congregating in one or two rooms for something to drink and light to eat. At a large party, guests will serve themselves or be served by a hired bartender or waiter. If you don't have a bartender, the host or hostess may pass drinks on a tray. The best choices for the tray are chilled white wine or champagne. It's fine for you to do this initial passing, and then direct guests to the bar for refills. If, as you are passing, someone asks for a nonalcholic drink, make a mental note and get it from the kitchen as soon as you have made the rounds with the tray.

When you are entertaining a large number of people, have two large plates of cold or room-temperature hors d'oeuvres set out where guests can help themselves. Don't forget to place small napkins and toothpicks nearby. Choose something that can be eaten without the benefit of a fork and plate, such as cheese and crackers or vegetables and dip. Hot hors d'oeuvres, which are not necessary but always welcome, should be passed on a tray along with napkins. Remember to canvass the room periodically for used napkins, toothpicks, and dirty glasses.

Allow an hour for this part of the meal. Since your guests will presumably be busy talking to each other you can slip out to arrange the food on the buffet table. Unless you have hired a server for the evening you should position yourself next to or behind the buffet table to help your guests serve themselves and to answer questions about the food: "The corn bread is already buttered" or "The green dish contains couscous, a grain I've mixed with curry and raisins." Remind your guests that they can help themselves to a drink at the bar or let them know you will be along soon to pour more wine. The host and/or hostess always serve themselves last.

If you have planned carefully, your guests will be able to find places to sit, lean, or perch to eat. If you find people looking helpless, offer to find them a comfortable place to sit.

When you notice that people have finished eating, wander through the room(s) and offer to bring them more or suggest they help themselves. If they indicate that they are through, take their plates (don't scrape or stack until you get to the kitchen) and flatware, leaving them their napkins unless you have used paper napkins, in which case take the napkins and offer replacements with dessert. Next offer more wine or water, removing the first glass if a guest has finished drinking.

Clear the serving dishes and utensils from the buffet table, plus any warming trays, condiments, etc. Shake or sweep any crumbs from the table and straighten out the table covering if there is one. Bring out the dessert, dessert plates, dessert forks, coffee spoons, extra napkins, and serving implements. Also bring out the coffee cups, sugar, a spoon, and milk or cream pitcher, plus a hot pad or warming tray for the coffeepot. Check the area one more time for dirty dishes, etc. and then call your guests in for dessert. Again the guests may serve themselves, or you or a server may help. If you are serving a cake, pie, or other dessert that needs to be cut, the line will go faster and the dessert will stay looking prettier if one person (the host or server) cuts it. Guests may wish to get their coffee at the same time, or return to get it after they finish dessert.

With the pressure of the meal over this is your time to relax and spend time with your guests. Don't forget, however, to offer more coffee or another helping of dessert (if there is any extra). Some guests may leave soon after dessert, so you'll have to juggle your time saying good-bye with picking up dishes. The good-byes definitely come before the clearing.

Open Houses

These are not so very different from buffets except that, by my definition, they are less formal and often accommodate more guests than a buffet. Even if you live in a small house or apartment you can give an open house party for thirty to fifty people. The key is to make it last for enough hours so that you can be sure that not everyone will show up at the same time. The invitation clearly states "open house" and most people know that means they are invited to stop by any time between the beginning and ending hours of the party.

While an open house is a great way to entertain a large number of people—and a good way to invite casual acquaintances to your home or introduce groups you think would enjoy each other—it has its share of unique responsibilities. First, you must see that food is constantly replenished and used glasses, plates, cups, and so forth are continually collected and replaced with fresh ones. It's fine to use paper plates and napkins and plastic glasses for an open house, but please buy the high-quality kind. They hold up very well and come in all sorts of pretty colors and patterns. It's especially nice to tie in a theme to the paper-ware and other decorations, particularly if you are giving a holiday open house.

Second, an open house puts responsibility on the host or hostess to circulate and make introductions, since one presumes that not all the guests will know each other at such a large party. You will have to move from group to group rather than linger for long conversations.

Most people usually set the food out on a large centrally located table or divide it among several tables in different rooms. You may also pass some platters. It's a good idea to stick to room-temperature or cold foods, since you'll have enough to juggle without worrying about last-minute heating or cooking. If you are offering finger foods that can be eaten without plates, make sure you have a supply of napkins and toothpicks nearby.

You should have a table with wine and soft drinks, or a large bowl of punch. If you are serving an alcoholic punch, be sure to offer non-alcoholic beverages as well. Place the glasses and some napkins next to the drinks, as well as a bucket of ice and tongs, ladle, or large spoon to use with the ice.

You should be completely set up and ready to go with the food out and the drinks ready at least fifteen minutes before the beginning of the party. This will give you a few minutes of quiet before the storm, and a chance to go over your guest list so introductions will be easier.

Outdoor Entertaining

Whether you are having a few friends over for a cookout or are planning a wedding luncheon al fresco, entertaining under the open sky takes as much planning as dining inside. True, the preparation is a lot easier (especially if someone else mows the lawn!) and you don't have to worry about fresh flowers, stains on the carpet, and whether you have enough square feet to squeeze in Cousin Adelaide's three step-children who are visiting from Piscataway. But there are some things about outdoor entertaining that are completely out of your control.

The most obvious variable is weather. Picking a date for the party when the weather should be nice does not mean it won't rain on a June evening or that the temperature won't plummet unseasonably on a September afternoon. One of the most important things I learned from my years as a caterer was to caution my clients planning an outdoor event to have an alternative plan ready to put into action—just in case. An informal barbecue can easily be moved inside and the food cooked under the shelter of a porch or in an open garage. It can even be cooked in the oven. But if you have invited more people than the house can possibly handle, consider rescheduling (called a rain date) or take everyone out for pizza.

For anything more formal, take a good, hard look at the guest list and then a good, hard look at the interior of your home. If it is not large enough to accommodate all your guests in case of inclement weather, your choices are to rent a tent (not an inexpensive proposition) or cut down the list. You don't want to end up like a woman I know whose early May garden wedding found her two hundred guests crammed into her tiny house because of a freak blizzard.

Bugs are another problem of outdoor party giving. Plan the event so that the meal is finished before those pesky no-see-ums and mosquitoes begin their nightly rampage. You can try lighting camphor candles and handing out bug spray if the party is informal, but at more formal affairs, very few guests want their party clothes smelling like insect repellent. If bugs are a problem at a certain time of year or because of your proximity to wetlands, you might want to rethink the outdoor party and content yourself with cocktails on the deck before retiring inside for a civilized and bug-free meal.

Most young people don't think twice about plopping down on a blanket to eat a picnic meal, but if you have invited folks whose hips and knees may not be as cooperative as they once were, be sure to scatter some chairs around the lawn or on the porch or deck. It's also helpful to place some small tables near these chairs. Older guests appreciate not having to balance a plate filled with coleslaw, potato salad, a sloppy burger, and several pickles on their laps.

Think about lighting. While the sun may be shining when the first guests arrive, it will go down eventually and therefore you should have ample outdoor lighting or a good supply of candles or lanterns set about the lawn, deck, or patio to illuminate the area. It's important to light steps and steep paths, particularly those that lead to the house (and the bathroom) and the driveway.

If your yard or outdoor space is more than a few steps from the kitchen, be sure to take the trek back and forth into account when planning your menu. At an informal event you no doubt will have eager volunteers to help you carry bowls, platters, and cold drinks to and fro, but for something fancier when you want your guests to relax and feel pampered, consider hiring an extra pair of hands and feet.

Wait until the last minute to set out perishable food. If possible, place it in a shaded area out of direct sunlight. Dishes made with mayonnaise, eggs, meat, fish, fowl, and dairy products (with the exception of cheese) should be kept in the refrigerator or ice chest until you serve them. Uncooked meats, poultry, and fish should be refrigerated until they're put on the grill and leftovers should be returned to the fridge soon after serving. Don't use cooking utensils that have been in contact with raw food, particularly those that have been used for raw chicken, unless they have first been washed with hot, soapy water. The same rule holds for cutting boards and trays. And finally, when you set the food on the table, be sure to cover it to keep flies away.

Entertaining in Restaurants

Sometimes it makes more sense to entertain in a restaurant rather than in your home. This may be because you don't have enough room to seat everyone comfortably, your schedule does not permit time for cooking, or you want the evening as special and nonwork-oriented for you as for your guests. When you issue invitations, be clear that this is your party. You can say something like "Joanne, Bill and I would love to have you and Tom join us as our guests for dinner at Chez Maison next Saturday at 8 o'clock."

Call ahead and make a reservation and then confirm it on the day of the party. American diners have abused the reservation system by double-booking: making reservations at two different restaurants and waiting until the last minute to decide where to go. They then forget or neglect to call one restaurant to cancel the unwanted reservations. This attitude has understandably left restaurant owners feeling burned. Because popular restaurants time their reservations carefully and systematically, be sure to show up on time. If you invite guests who are perpetually late, make the reservations a half hour later than you tell them or offer to pick them up on the way to the restaurant.

If this is a really big deal dinner, be sure to try the restaurant before taking guests to it. This gives you an idea of the menu, the cost, the ambiance, and the attitude of the serving staff. It might also give you a chance to develop a relationship with a certain waiter—be sure to request his or her table when making the reservation for the party.

If you prefer to have the check a non-issue, give the person who takes the reservation your credit card number and request that the check not be presented—just the charge slip handed discreetly to you to sign at the end of the meal. If the restaurant will not do this, at some point during the evening ask the waiter or maître d' to be sure the check goes to you, and you only. Another way to deal with the check is to excuse yourself from the table and slip the waiter your credit card on your way to the rest room. All three strategies avoid any confusion about who is to pay, and your guests will feel under no pressure to offer.

If you discover you have been given a bad table—next to the kitchen or bathroom door, for instance—and you can see there are other tables, you have every right to ask to be moved. Of course, the restaurant may say the other tables are reserved for other guests, but that should not prevent you from politely and graciously requesting a switch.

If you happen to run into someone you know on the way to your table, give him or her a brief hello and keep moving. There is nothing as awkward or tedious as standing behind Chatty Cathy as she catches up with a long-lost friend with news of her college roommate's ex-sister-in-law.

Once you're seated, the waiter will supply you with menus and a wine list. (The latter may come from the wine steward if the restaurant has one.) It's polite to confer with your guests whether you want to order cocktails or a bottle of wine to drink before dinner rather than making the decision yourself.

Ordering wine is stressful for many of us, particularly for those who are new to the game. If you are in over your head, it's appropriate to ask the waiter or wine steward to select a bottle or two. You can quietly indicate the price range by pointing to a selection on the list—remember, this is one of the most important aspects of the steward's job and he is skillful at providing quick and discreet help.

The waiter or steward will present the bottle to you, unopened, so that you can check that it is indeed the bottle you ordered. Nod and smile and he will proceed to uncork it. He will then pour a little for you to taste. Do so, nod and smile again, and pronounce the wine "fine." He will then pour it for everyone at the table who is drinking wine. If there is something really horrible about the wine—it tastes vinegary or sour, for instance—ask the steward to taste it too. You and he will then make a determination if the wine is "off" or if you are simply unfamiliar with that particular taste.

If the wine is red, the steward may suggest letting the bottle breathe for a few minutes so that the wine can develop its full flavor. He should return shortly to let you taste the wine and to pour it. I have a pet peeve about restaurants that don't automatically bring an ice bucket for white wine. By all means, ask for one if it does not arrive. White wine is much better chilled than lukewarm.

The key to getting good service in a restaurant is to treat the staff politely without ever being bossy, condescending, or obsequious. If you need attention, first try catching the waiter's eye. If that doesn't work, try raising your hand to just above shoulder height and signaling in an understated manner. Please, no waving arms or yelling out "garçon!" or "waiter!" I promise, this behavior assures that the steak will be overcooked and the soup cold.

Good manners dictate that unless the food is really inedible or there are foreign bodies lurking in the salad, say nothing but vow never to eat there again. If your fish is raw, tell the waiter you would like it cooked a little more. Don't make a scene; your guests will be embarrassed. If you have a serious complaint, excuse yourself and have a quiet word with the manager or maître d'. If he has an attitude problem, you can try telling him the woman at your table writes a column for a major food magazine. That should get his attention!

Good service deserves a 15 percent tip, the customary amount in nearly all cases. But great service warrants a 20 percent tip. If the service has been great but the food poor, don't punish the serving staff (they aren't cooking the stuff!) by leaving a measly tip. If the wine steward has been especially attentive and helpful, give him a tip as well. Fifteen percent of the price of the wine is a good rule of thumb.

If you plan to entertain in restaurants frequently, find two or three places that you really like and patronize them regularly. Your repeat business will win you a special place in the hearts of the owners and staff and I guarantee that the service will reflect this.

The All-Important Guests

When you were a little kid you got to invite all your friends to your birthday party. Now that you're a grown-up, all your friends don't know each other, space is limited, and you (not your mother) are doing the work—all of which means this "all or nothing" strategy won't fly.

⌇ **GUEST LISTS:** When planning the guest list, begin by deciding how many people to invite (determined by the type of party you are giving). Next, choose people you think might get along and enjoy each other's company. You don't have to make perfect matches, this is not *The Dating Game* (unless, in fact, you are fixing up a friend with a friend, in which case you're on your own!). You don't have to obsess about equal numbers of men and women or even numbers of guests, although I would be sure that the one woman I've invited to watch the Super Bowl with twelve guys is up to the task. Simply think of people who know and like each other, or who have indicated they would like to know each other better, or who you think would truly enjoy each other's company.

Don't assume that just because someone is *your* friend he or she will get along with all your other friends. Some mixes don't work, and I'm not talking about food fights or pouting bouts. I'm talking about verbal fireworks or (worse) deadly silence, with you chattering foolishly into thin air. I would not invite my friend the radical lesbian economist to eat at the same table as my brother-in-law the banker who is slightly to the right of Attila the Hun, nor would I invite one highly opinionated person with five mild, meek, head-nodding folks. I would not ask six of the shyest people I know for dinner with the hope that my great food and scintillating conversation would miraculously bring them out of their shells. I steer clear of inviting couples who are having serious trouble with their relationships, too. There is enough challenge to being the host when everyone gets along, why ask for trouble?

When you plan the list, be sure to have a reserve list (also called the B list) in mind. This way, if not everyone can come, you have other people to call. If a guest cancels at the last minute, either resign yourself to a smaller party or ask a good friend, who won't be insulted, to fill in. Be sure to put this generous soul on the top of your next A list—he is doing you a favor this time.

And finally, be sure to go over the list just before the guests arrive. This may sound crazy, especially if you are giving a small party, but you could forget someone's name—something the host should never do!

INVITATIONS: Invitations play a key role in entertaining. All the information you need to convey to the person you are inviting comes in the form of a phone call or piece of mail. Usually, written invitations are reserved for special occasions such as birthday parties, showers, graduation parties, or open houses when you are inviting a large number of people. However, quite often I send invitations written on pretty note cards to invite friends for a non-event dinner. It gives a special festivity to the occasion.

It's acceptable to phone people to invite them to dinner. Be sure to convey in the phone message all the information you would print on a written invitation. I suggest jotting down the particulars (time, date, reason, dress) for reference before making the phone calls. This may sound ridiculous, but if, as soon as she hears about the upcoming party, Betty launches into an ecstatic description of the "to die for" dessert she had at Wilma's house last month, you might forget to deliver the complete message in your eagerness to get off the telephone. Finally, be sure to talk with the person you are inviting. Don't invite people by leaving messages with children or babysitters.

I know people do it, but I do not want to get reports of any of my readers delivering invitations by phone machine or fax! Invitations issued this way have a habit of being eaten by the machine, and then when you don't hear from them, you never know whether the invitees did not get the invitation or are simply ignoring you.

Card shops sell a confusing array of invitations. Unless you are giving a specific kind of party (birthday, surprise party, etc.), buy the simplest, cleanest-looking invitations with ample room to write the information you need to convey—without it getting confused with the information Hallmark thinks you should convey. If your handwriting is as awful as mine is, print the invitation and address, or have your ten-year-old do it for you. Be sure to write your return addess and last name on the envelope. I have received invitations to dinner from "Sue and Howie" without having a clue about which Sue and Howie were inviting me.

Mail invitations no later than two weeks before the party and, unless you're hosting a wedding or coronation, no more than four weeks.

Regardless of the form the invitation takes, the pertinent information must include where, when, the occasion, and any particulars such as "surprise party," "no gifts, please," "bring a bathing suit," or "black tie." If the party is a surprise party for someone you live with, be sure to indicate a specific telephone number or the best time of day to respond, or both, on the invitation.

The "where" should include your full address and directions if necessary. Sometimes it's helpful to include a map, which can be Xeroxed on a separate sheet of paper. Don't just say "Jack's house" unless you are inviting Jack's family only. As unlikely as it may seem to you, someone may be confused by such scant information. If you supply written directions, without a map, make them clear and concise. I have found it helpful over the years to keep a set of directions to our house on the computer for easy printout whenever they are needed. You can also type or handwrite them once and make a number of Xeroxed copies, passing them out as needed. Put your name, address, and phone number directly on the sheet of paper with the directions (people often leave the invitation at home but clutch the directions to their breast when leaving their house for yours). Give a little description of the house ("a two-story, white brick house with a hedge in front") and if you live on a heavily trafficked street, give a signpost or two when the turnoff is near ("after the Citgo station on the left, start looking for Broad Street, about a quarter mile on the right").

Be as exact as you can about when the party is. Most parties don't have an ending time unless they are open houses or children's birthday parties, but all have starting times. It's also a good idea to include the day of the week next to the day of the month: Friday, April 12. You'd be surprised how many people have it fixed in their mind that April 12 (or whatever) is a Saturday night. And they'll show up, dressed to the nines, the day after the party only to catch you in your bathrobe and slippers vegging out in front of reruns of The Brady Bunch.

When describing the occasion, say something like "Betsy's Baby Shower" or "Come celebrate Harry and Ethel's Fortieth Anniversary." You should also indicate the occasion of more general parties, such as "an informal brunch" "lunch by the pool" "supper after the hockey game" or, simply, "dinner."

Finally, be sure to ask the invitees to respond to the invitation. The letters R.S.V.P. stand for the French phrase _répondez s'il vous plaît_, which translates to "please reply." This is the most common way to remind folks you want to hear from them and is usually followed by a phone number or numbers and perhaps the best time to call. You can also write "regrets only," but since people seem to respond better to an R.S.V.P., I suggest using "regrets only" for large parties where you don't need an exact head count. For large seated affairs or catered ones where you are charged by the person, consider putting a date by which to respond on the invitation: "R.S.V.P. by October 1."

There are always those lazy people who never respond. Maybe they are waiting for a better offer or are so consumed by their dog's obedience classes they don't have a minute to call, but regardless of the reason, they are being rude. I suggest calling if you don't hear from them within a reasonable amount of time (at least a day or two before the party). They'll swear they were on their way to the phone just as you rang or insist they left a message on your machine, and your job is to be gracious and overlook such obvious tall tales. At least you have an accurate head count.

Dealing with those people who put you off with some not-so-urgent excuse ("We'd love to come but Junior might be inviting Big John's boss's son to spend the night. Can I let you know when we know?") is a sticky problem. My advice is if you have the ability to be flexible, cut them some slack; if not, simply say, "Sorry, but I really need to know. We'll plan to have dinner together another time."

If you choose not to use the fill-in-the-blanks sort of invitation, here are some ways to word written invitations:

Our pool is Finished At Last!
Help us celebrate at a poolside barbecue
Saturday evening, July 9, 1994
7:00 P.M.
Bill and Sara Nade
440 Weathervane Terrace
Buena Vista Heights
R.S.V.P. 555-2323
Bring your bathing suit!

꒰

Clark Street Annual Neighborhood Potluck Family Supper
Friday, January 14, 1994
6:30–9:30
At the Esthers'
42 Clark Street
Please call Polly at 555-2345 for your food assignment

꒰

It's Aunt Sue's 80th Birthday!
Please come for drinks and dessert
Saturday evening, April 23, 1994
7:00 P.M.
The Pink Flamingo
223 West Street
Bloomfield, Connecticut
Please respond to Vinnie Lee at (203) 555-6706
by April 12
No gifts please, but please write a funny poem
in tribute to Aunt Sue

꒰ **DRESS:** Usually the invitation implies the dress. If you ask me for a cookout in your backyard with the kids, I know not to wear a strapless evening gown. But some people need to have these things spelled out for them, and it's only considerate to do so. Be prepared to answer questions about what to wear when your friends call to respond to the invitation. I once invited a couple to a very casual supper. "How casual?" I was asked. "You can wear your pajamas, if you want," I joked. Sure enough, the next Saturday night, here's this guy standing at my door in his blue flannel pj's. It's appropriate to write the dress expected on the invitation, such as "please wear shorts" or "informal attire."

Remember that what you decide to wear will make your guests

feel comfortable—or maybe not. If you insist they should wear jeans and sneakers and then at the last minute you decide to don a tiara or your new ultrasuede pants suit, they will surely feel awkward the minute you answer the door. On the other hand, be sure to leave time to change into something clean and fresh before the party rather than wearing the same grubby sweatshirt you wore all day while cooking and cleaning.

If you will be doing last-minute cooking, remember the Rules of Attire in the Kitchen: Tie back your hair and forgo billowing sleeves and flowing cuffs. Invest in two large aprons, one to wear while doing your advance preparation and a clean one to tie on when the company arrives. I always buy navy blue aprons—years of stained white aprons taught me a lesson. Aprons are not silly— they can save your silk blouse or tie from being splattered. Wear comfortable shoes (high heels and full platters don't always agree) and clothing that won't make you sweat over the grill or stove. Avoid slipping straps, armloads of bracelets, and glasses perched on top of your head from where they can tumble into the soup. I also don't recommend clouds of perfume, cologne, or hair spray. They will throw off your sense of smell and taste, annoy your dinner partner, and some foods, such as chocolate, actually absorb strong odors such as perfume. Same goes for cigarette smoke.

⌐⌐ **OFFERS OF HELP:** The thoughtful guest often asks what he or she can bring to the party. You, as host, have the choice of graciously refusing by saying something like "How kind of you, but I think I have everything under control." If you feel your friend would be hurt unless permitted to bring something, ask for a bottle of wine, specifying red or white. This implies that the wine will be served that evening and won't end up in your wine cellar waiting for the next party.

It's fine to accept offers of help from people you know, but if you are inviting mere acquaintances or, for whatever reason, people you have yet to meet, I advise against it. If you are accepting offers, keep time and budget in mind, and remember whose party this is: yours. I would never ask anyone, not even my best friend the pastry chef, to bring a drop-dead chocolate dessert for twenty. A loaf of bread or a salad is more in keeping with the expectations of the person making the offer. If people in your family offer to bring something for a holiday meal, they may expect to bring a dish for which they are noted. In this case, say, "Gee, Grandma, Thanksgiving wouldn't be the same without your sweet potato pie."

〜 **HANDICAPPED GUESTS:** As the host or hostess you need to develop a sensitivity for ways that you can make handicapped guests feel comfortable without being doting or overly attentive. While a friend recovering from knee surgery or whiplash may enjoy extra attention lavished on him during recovery, someone with a permanent handicap does not.

Arrange parking and easy access to your home for anyone in a wheelchair or on crutches. We often entertain a friend in a wheelchair and have a portable ramp that allows her access to our back door. Offer a footstool to someone in a leg cast and personally escort the person on crutches to his or her seat at the table, placing the crutches (or cane) nearby. Keep an eye out for the time when the person may need them retrieved. If you are having a buffet, offer to bring this guest his or her food. Be sure to leave ample space at the table for the wheelchair, thus avoiding the bothersome and perhaps embarrassing task of moving chairs when it's time for dinner.

Be considerate, too, of the physical limitations other than those necessitating crutches and wheelchairs. Think about background noise and dim lights. I usually place anyone with a hearing loss next to me at the table so that I can relay or repeat conversation if necessary. When entertaining someone with impaired vision, I raise the lights in the dining room higher than I might otherwise. Consider the menu, too, when inviting guests with physical limitations. Grandpa may have trouble cutting steak with a steak knife because of his arthritis. How about salmon or pasta instead?

〜 **UNEXPECTED GUESTS:** Extra guests who turn up at the last minute are more of a problem at a sit-down dinner than a buffet or open house. Sit-down dinners require more precise amounts of food and you may simply not have enough. At buffets, you probably will have enough for another person or even two, but if you are in doubt, serve the food yourself (don't make it self-serve) so that you can monitor portions.

"May I bring a date?" is exactly the sort of question hosts and hostesses should expect to get when someone responds to the invitation—not later. Often when you issue an invitation, you suggest that your friend may bring a date. But if your friend, out of the blue, says he's met this terrific woman and would like to bring her, you may have to give up the notion of introducing him to your sister's best friend and graciously respond with "Sure, I'd love to have her come." If you've already invited your sister's pal, find another guy—fast!

There are always those dreaded last-minute calls from friends saying that Uncle Joe just blew into town and they cannot leave him alone. Can he come along? You've met Uncle Joe and find him delightful, but it's 5:00 P.M. and the fish store is closed and you have enough salmon only for eight. Help! Make some extra rice or pasta (you have extra in the cupboard if you stock it as I instruct on pages 94–96), and when you serve the salmon, slice it into five- or six-inch-long strips and divide these among nine plates. If you're still short of food, give yourself the least. In the future you will follow my number one rule of extras: Always cook for at least two "invisible" guests.

Be sure to make Uncle Joe feel welcome in your home and let him know you are not in the least put out by his unexpected presence. On the contrary, you are thrilled to see him again. And if this extra guest means a little more last-minute time in the kitchen and perhaps a little less food on your plate, don't be grumpy. If you are, you should have refused your friends' request in the first place.

Saying no is your right if you cannot or don't want to accommodate an unexpected guest. If your dining room table seats eight and an extra body will mean everyone will be uncomfortably crowded, you can say no. If you have eight place settings and a ninth person will mean you have to serve someone's meal on a paper plate (yours, by the way), you can say no. A polite but firm "Gee, I'm awfully sorry but there's not enough room (or food)" is all you have to say.

If, God forbid, a guest shows up at your door with an extra person, smile nicely during introductions and then take the offending invited guest aside and explain that you are completely unprepared to handle extras and therefore you are sure he or she won't mind getting last night's leftovers or a large helping of cottage cheese. When you serve this person his special meal, sweetly explain to everyone else that he or she is on a strictly kosher vegetarian diet.

Of course, you may have plenty of food and room and there will be no need for such drastic action. But I would still make it clear to your friend that you don't like surprises.

When your husband, wife, or some other significant relationship shows up with extra mouths to feed, take a deep breath and smile. This is not the time for histrionics or threats of divorce or murder. That comes later in the evening when the company has left. Either whip up a simple pasta dish or call out for Chinese food. Don't show any hostility by plunking the takeout on the table still in its cardboard cartons. Spoon it into serving dishes and warm it up in the microwave. Stifle your temptation to use paper plates. You won't be doing the dishes tonight! Keep your chin up and smile broadly. Perhaps the unexpected guest is a judge for the MacArthur Genius Awards and will be so impressed with your inventiveness she will nominate you. Think of this as the ultimate test: If you handle it, you are ready for anything fate throws your way.

Preparing Your Home for the Party

Nothing inspires a good housecleaning like giving a party. If you don't have regular help in this department, brace yourself for a full day of preparation. And this does not include cooking and setting the table. I highly recommend you comandeer children and spouse to help. If you have none, pull on the rubber gloves and get cracking.

CLEANING THE KITCHEN: If you are following the menus in this book or any other menu that allows you the luxury of cooking dishes ahead of time, begin by cleaning out the refrigerator. How annoying to have the pasta salad, the lemon mousse, and the marinating chicken all ready for chilling only to open the fridge and find it stuffed with cartons of aging Chinese food, barely filled orange juice containers, and wilted bunches of carrots and celery. Toss the expired and half-eaten cartons of yogurt and cottage cheese and stash the mustard and other condiments on a low shelf out of the way (you might also consolidate these, scraping the last tablespoon of Dijon mustard into the almost full jar and mixing the strawberry preserves with the strawberry jam—who will know?). Wash out the plastic containers holding forgotten leftovers, and wash out and rinse the vegetable bins and line them with fresh paper towels. Take a hot, wet cloth to sticky spills, and shove an opened box of baking soda in the back of the refrigerator to absorb odors (this should be discarded and replaced every eight to ten weeks).

I feel morally obligated to ask you to take a good look at your oven. Turn on the kitchen light and be honest about what you see. Are the racks shiny and the bottom free of the remnants of last Thanksgiving's apple pie attempt? If the prognosis is poor, do not despair. You can and should clean your oven because food cooked in a dirty one tastes and smells burned. Lucky you if you have a self-cleaning oven, but if not, hightail it to the supermarket or hardware store and buy some oven cleaner. I know the television commercials make this sound like a grim job, and in some ways they are right. But as with all cleaning jobs, it doesn't take long to figure out how to do it, and then it only takes elbow grease to accomplish the task.

Buy oven cleaner in a nonaerosol can (better for the environment), read the directions, and let the stuff sit on the grimy surfaces for the allotted time. Spread newspaper on the floor beneath the oven—this is a messy job. Next, take a well-wrung-out sponge (big is better) and start wiping the cleaner away. The baked-on residue won't slide off like applesauce from a baby's chin, but with a little pressure and rubbing, it will disappear. The job is repugnant enough so that the next time you notice a fresh spill on the oven floor, you will be quick with the damp sponge. Clean the top of the stove, too, with oven cleaner or nonchlorine abrasive cleanser. Lift off the burners and be sure to check the drip pans if you have them. You can buy foil liners for the burners, which will make cleanup easier next time. Finally, don't attempt this the day of the party. It takes too long and the fumes will linger in the kitchen. Also, it's recommended to turn the oven on for a while to rid it of fumes before attempting to cook in it.

I don't care how big your kitchen is, it does not have enough counter space! You need all you can get when giving a party, so clear away the hot-air popcorn popper, last Sunday's paper, your kid's math book, and the bucket of cat treats from the countertops. Remove the food processor, standing mixer, and blender while cleaning the counter and, once you have finished using them, plan to stow them in the garage or basement for the duration of the party. Scrub down the now-clear counters with a weak solution of bleach and warm water (one part bleach to six parts water) and then rinse the surfaces with lots of hot water. Wash your dish towels and pot holders (pot holders go in the washing machine) and run your sponges through the dishwasher with the dishes (yes! it works).

〜 **CLEANING THE BATHROOM:** You've cleaned the kitchen, now it's time for the bathroom. Even if you expect your guests to restrict themselves to the downstairs half bath (if you have one), don't count on it. Some will venture into the rest of the house looking for a bathroom, and you better be ready!

Rearm yourself with your abrasive cleanser and sponges, plus glass and tile cleaner, toilet cleaner, paper towels, a toilet brush (also called a johnny mop), and a floor mop. Clean the toilet inside and out, scrub the sink with cleanser, taking care to wipe the soap dish clean and making sure the toothbrush rack looks presentable—not stuffed with toothbrushes so that it looks as though the entire seventh grade class stops by your house to brush their pearly whites. I know no one will be showering during your party, but I strongly advise cleaning the tub and shower stall with cleanser. Lots of people like to "peek." If there are rust stains on the porcelain sink or tub, dampen them slightly and sprinkle them with cleanser. Let the cleanser stand on the stains for several hours; the stains will lighten considerably.

Toss out those virtually empty bottles of shampoo or combine them in one bottle. Remove the dirty towels and bath mats and replace the towels with clean ones, particularly hand towels. I suggest you avoid the dainty embroidered jobs you inherited from Great-aunt Tess. They are worthless in the absorbing department and (worse!) have to be ironed. Put a fresh bar of soap in the soap dish (not on the rim of the sink). This is a good opportunity to use "real" guest soap instead of deodorant bath soap. It looks pretty, too.

Supply the bathroom with extra toilet paper, either under the sink or on an obvious shelf. It's also nice to put out tissues and hand cream. I make sure there is aspirin and a box of tampons easily accessible under the vanity in my guest bathroom. If your bathroom has poor ventilation, put unscented bathroom deodorizer on the countertop.

If your toilet runs or sometimes overflows or your faucet drips or otherwise misbehaves, either leave clearly written instructions for your guests on how to handle the situation or, better yet, get the problem fixed *before* the party.

I suggest checking the bathroom once or twice during the party to fold hand towels or provide more toilet paper. This is especially important if you are entertaining a crowd.

〜 **CLEANING THE REST OF THE HOUSE:** Drag out the vacuum cleaner and attack the rugs and hardwood floors throughout the house. It's better to vacuum before dusting, as the powerful machine stirs up dust, which you can later wipe away. Don't forget the stairs, the floor of the coat closet, and underneath and behind the furniture.

Dust windowsills, venetian-style blinds, and the tops of books and picture frames. Look up to locate dust webs in high corners and around light fixtures. If you are into furniture polish, polish away. Avoid heavily perfumed polishes and never, never set out scented air fresheners. Your house will not smell like a field of freshly mown hay or a Northwestern pine forest. It will smell like you are trying to hide a bad odor. If there is a litter box for your cat, replace the litter and move the box to a room where no guest is expected to wander. And be sure to show Felix where his box is temporarily residing.

Discard the piles of magazines in back hall. Put the squash rackets, umbrellas, and galoshes cluttering the entryway in a back closet or under your bed. Is there a ledge or small table in the entryway that might hold a vase of fresh flowers? What a nice way to greet your guests.

Shake out the welcome mat and sweep the entire porch. Shovel the walk if there's snow on it, and sand or salt it to prevent slips and spills. Store bicycles, rollerblades, skateboards, and trash cans in the garage or backyard. Take some glass cleanser to the soot and spots on the storm door and remove the dead moths from inside the porch ceiling fixture. Be sure all outdoor lights work, and that your house number is clearly visible from the street.

⌐ **MAKING ROOM FOR COATS, UMBRELLAS, ETC.:** If you are having a really big bash and decide to store guests' coats in a bedroom, make sure the bed is made and the room straightened up. If you have children, don't decide to use one of their rooms unless the tyke won't be going to bed before the last guest leaves. If you have room for it, a rented coatrack in the back hall or utility room is great. If it's raining outside, it's far better to hang coats up instead of piling them on a bed. Designate a place for boots, too. For large parties, shallow, plastic garden trays are perfect.

If you are having a small party, you may have room for coats in the front hall coat closet. Make sure it is straightened up—you don't want tennis balls bouncing off your head as you open the door to hang up someone's coat. Put extra coat hangers in the closet; heavy wood or plastic ones are best. If need be, you can double-hang (dry, not rain-drenched) coats on them. Even if you plan a summer party, think about coats. It may rain and your guests will arrive wearing raincoats and carrying umbrellas that need to go somewhere.

⌐ **REARRANGING FURNITURE TO ACCOMMODATE GUESTS:** If you are inviting a few people to dinner, you probably won't have to move furniture to make the party comfortable. But whether you are expecting two or twenty guests, walk the path that your guests will take. Is there an electric cord you are conditioned to step over that might trip an unsuspecting guest? Have you *almost* slipped on that tiny rug in the front hall so many times you suspect it might be lethal? How about the pile of telephone books in the corner—are they an accident waiting to happen? If you have priceless pre-Columbian relics perched on end tables, you had better opt for only a few people and make sure they leave the kids at home. Or, put the valuable pieces away for the evening, just as you move the electric cord, roll up the rug, and cart the telephone books to the recyling station or the basement.

For a buffet or open house, check that you have enough spots throughout the living rooms (the living room, den, family room, etc.) where guests can sit as they eat. Several well-placed folding chairs, ottomans, and even large floor cushions do the trick. To ease traffic flow, consider pushing the couch against the wall, moving the coffee table, and carrying the rubber tree plant upstairs. If you move the dining table against a wall and it generally sits in the middle of the room with a chandelier suspended over it, raise the chandelier so that guests won't bonk their heads on their way to dinner.

↩ **LIGHTING AND CANDLES:** For daytime parties, the best light is natural light flooding in through clean windows. If the day is dreary, turn on a few table or floor lamps. At night, the light should be bright enough to see but not harsh or glaring—your guests might tolerate that sort of light all day long in office buildings but in the evening and at a party the light should be soft, flattering, and cozy. Turn off overhead lights and turn on table and floor lamps. Turn the dimmer switch to medium instead of high. And before the party, be sure to check that none of the bulbs are burned out. Even check lamps you may not plan to turn on; you never know when a guest will lean over to switch it on. Make sure all the little bulbs in the dining room chandelier work too—one dead bulb out of eight may not bother your family on a day-to-day basis, but it looks slipshod at a party.

Consider supplementing the lighting with candles strategically and safely positioned on the mantel, side tables, and windowsills. I have a friend who arranges votive candles (the sturdy white candles in stubby glass containers) on a flat plate and puts them in the middle of the coffee table. When selecting candles, buy fragrance-free ones—you don't want your house smelling like Ye Olde Handicrafts Shoppe—and, if using traditional tapers, make sure they are dripless. This prevents a mess to clean up the next day.

Candles are lovely in the dining room and if you haven't room for them on the table, put them on a sideboard or side table. I think nothing is as romantic as a room lit completely by candlelight. Don't worry about having all the candles and candlesticks match. In this case, mix and match is definitely in vogue.

↩ **PARKING:** If you live in an urban area or in any large, busy city where parking is known to be difficult, how your guests deal with it is not your responsibility. But if you live anywhere else, you should think about parking when planning a party.

If your apartment complex has assigned parking spaces for residents and very few for guests, make arrangements with the management or your neighbors to accommodate your guests. You might have to ask your teenage son to operate a shuttle service between your front door and a nearby parking lot—in which case alert your guests to this convenience. Some small cities require street parking permits and you will have to ascertain how to get guest parking passes for the evening in question. When you're planning to have a crowd, it's usually a good idea to notify the local police department of the temporary increase in traffic you will be generating. Some towns require that you hire an off-duty cop to direct traffic and parking, others make the service available. It doesn't cost much and often makes your guests feel at ease to see a blue uniform taking charge.

You may live on a quiet residential street where parking is no problem. If so, warn your guests about any hidden driveways or handicap access routes in the neighborhood. Not only will they appreciate this, but it is a good way to remind them subtly to be considerate of your neighbors when they park. Finally, if you are expecting a handicapped guest, make sure to explain the best place to park—and then make sure no one else parks there. One way to do this is to put a sawhorse or picnic table bench in the spot with a big "reserved parking" sign taped to it.

NEIGHBORS: When you're planning a big party that may result in loud music, boisterous conversation, and constant comings and goings of people and automobiles, it's courteous to let your neighbors know about the party ahead of time. If you like your neighbors, invite them and your problems will be solved—but if you don't, forewarned is forearmed. Running interference ahead of time is preferable to getting an angry phone call during the party. Tone down the music about the time that most people go to bed (ten or eleven on a weeknight, no more than an hour or so later on a weekend) and remind your guests to keep their voices down when they leave. This is especially important if you live in an apartment or a two-family house.

Final Touches

Once the house is clean and you have taken care of parking arrangements, shoveling the front walk, and replacing burned out light bulbs, it's time to have some fun. Setting the table, arranging flowers, and planning the music all fall in this category. Carrying out these necessary duties is guaranteed to put you in a festive and happy mood.

FLOWERS: Flowers can transform the atmosphere of your home be it a studio apartment or a castle by the sea. They have nothing to do with the mundane mechanics of party giving (where to hand coats, when to take the roast from the oven) and everything to do with grace, beauty, and welcome. Set a simple bouquet in a vase in the living room and arrange a centerpiece for the dining table. For everything but the most formal affairs, I prefer loose cut flowers to an arrangement from the florist. If you decide to buy an arrangement—and it might be easier for you in the long run—ask the florist for something simple. "Less" tends to be in better taste in the home.

If you are lucky enough with the time of year and your access to a cutting garden or field of wildflowers, pick your own and set them around the house. Be careful not to pick any that may cause an allergic reaction, such as lilacs, goldenrod, Queen Anne's lace, and poison sumac. Otherwise, I find that scouting out the flower departments of the supermarket is a great way to find fantastic buys. I have bought long-stem roses, daffodils, irises, and daisies for a fraction of the price charged by the florist.

When you bring flowers home, cut the stems under running water (especially important with roses) and place them immediately in water. This can be a large bucket you then store on the porch until you are ready to arrange the flowers in individual vases. It's best to keep the flowers cool until shortly before the party—but make sure that if they are set outside on the back porch on a warm fall afternoon you bring them inside before it rapidly turns into a freezing fall evening. Otherwise, you will have a bucket full of dead flowers. Mud rooms, garages, and basements usually are good choices for cool storage.

If you want to decorate a cake or platter with fresh flowers, wait until the last moment to put them in place and make sure they are edible. Obviously, you don't expect your guests to eat the blooms, but a petal or two might get speared with the cake and if the flower is poisonous, this could be real trouble. Some plants that are highly toxic and should be avoided at all costs are poinsettia, lily of the valley, hemlock, holly, and yew (particularly the berries). If in doubt, forget the flowers or call local poison control for exact information.

MUSIC: Unless a concert or recital is the purpose of your gathering, music should be a pleasant sound in the background. You don't have to dish up Muzak or turn the radio dial to the "easy listening" station. Instead, select the kind of music you and your friends like. Opera, rock, country, country and western, and jazz all provide great background entertainment if the volume is right. It should be loud enough to be heard (it's annoying for your guests if the music is so low that they think they hear music coming from somewhere) but not so loud as to drown out conversation. If anyone seems to be feel the need to raise his or her voice to compete with the music, turn it down—or off.

I always give some thought to pairing the music with the mood of the party and the food. I've had funky Neapolitan dinners— checked tablecloth, Chianti in straw-covered bottles, and spaghetti with red sauce—with Dean Martin softly crooning "That's Amore" in the background. The music cemented the mood nicely, thank you very much. You may find something more subtle to go with your party—or maybe not. Remember, you're in this to have fun!

SETTING THE TABLE: I don't know who made up the rules about forks and napkins on the left and spoons and knives on the right, but those are the rules. If you need to be creative, buy a red lace tablecloth, but don't play fast and loose with these rules. You will confuse your guests.

You can set the table a day before the party, if you have a quiet household. If there's a possibility that Rover will wag a glass off the table or Felix will leave paw prints on the linens, wait until the morning or afternoon of the event. Remember back in Chapter 2 when I exhorted you to iron the tablecloth before smoothing it over the table? I stand by that advice. If you are not using a tablecloth, choose place mats and napkins, making sure they are clean and that the napkins are neatly folded (you don't have to be fancy when it comes to folding them). Position the cutlery in the correct sequence and set a plate between the forks and the knives. You might decide to serve the dinner from the kitchen, in which case leave the plates off the table for the time being.

The correct order for the cutlery is to line up it with the pieces your guests will use first on the outside. This means dinner forks are to the left of dessert forks; soup spoons are to the right of teaspoons—and knives always (cutting edges turned toward the plate) to the left of the spoons. If you are serving salad before the main course, place salad forks to the left of the dinner forks. if you are serving it between dinner and dessert, position the salad forks to the right of the dinner forks. This last instruction is moot if you are going to use the same forks for salad and dessert. Put the salad fork to the right of the dinner fork, and forget about a dessert fork. You will have to wash the salad forks before dessert anyway. If you are using butter knives, it's acceptable to lay them on the butter plates or to set them above the dinner plate, centered between the forks and spoons.

Put the water and wineglasses above the spoons, to the right of the plate. Water glasses should sit to the left of the wineglasses. If you are setting the table ahead of time, turn the glasses upside down to keep dust out, but remember to turn them upright before the guests arrive.

Arrange trivets and hot pads in strategic places on the table and lay serving implements nearby. Put out spoons for sauces, jams, or chutneys. Set the candlesticks on the table if you are using them, being sure to replace any burned-down candles with fresh tapers. It's tacky, except with the best of friends and at the most casual gathering, to use burned candles. Always light fresh, uncharred wicks.

↪ **CENTERPIECES**: My grandmother had a bowl of waxed fruit in the center of the table at every meal. No one ever noticed it and it became the repository for bits and pieces of food I couldn't finish—not the ideal role for a centerpiece. A centerpiece is meant to enhance the beauty of your table, not simply take up empty space.

Understatement is the key here and you don't have be a decorator to make it look good. I have pretty traditional taste when it comes to the centerpiece: candles and flowers, or candles and flowers. The flowers should be real, not plastic, although silk ones are acceptable. They should have very little scent so that they don't war with the food, and should be arranged so that they are low enough for your guests to see and talk across.

Simple is the operative word here. No need for your guests to crane their necks around an arrangement more appropriate for a royal wedding or funeral. Put the flowers in the center of the table with the candles on each side, but not so close as to endanger the flowers. Light the candles just before sitting down. I suggest keeping the matches next to your plate so that you don't run around looking for them at the last minute.

For holidays, I put a large china or wooden bowl heaped with fresh fruit and nuts in the shell in the middle of the table and arrange some pine boughs around it. The whole thing is punctuated with red, dripless candles firmly stuck into appropriate-sized candlesticks. And I make sure the candles have no scent.

For large, fancy buffets, go to town on the centerpiece if you want. Unless you are skilled at flower arranging, I suggest talking with the local florist. Explain the size of your table (a sketch helps) and the amount of room you will allow the centerpiece. Ask for something seasonal (it's more affordable) that won't look out of place or ostentatious. An alternative is to buy four to six small African violets or other pretty flowering plants and, after removing the foil, place the pots in one basket or on a large platter. If the pots are plastic, I highly recommend a basket or deep dish to hide them.

SEATING PLANS, PLACE CARDS, AND NAME TAGS: Control freak that I admittedly am, you might be surprised to hear that I rarely use seating plans. The end of the table closest to the kitchen is my place and my husband, David, sits at the opposite end. I tell guests to seat themselves and folks seem to sort themselves out, hardly ever sitting next to the people with whom they have arrived. They usually alternate male, female, too.

I use seating plans when I have invited someone I particularly want to sit next to. This may be when a guest is hard of hearing and I want to make sure I can relay the conversation, or when someone is especially quiet and I want to draw him (or her) into the conversation by placing him next to me and another equally garrulous person. When we have a large group at the table, David and I switch places just before dessert so that we have the opportunity to talk with guests we weren't seated near in the first place.

Seating plans can be instituted in a few ways. You can make up a little chart and refer to it, discreetly, as you direct guests to their places. "Kate, please sit on my left. John, you go next to Kate," and so on. Or, you can use place cards on which you write the guests' first names, then put them at specific places as you wish the seating to be. The guests mill around the table (you can help them) until they find their seats. The traditional way to arrange seating is to alternate men and women—but don't worry if you have an uneven number of one sex. This is the nineties and it's definitely passé to scrounge around among your acquaintances and distant relatives to find "an extra" man or woman. Just invite whom you want and let the chips (sexes) fall where they may. Finally, the host and hostess sit at the opposite ends of the table and do not sit down until everyone else is seated.

Name tags have their place at business functions when people do not know each other by name. The only time I can imagine they would have a place in a social setting would be at large family reunion where there is a legitimate reason for people to display this information. In that circumstance, I would go so far as to include the branch of the family and the hometown on the name tag.

Party Etiquette

In this section I will guide you through a party in full swing. Regardless of my advice and your bravado, a party assumes a life of its own and you may not be able to control every incident. It goes without saying no one expects unpleasant behavior during a party, and by controlling your guest list you can pretty much avoid this. But there are far more subtle ways your party may not turn out precisely as you imagined. This is neither good nor bad. It just is. For example, you may have imagined that your friend the biology professor and your old buddy the veterinarian would interact in such a way that the entire party would enter into a heady discussion of bioengineering, but instead they spent the evening talking golf scores. Don't be disappointed; are they having a good time? Great!

⌐ **ARRIVALS:** Every corner of the world has its own idea of what "on time" means. In the United States, you are generally expected to arrive at a party fifteen to twenty minutes later than the designated time. In some rural areas and at Grandma's, eight o'clock means eight o'clock unless a blizzard holds up the sleigh or four-wheel drive. In the fashionable sections of large cities, where an invitation to dinner is an invitation to make an entrance, there is the not-so-quaint custom of arriving "fashionably late"—an oxymoron if I ever heard one. But every region of the world shares one common rule about arrivals: Don't show up early. The hostess then has every right to leave you sitting in the living room being entertained by her two-year-old while she finishes dressing.

As the hostess you should be dressed and ready to rock and roll a good twenty minutes before the guests are expected. You should be well organized, with glasses set out, the cheese coming to room temperature, and the olives or nuts in bowls in the living room so that you don't have to disappear for any length of time soon after your company gets there. Remember, it is not necessary to assault your guests with food the minute they walk though the door.

If, as a guest, you will be more than twenty or thirty minutes late, call the host or hostess to explain why. "The baby-sitter was late" is an acceptable excuse; "Martha couldn't find her other pearl earring" or "Joe was late getting home from the tennis court" is not.

⌐ **HOSTESS GIFTS:** While it's certainly not obligatory, it's a lovely and thoughtful gesture to bring a small gift when you are invited to someone's house. A small plant, a bottle of wine, a jar of jam, or some chocolate are all nice gifts. Homemade things are especially nice if they do not have to be eaten immediately. In other words, unless you have double-checked first with the hostess, don't bring food or even a bottle of wine that you expect to be consumed that evening. As the hostess, you should accept the gift at the door with a gracious thank-you and—except for flowers, which you should soon after bring out in a vase—put it away to open later after everyone has gone home. This avoids embarrassing other guests who might not have brought a gift.

⤷ **CONVERSATION:** Introductions are the responsibility of the host or hostess; though when the party is large, it is also the responsibility of the guests to introduce themselves to each other as well. It is also up to the host and hostess to initiate conversation. Most often you do this when you first make introductions: "Jane, I'd like you to meet Wendy. Wendy is a silversmith. I know you'd love the earrings Wendy makes." At this point, you can leave Jane and Wendy discussing silver jewelry while you move on to talk to other guests.

Beyond introductions and initiating conversations, it is up to you to keep the conversation going if it lags during the evening. Never get so engrossed in a conversation at one end of the room that you neglect to notice that things are very quiet at the other end. When you do notice this, move to the quiet zone and inject some chatter. The same goes when you're seated at the table; address a question to someone at the quiet other end. Make it a question that will grab your other guests' interest: "John, I understand you just returned from a manned space flight. How was the food on Venus?" is a far better choice than "John, how are those light treatments working for your psoriasis?" Obviously, you have to do a little homework to keep the conversation lively. Finally, whispered conversations spoken behind one's hand to the person next to you at dinner are strictly verboten. If you notice a clandestine chat at the table, don't behave like a schoolmarm with stern warnings. Instead, jolt one (or both) of the culprits back to the mainstream by directing a friendly, upbeat question at him or her that can't be ignored.

⤷ **THE TELEPHONE:** I often wish I could unplug the telephone during a party, but because in the real world there are problems with baby-sitters, teenage children whose rides fail to materialize, business crises, and the like, this is not possible. If you get a call during the party, deal with it swiftly by explaining that you will have to return the call the next day. If it's an emergency, take the call in private so that you can make decisions and answer questions without involving your guests in your problems. If a guest gets a phone call during the evening, offer an extension in a private place for him to deal with the caller. Don't hand him the portable phone as he stands surrounded by half a dozen people, or stretch the kitchen wall phone with the extra-long cord to the table.

I have yet to face the situation of guests who bring cellular telephones to my house. If this was absolutely necessary, I trust the person would have the good manners to explain to me that she was expecting some world-stopping communication on this objectionable gadget and when the call came, to have the decency to excuse herself from the table. If not, I expect the proper protocol for me, as the hostess, would be to suggest to the guest with the cellular phone that she would no doubt find it more private to take the call in another room.

↩ **ANIMALS:** I am not talking about "party animals" but the kind with four paws and warm noses. I love dogs. I have two of them and even though they are well behaved, I make sure that the people I invite to my house are not allergic to or terrified of dogs. The same holds true for cats. If either is the case, a good hostess will put Rover or Felix in another room—and one far enough away from the party so that no one will hear his pitiful whining. If your pets shed and you notice a guest starts sneezing, remove the animal immediately. (An allergic guest with half a brain should, of course, let you know ahead of time if he or she is allergic—and you, as host, can look forward to a serious vacuuming job. You might also offer to entertain the seriously allergic person in a restaurant.) Keep Junior's pet rabbit or guinea pig in its cage, and all reptiles far away from the party.

If your dogs are full of enthusiastic energy whenever the doorbell rings, restrain them. From the guest's point of view, nothing is less inviting than watching Rover drool on his new blue suit. Dogs should be taught not to beg for food, and kept out from underfoot during the party. You may be used to maneuvering around a two-hundred-pound Saint Bernard, but your guest, who is balancing a full plate of food and glass of wine, is not.

Actively discourage dogs from circling the table while you are eating, and try not to reenact King Arthur's court by throwing a haunch of venison or even a gnawed lamb chop to the salivating dog next to your chair.

⌒⊃ **STAINS, SPILLS, AND SMASHED CHINA:** Accidents happen. That's a fact of life. When I was about ten years old my parents took me to dinner at some friends' house who had no children of their own. The house was filled with original art and fragile furniture positioned as an obstacle course on rare Oriental rugs. I sat on the edge of a dark green velvet sofa, feet dangling, arms crossed tightly over my chest, and my hands anchored securely into my armpits lest I inadvertently fling one of them out and take down a Ming vase. Whatever possessed our hostess to serve grape juice to me in the same kind of delicate goblet she used for my parents' wine, I'll never know. What I do know is that I will never forget the look of horror on her face when in one careless moment I sent the glass flying, giving her wallpaper a hideous purple stain. It's been almost forty years and I still cringe when I think about it.

Your job as a host or hostess is to minimize the chances that something equally devastating—or even slightly upsetting—happens to one of your guests. Naturally, I strongly advise against serving grape juice to children. Also, don't serve drinks in glasses that tip easily or food on plates that are too small. Don't overcrowd the table or cram so many people into one space that elbow room is scarcer than an empty seat on the subway at rush hour. Remove obstacles such as stacks of books or a chair that blocks a doorway or stairway. Put away fragile knickknacks and precious artwork, especially if children are on the guest list. Serve food that can be cleaned up easily in case of spills.

If someone does spill, calmly wipe it up with the least amount of fuss possible. If overly helpful guests rally round tut-tutting and offering words of wisdom on housecleaning, gently persuade them that you are capable of taking care of the mishap. Their concern will only draw attention to it and embarrass your guest further. If a glass or piece of china crashes to the floor, stay calm (even if the china was a gift from Great-grandmother Letty on the occasion of your birth), collect the broom and dustpan, and remove the broken pieces quickly. Be sure to wipe up any food or liquid, too, and to warn nearby guests to tread carefully until all is cleared away.

If someone spills something at the table, wipe it up and place a clean napkin over the remaining stain. It's better if the stain is hidden instead of being a constant reminder of the accident. If red wine or another stain-making food is spilled on a rug or tablecloth, use selt-zer to dampen the area and then sprinkle it with a generous layer of salt. Let the salt stay in place for several hours before vacuuming or brushing it away. Treat the stain with rug cleaner or spot remover.

📖 **OFFERS TO HELP CLEAR THE TABLE:** One of my pet peeves is people who insist on helping. It's okay, of course, if the meal is very informal (a potluck or barbecue) or a family meal where everyone pitches in because it's tradition, but at the dinner party, the only people who should clear the table are the host and hostess, or someone you may have hired to help out in the kitchen. Nothing is more disruptive than two or three guests leaping up from the table to stack dishes and toddle off to the kitchen with them. Nip this behavior in the bud. It only makes the other guests feel awkward and is really unnecessary. As soon as someone makes a grab for the dishes, firmly but politely say that you prefer that he or she sits at the table. "I have it under control, but thanks for offering" is all you need to say. If the person insists, insist right back that "it's really easier for one person to take care of this job."

Clear away the dishes from each course only after everyone is finished eating. If someone is lagging behind, it's acceptable to ask if he or she would like a few more minutes to finish. This gives the person a chance either to eat what is left or indicate that he or she has had enough. Clear the dishes from the left—if you care that much about etiquette. Never, never scrape food from one plate to another at the table and stack the plates. Nothing is more unappe-tizing.

If you served a first course such as soup and the bowl was de-livered on a plate, then the bowl and plate are removed together, along with the spoon. Between dinner and dessert, remove all serv-ing dishes, the salt and pepper shakers, the bread basket, and the butter dish, as well as any empty wineglasses and bottles. However, if there is wine left in the bottles, offer it to your guests so that they can enjoy it while you organize coffee and dessert. Finally, do a quick check to make sure everyone has the right number of forks and spoons left and quietly replace them if need be.

📖 **COFFEE AND TEA:** If you heeded my advice in *The Kitchen Survival Guide*, you have relegated the jar of instant coffee to the baking shelf and use it only to make mocha mousse and similar desserts. Regardless of what the TV ads say, instant coffee insults a good meal and now that you're a grown-up it's time to make grown-up coffee.

The most foolproof way to accomplish this is to use an electric drip coffeemaker. With one of these, you measure the water in a glass carafe, pour it into the reservoir through the top of the machine, measure ground coffee into a filter-lined basket, and then set the basket on top of the carafe so that the water can drip through it. The carafe sits on a heating base so that the coffee stays hot. You can set this up a good hour before your guests arrive and then switch it on about fifteen minutes before you want to serve the coffee. You can also measure out the ground coffee the day before and store it in the freezer in a plastic bag. If you think you will make more than one pot in an evening, measure out several bags. Take care to label the bags "caffeinated" and "decaffeinated"—your caffeine-sensitive friends will not thank you for carelessness! If you are serving a crowd, borrow or rent a thirty- or sixty-cup percolator. The towering apparatus requires about twenty minutes to perk but the coffee and water can be measured in advance. And if you use freshly ground beans, the coffee tastes pretty good. Smaller percolators, which by design force the water through the grinds over and over, produce bitter-tasting coffee, I think. Plunger-style coffeepots make good coffee but are a little bothersome to use.

For success with any kind of coffeemaker, please use coffee beans freshly ground to the right texture for the kind of machine you own (electric drip coffeemakers call for "auto-drip" or simply "drip"; percolators call for "percolator grind"). If you don't own a coffee grinder, I suggest buying one. Or you can have the coffee beans ground at the store where you purchase them—just do so the day of the party.

Begin with a clean coffeemaker. This means washing the removable parts in soapy water and rinsing them well. It's a good idea to run some coffeepot cleaner (sold in supermarkets) or a weak solution of vinegar and water (one to eight parts) through the machine every month or so. For the coffee, use cold tap water or bottled water if your city water doesn't taste good, the right-size coffee filter for the basket, and a bona fide coffee measure, sold in supermarkets, coffee emporiums, and kitchenware shops. Use one measuring spoon for every eight-ounce cup of coffee. If you like strong coffee (as I do), use a heaping spoonful for each cup and then toss in an extra one "for the pot." Never let the coffee boil and never reheat cold coffee (yuck!). If it sits too long in the coffeepot, it will begin to taste bitter and burned.

Because so many people prefer decaffeinated coffee at the end of the meal, be prepared to offer it. Water-processed, freshly ground decaf beans taste great—almost like the real thing. Many hosts serve only decaffeinated coffee and thus avoid the hassle of making two separate pots. If you decide to make two pots, brew the caffeinated coffee first and pour it into a heat-proof pitcher (not plastic). Set the pitcher in a pan of water so that the water comes two or three inches up the sides of the pitcher. Put the pan on the stove and turn the burner to low simmer. This will keep the coffee piping hot while you brew the decaf.

When you bring the coffee to the table, remember to set out cream and sugar too. While very few people expect heavy cream in the pitcher, most prefer whole milk or half-and-half. Don't serve blue (skim) milk to company. If the cream smells "off," pour a little into a cup and sniff it. Often it's the caked and partially dried cream or milk near the pouring spout that smells sour. And, since someone will no doubt request it, put out the sugar substitute along with the sugar.

For ice coffee, double the amount of ground coffee (sixteen spoonfuls for eight cups of coffee), let the freshly brewed coffee cool, and then add ice. If you are really clever and organized, pour that morning's leftover coffee into ice cube trays and use that ice with the ice coffee.

When you walk into a specialty coffee shop or gourmet store that sells a wide variety of beans, you may be enticed by the array of flavored coffees. My personal preference is for straight coffee that tastes like coffee—not like almonds or vanilla. Therefore, unless you know the crowd very well, I advise sticking to the real thing; save the snickerdoodle coffee (swear to God, I saw it in the local deli) for your best and most forgiving friends.

When brewing tea, give the process the respect it deserves— don't swish a generic tea bag around in a mug of boiling water and have done with it. Instead, begin with loose tea or quality tea bags. Those wrapped in foil or plastic are apt to be fresher than the sort stacked cheek by jowl in a thin cardboard box. When shopping for tea, buy some decaffeinated and herbal teas too.

Begin the tea-making process by boiling fresh cold water. When it boils, rinse the cup with the boiling water to heat it up, spill out the water, place the tea bag in the hot cup, and pour boiling water over it. Leave it in the cup for about sixty seconds if a guest requests weak tea and for two to three minutes if the person likes tea strong. Fill the cup only about two-thirds full if your guest likes milk, and be sure to offer whole milk. Half-and-half and cream are not traditionally served with tea. If lemon is requested, put the slice or wedge on the saucer or a separate plate. Don't suggest both milk and lemon—the acid will curdle the milk.

When more than one or two people request tea, make a pot. Rinse the pot with the boiling water to heat it up and then put one tea bag for every two eight-ounce cups into the pot and pour boiling water over them. If using loose tea, put one teaspoon for every cup into the pot and add an extra one "for the pot." Cover the pot and let the tea steep for three to five minutes. Stir it once during steeping. Remove the tangle of tea bags before pouring the tea. If you have used loose tea, remember to strain the tea as you pour it into the cups. You may choose to use a tea ball if you prefer loose tea. This gadget holds the tea inside a perforated stainless steel ball that you can remove before pouring the tea.

AFTER-DINNER DRINKS: Serving cordials or brandy is a lovely way to end an evening. After-dinner drinks usually follow coffee and may be served at the table or back in the living room or den. It's customary to offer cordials such as Grand Marnier, amaretto, cognac, cream and flavored liqueurs, and perhaps sambuca with a coffee bean in the glass. These are potent drinks and therefore are poured into small cordial glasses in one- and two-ounce amounts. If you don't have cordial glasses, use small wineglasses. Brandy and cognac are traditionally served in bowl-shaped brandy snifters.

EARLY AND LATE DEPARTURES: Because many guests have lemminglike qualities, when one has to leave long before you expect everyone else to, it's advisable to keep the departure as low-key as possible. There should be gracious but quick good-byes as the guest(s) is escorted to the door by the host or hostess. Both do not have to go to the door; one can stay behind to keep the party going. The trick is to disrupt the mood of the evening as little as possible. If a guest knows ahead of time that he or she has to leave early, then he or she has the obligation of letting the host know so that the exit can be orchestrated gracefully. Otherwise, everyone else may suppose the guest in question is having a lousy time.

Exceptions, such as sudden illness or a baby-sitter emergency, cannot be avoided. In these cases, the guest should make his or her quiet apologies to the host or hostess, say goodnight to the remaining guests, and leave without fanfare. Other guests may be paying a small fortune for a sitter to care for the triplets while they finally get a night out and the last thing they need is to hear the grisly details about the kitchen catching on fire when MaryJane attempted to teach your kids how to roast marshmallows on the stove.

There is an appropriate time for company to depart and in many cases they will know when it is. If the clock is saying eleven and you are thinking of tomorrow's dawn-patrol carpool to the hockey rink but your guests show no signs of leaving, lean back in your chair and enjoy the moment—for a moment. It's a compliment and means the party is a success. But after a few minutes of basking in this rosy glow of accomplishment, you may bring the evening to a close in one of several ways.

Clap your hands together while you try unsuccessfully to stifle a small but definite yawn. Give a little stretch (arms up so that everyone notices) and start to get up, saying, "Wow, this has been a terrific evening." If your guests stare at you blankly, add something like "I hate to break up the party but I have a sunrise meeting with the Joint Chiefs of Staff." As you rise, your guests will too, and you can immediately start herding them to the door. We once had a guest who absolutely did not get it. Finally, after taking the dogs for their nightly constitutional, my husband and I went to bed, telling him to lock up on his way out. He was gone the next morning.

⌐ **THANK-YOU NOTES:** Even before they learned to hit a baseball, my kids learned to write thank-you notes. Both my husband and I and our sons write notes every time we receive a gift or are entertained. Informal events get a phone call. If a guest is thoughtful enough to bring me a hostess gift, a note goes out the next day.

Now that you are a host or hostess, think about how hard you worked to pull off the party and how much it mattered to you that everyone had a wonderful time. Think how great you will feel if you receive a note or telephone call saying just how much fun the evening was and how delicious the food was. And the next time someone entertains you, don't forget to write the note or make the call.

CHAPTER FOUR

General Advice: Or Everything You Need to Know About Entertaining That I Haven't Already Told You

This is the chapter to turn to for general, overall advice—the sort you might solicit from your mother or aunt if she were around. I will tell you how to stock a bar, when to hire a caterer, and once you have, how to instruct the caterer to meet your needs. I will explain some basic cooking skills and help you deal with possible disasters. I'll also address entertaining children—and how to handle unexpected guests. Finally, I will advise you on "other" types of entertaining, such as overnight and weekend parties and condolence calls.

Food and Drink

In the next chapter I get into the nitty-gritty of menu planning, shopping lists, and timetables. Here, I examine more general topics such as serving sizes, taking advantage of take-out food, and stocking your bar.

SERVING SIZES: If you were raised in a family where Mom piled food on your plate and reminded you of the starving children in some third world country (while you silently wished she would just pack up those peas and scalloped potatoes and send them there!), you will have to regroup before you start feeding your guests. It is not your job to overload their plates and then glare at them accusingly when they don't eat every morsel. On the other hand, don't deprive them. You may think it trendy to fan a few snow peas beside the tiny fillet of poached chicken and call it a meal, but your guests will not kick up their heels with delight if they need a magnifying glass to locate their dinner.

Prepare eight ounces of *uncooked* protein (meat, fish, or poultry) per person, not counting the weight of the bones, or the equivalent amount of a vegetarian entrée. Figure on one cup of complex carbohydrates (what used to be called starch), a half to two thirds of a cup of vegetables, and a cup of salad for each person. If you are serving family style, with platters passed around the table, or buffet style, cook for three to four "invisible" guests, using the same per-person amounts. When they serve themselves, folks tend to eat more. For children, estimate about two thirds of the above amounts; for teenagers and marathon runners, double them.

APPETIZERS AND FINGER FOODS: The terms *appetizers* and *hors d'oeuvres* are used interchangeably in our American argot and so I will not quibble about the subtle differences. Both are served before the meal and are meant to whet the palate, pick up the appetite, and make guests eager for the good food to come.

These starters can be served in the living room or den before the meal, or if the party is very informal, in the kitchen. If you are having a buffet or open house, appetizers may fall into the category of passed foods or may be set on the table with the main course, as you make no distinction between courses (except dessert) at this sort of meal.

When I have prepared a full dinner, I keep the appetizers light— I don't want my guests to fill up before they come to the table. I set out a bowl of olives (and a saucer for the pits) and perhaps some nuts for munching. I may also serve a platter of vegetables with a yogurt dip. If I am having the kind of party where the whole meal is made up of appetizers, I serve breaded, creamy, and rich cheese tidbits. (By the way, these more substantial appetizers are often more economical than lighter fare that may involve seafood and meat, so if you are on a budget, consider breaded and stuffed goodies.)

Finger foods are often translated in our minds to be appetizers. But I think they fall into three categories with only the first being appetizers. This includes canapés—elegant small creations that are served on tiny slices of bread or skewered with toothpicks—and chips and dips, a far less elegant variation on the finger food theme.

The second category of finger foods includes informal fare such as pizza, hamburgers, sandwiches, hot dogs, fried chicken, ribs, lobster, shrimp, and so on. The third includes foods from other countries, such as sushi, Indian food eaten with flat bread called poori or nan, and Moroccan food such as b'stilla, which is a chicken and sweet almond pie made with rice and encased in a flaky dough. You make the call about this last category—you may decide to put out forks or chopsticks since many Americans are not completely comfortable eating main course dishes with their fingers.

When serving appetizers before a meal or main course finger foods, be sure to have plenty of napkins and assume that each guest will need several. Use cocktail-size napkins for canapés and oversized paper or cloth for other food. After the meal is consumed, it's a nice touch to pass around warm, moist washcloths—an updated version of old-fashioned finger bowls. The easiest way to prepare the washcloths is to do what the airlines do: Fold each washcloth in half and then roll it into a compact cylinder. Lay the cylinders in a single layer on a microwave-safe plate or tray. Sprinkle them generously with water and then microwave them on high for two minutes, turning the plate if necessary to heat them all.

One final word of advice: If you are planning to serve finger foods other than the expected canapés or chips and dip, let your guests know so that they can dress appropriately. You don't want anyone arriving in a silk dress for a clambake.

〰️ **TAKE-OUT FOOD:** First, let me differentiate between fast food and take-out food. Fast food is McDonald's and pizza from a chain. It's anything that comes in a paper bag, cardboard box, or Styrofoam container and gets passed to you through a window by a fifteen-year-old kid wearing earphones and a headset. Fast food leaves your car smelling like a Fry-O-Lator and a trail of flotsam and jetsam of straw wrappers and little plastic toys stuck between the seats.

Take-out food is from a real restaurant: Chinese, Indian, Korean, Japanese, Thai, Italian, Greek, etc. Pizza from Pizza Hut is fast food; pizza from the pizzeria with a wood-burning oven on the corner is takeout. If you don't get the subtlety, don't worry about it. Just remember that fast food is the stuff you and your kids eat when you can't cope with anything resembling cooking, but takeout is acceptable for company.

Take-out food can also come from the local gourmet shop in the form of salads, pasta sauces, soups, and freshly baked breads. All take-out food is a boon for last-minute or weeknight entertaining. For instance, serve it when you invite your neighbors over, saying, "Joan and I were wondering if you and Bill wanted to come over and see our wedding slides and have Chinese food?" Make it clear that you haven't just completed an intensive course at Sun Yee Culinary School—the food will be from a local Chinese restaurant. It's fine to pick up some tasty soup or loaf of bread on your way home from the office if you are running late. Or buy a container of *pad thai* (Thai noodles) to go with grilled shrimp, or fried rice or wonton soup to serve with your own stir-fry or Mongolian hot pot.

It's essential that you transfer the food from the container it comes in to dishes and bowls. This can be done before or after reheating, and reheating can be done on top of the stove or in the microwave. You don't serve the food in pretty bowls to hoodwink your guests into thinking you prepared it yourself. You do it because it looks nice. Judicious use of take-out food can save you time (although not money, since it's definitely less expensive to make it yourself) and can help a lot in a pinch.

STOCKING THE BAR: I am not talking about a bar similar to the one where the crew from *Cheers* hangs out, or even the built-in bars common in 1950s-style rec rooms. I am talking about your supply of hard liquor, cordials, wines, and beer. If you consume no alcoholic beverages, there is no reason to have any in the house. Offer your guests soft drinks or cider. But if you do drink or serve alcohol, you will want to have a bar. In most homes, the bar is stored in a cabinet and then brought out onto a counter or table to offer to guests.

Choose a cool, dark place for bar storage. This is especially important if you plan to store wines, but no alcoholic beverages should be exposed to sunlight for any length of time or to extremes in temperature.

Because mixed drinks are rarely offered anymore (you know, daiquiris, whiskey sours, and pink ladies), the choices for hard liquor usually are gin, scotch, rum, and vodka. Cordials generally include selections such as Grand Marnier, amaretto, and crème de cacao, and fortified wines such as vermouth and marsala. All the above can be served straight up (plain), or with water, seltzer, or tonic, or on the rocks (ice).

With the help of my good friend at the local liquor store, I compiled the following list of items for your bar. Don't run out and buy a bottle of each liquor listed here; start with a few you like and add others when you can.

HARD LIQUOR

Vodka	*Bourbon*	*Scotch*
Gin	*Whiskey*	*Tequila*
Rum		

CORDIALS AND COGNAC (USED FOR BEFORE- AND AFTER-DINNER DRINKS AND IN COOKING)

Coffee liqueur such
as Kahlúa
Orange liqueur such
as Grand Marnier
Almond-flavored liqueur
such as amaretto

Cognac
Sherry, medium, dry or cream,
depending on your taste
Sweet and dry
vermouth
Marsala

It is more economical to buy larger bottles, and everything except cream-based liquors (Bailey's Original Irish Cream, for example) has an indefinite shelflife. Cream liquors keep in a cool, dry place for about six months and refrigerated for up to eight months.

Do you suffer from oenophobia? Have you developed a fear of wine because of all the pretentious nonsense that some folks attach to the fruit of the vine? If you are interested and want to learn more about wine, that's great. There are many excellent books on the subject. But saying you have to be an expert to enjoy it is like saying you have to be Bobby Fischer to play a game of chess with your ten-year-old nephew. If all you know is white, red, and blush and don't want to know more, find yourself a good liquor store with a large selection of wines and spirits that employs a wine person who will help you with your selections. Tell this person what you are serving, how many are drinking, what your budget is (this can be from four dollars a bottle to fifty or more dollars a bottle, and if it's in that last range, please let me know what time I should be there). Any merchant who wants your repeat business will treat you respectfully without making you feel like a complete moron. Your job is to be up front and say you don't know much about wine. The wine person will ask you some questions about your preferences, and what kind of occasion you are planning. If you have given yourself enough time, ask the wine person to recommend several bottles for you to bring home and taste. You could even invite some friends over and ask their opinions. When you find the wine you like best, return to the store and buy it by the case (twelve bottles), for which you will most likely receive a discounted price.

If you have waited until the last minute and find yourself buying wine in the supermarket for that night's dinner, here are some guidelines:

White wine is served chilled, but not ice-cold. Don't make the mistake of storing wine in the freezer to hasten its chilling and then forget to remove it—frozen wine is good for nothing. Traditionally white wine is served with "lighter" dishes such as chicken, fish, veal, many pastas, and vegetarian dishes. You want to look for something "dry" (as opposed to "sweet"). Look for wines like chardonnay or Chablis.

Red wine is most often paired with "heavier" dishes such as beef, game (venison, duck), and lamb. Turkey and pork can go either way, and my preference is red.

There are several tricks for finding an appropriate wine when you don't know what you're doing and have no one to help you. First, stay away from anything imported. Go straight to the domestic wines and look for bottles with labels that describe what the wine tastes like. Don't be tempted to use your guests as guinea pigs for experiments with bottles you bought because you fell in love with the label or the name. If you want to experiment, buy a a bottle and taste it when you are alone or with someone who won't leave you, no matter what.

While it is far more economical to buy wine in large bottles, keep in mind that jug wines are appropriate only at casual and very informal affairs. I suppose you could always pour this kind of inexpensive wine into a carafe in hopes that your guests think you're serving something rare, but most likely they'll confuse your house with a cheap restaurant. And if you don't finish a jug of white wine, it needs to be refrigerated or it will go bad. Most of the big jugs don't fit in most refrigerators.

Champagne is a sparkling wine from a certain region of France that can be served as an elegant before-dinner beverage or with dessert. Occasionally champagne is used as an ingredient in champagne punch or certain sauces for food. Some very dry champagnes can be served with certain dishes as well. Many sparkling wines that do not come from the Champagne region in France are just as good and often far less expensive. Champagnes and sparkling wines range widely in taste in part because of the methods used to make them and in the amount of sugar they contain. While some people like sweet champagne or sparkling wine (Asti Spumante, for instance), I much prefer an extra dry or brut. I recommend saving the sweet (and usually far less expensive) champagnes for champagne punch or mimosas (a brunch drink made with champagne and orange juice).

Wine needs to be stored in a cool, dry place, out of direct sunlight where the temperature is constant. Wine bottles should be stored on their sides so that the cork remains wet. The exceptions are jug wines and wines with screw-off caps. My wine expert says that short of a wine rack the best way to store wine is in cardboard boxes with dividers that come from the liquor store. If you are storing bottles in the basement, make sure you don't have mice in the house. They will eat right through the metal and cork of your wine bottles. Don't store wines in the liquor cabinet for longer than six months. Longer storage demands a climate-controlled wine cellar.

Back when I was a kid (before electricity according to my progeny), in the world of beer there was Miller and there was Bud. Now you can have a nervous breakdown trying to pick between light, dark, pasteurized, home-brewed, imported, Occidental, Oriental, above the equator and below it. There is also nonalcoholic beer and diet beer. I have to confess; I am not a beer drinker but because I have friends who are, I usually buy several different kinds when I'm planning a party: one straightforward brand like Michelob and one yuppie type (you know what I mean) like Sam Adams. If I am planning an ethnic meal that cries out for beer, I pair the beer ethnically with the food; Dos Equis with Mexican, Sapporo with Japanese, Singha with Thai, etc. Beer is also a fantastic ingredient to use in cooking.

SERVING ALCOHOLIC BEVERAGES: When your guests arrive, offer them a drink. If you are serving only wine and beer, make this clear. Otherwise, leave the offer open.

If you are serving hard liquor, you will need low and high (or short and tall) glasses. It's not the capacity that makes the difference, it's the height of the glass. When liquor is served straight up or on the rocks, you use a short (old-fashioned) glass. When it's mixed with tonic or seltzer and ice is added, you use a highball glass. There's no reason to spend a lot of money on bar glasses. Go to a seconds store or china warehouse and buy a dozen simple glasses that will be easy to replace.

If in doubt about how much liquor to pour into a glass, you can use a jigger (one and a half ounces) or rely on the "finger method."

For this, hold the bottom of the glass with your thumb on one side and your index and middle finger wrapped around the other. Pour liquor into the glass until it is level with your index finger. Remember, this isn't orange juice; two fingers is the right amount. If someone asks for the liquor "with a splash" of water, tonic, or whatever, this means a quick tilt of the mixer bottle or pitcher of ice water. Ice should be added last and unless this is an extremely casual affair, please use tongs or a large spoon for the ice—not your fingers.

I have discussed wineglasses at some length in Chapter 2 and also talked about the different shapes for champagne glasses. Champagne, like white wine, should be served chilled. If you forget to put it in the refrigerator and want to try a quick chill-down in the freezer, don't leave it there for more than thirty minutes or it may explode. Never shake a bottle of sparkling wine. The cork is already under tremendous pressure and may come flying out. When opening a bottle, keep one hand on the cork while removing the wire and foil with your other hand, keeping the cork pointing away from your—and anyone else's—face. Drape a cloth napkin or dish towel over the top of the bottle and hold the bottle away from people, pets, and open shelves filled with crystal. Place one hand on the bottom (thumb inside the well) and grasp the cloth-covered cork. Slowly turn the bottle from the bottom until you feel the cork move. Rotate the bottle until the cork comes loose and then immediately pour champagne into the glasses. The object is not to create high drama by having the cork fly through the air and also waste half the champagne as it foams from the bottle. If the sparkling wine is of good quality, is chilled and unagitated, opening it is no problem.

Keep beer chilled and don't hesitate to offer it to guests in place of wine. During extremely casual entertaining, it's okay to serve the beer in its bottle or can. The next step up is to pour it into plastic tumblers. When serving beer at the dinner table, use large glass mugs or tall glasses.

For any number of reasons, a guest may decline your offer of an alcoholic beverage. The reason does not need to be explained to anyone, including you. Because this is not an uncommon occurrence, have club soda, ginger ale, cider, and nonalcoholic punch and nonalcoholic beer on hand. When you offer your guests drinks before dinner, be sure to include a few of the nonalcoholic beverages in your litany of choices: "Can I get you something to drink? I have white wine, beer, seltzer, and juice." When you sit down to dinner and a guest passes on the wine, offer him or her a soft drink.

Inherent in serving alcohol in your home is the responsibility of knowing when someone has had enough. Indeed, should an intoxicated guest leave your house and have an automobile accident, in many states you, as the one who provided the alcohol, are just as guilty as whoever was behind the wheel. Do not push alcohol on your guests. There should be no "happy meter" connected to a guest's level or lack of sobriety. It's up to you to know when to stop pouring, and it's better to err on the side of too little rather than too much.

If you suspect someone has crossed the line, there are some tactics you can employ to help that person slow down and sober up. First, stall: Take the glass and wander away, forgetting for a while to refill it. Return the glass full of soda or seltzer and pretend you forgot what the guest was drinking. If he or she doesn't get this subtle hint, it's time to say, "I thought you'd want to stop drinking in time to be able to drive home." You don't have to be coy. This is serious business. Look your guest straight in the eye when addressing him or her—and remember that anyone so far gone that he or she can't understand this warning should have been stopped much earlier in the evening. If this is the case, explain that you have to move his or her car—anything to get the keys—and keep the car keys until the guest can drive home or you can call a taxi (slip the cabbie the keys). Don't make an instant enemy by asking another guest to escort the inebriated guest home.

Cooking Disasters

Here is where I come to your aid, my blue cape billowing in the wind as I swoop into your kitchen and help you solve those culinary crises that plague us all at one time or another ("it burned!" or "it curdled!" for example). But before I begin I have some words of wisdom: First, keep your cool at all times. Chances are no one will know you're dealing with a "disaster" unless you draw attention to it. Second, keep the menus from your favorite take-out establishments in the kitchen drawer. When all else fails, push the buttons on the kitchen phone and order away.

Very few mistakes are out-and-out disasters. Most can be fixed or transformed into something else that's fit to eat. Read through this section *before* you issue your first invitation and *before* you crack a cookbook. There is no test at the end, so don't worry about absorbing every detail. It's more important that you get a feel for the kind of information I provide here so you will know where to turn when you start to panic.

It takes lots of years to get good at punting—to be so relaxed in the kitchen that you can shrug and laugh it off. Julia Child has a wonderful philosphy about things that run amok. She simply grins and says with great authority, "That's exactly the way I meant it to be." You will have disasters, and the trick is to keep your wits about you so that you can remember to pull the cord on your spare parachute, as it were.

I have four edicts for avoiding cooking disasters. Read carefully:

1. Keep spare ingredients on hand. I never buy "just enough," preferring to feed one or two "imaginary" extra guests (who, God knows, could materialize in the form of *unexpected* guests!). Also, keep your pantry well stocked with the essentials I list later in this section beginning on page 94.

2. Do not prepare an elaborate or expensive recipe that you have never made before. I'm sure your family or next-door neighbors would be delighted to sample your first attempt at rack of lamb or an elaborate chocolate cake. You think this is a costly experiment? I call it great insurance. When you begin to cook, read the recipe through at least twice and then assemble all the ingredients and equipment you will need. It's helpful to line them up in the order required if you have space, and I highly recommend doing as much prep work as you possibly can before you begin combining ingredients: chopping, sifting, measuring, etc.

3. Never tamper with, adjust, or experiment with a recipe until you have made it at least once exactly how it is written. Of course, you should season a dish with salt and pepper as you please, but don't substitute major ingredients or change proportions until you have some serious cooking experience under your belt. This goes for the techniques and equipment as well as ingredients. If a recipe says to cook over low heat, don't try to hurry things along by raising the flame; you'll end up with burned or curdled food. If a recipe calls for a ten-inch spring-form pan, don't substitute a tube pan or soufflé dish. And if you don't know what a springform pan is, ask your mother or the salesclerk at a kitchenware shop. (It's a round cake pan with a removable bottom and a spring clip on the side.)

4. Take the health issues of food preparation very seriously. You can make your guests very, very happy or you can make them sick enough to have to go to the hospital, or worse. Food poisoning is no joke. Utmost care and meticulousness must be maintained in the course of food preparation, handling, and storage. I urge you to refer to the *The Kitchen Survival Guide* to familiarize yourself with basic food safety rules. If you don't have a copy, I recap the most important points here:

- Foods that are not canned, boxed, bagged, or bottled usually need to be refrigerated or frozen. Some fruits are the major exceptions. And many canned, boxed, bagged, or bottled foods need refrigeration once they are opened.

- Don't leave uncooked meat or fish on the countertop for any length of time. Store it in the refrigerator (the back of the bottom shelf is the coolest and best place). Refrigerate cooked foods and dairy products as quickly as possible. Bacteria grows most rapidly at room temperature—which means cold and hot foods are safer than tepid or lukewarm foods.

- Keep utensils, work spaces, and storage areas clean. Wash with hot soapy water and rinse well. This reduces the chances for food poisoning considerably.

- Before you start cooking, wash your hands thoroughly with soap and hot water and dry them on a clean dish towel or paper towels.

- Don't use the same knife to cut up chicken or fish and other food without washing it first in hot, soapy water. Salmonella and other dangerous bacteria are often found in uncooked food and you must take extra care to keep work areas and utensils that come in contact with raw poultry especially clean.

- Don't reuse the same bowls for food preparation and serving until you scrub them first.

- Cook meat, poultry, and fish to the correct temperature. Follow tests for doneness provided in the recipe as well as cooking time estimations. And invest in an accurate, easy-to-read meat thermometer.

I promise, if you take the four preceding edicts to heart, you will avoid many pitfalls. However, accidents happen, as we know all too well. Read on and sleep better the night before your party.

↪ **HOW DO I MAKE A DISH LOOK MORE APPETIZ-ING?** This may not sound like a major crisis, but if you end up with a dull, plain-looking main course, you may be less than proud to carry it to the table. The art of decorating food is called garnishing and all those seemingly silly ingredients like parsley, lemon wedges, and confectioners' sugar come in handy when you want to turn the ordinary-looking into something special. You can sprinkle chopped parsley on top of meat, fish, or vegetables, or decorate the serving platter with sprigs of parsley, watercress, or slices of lemon. You can dust the tops of cakes with confectioners' sugar, cocoa powder, chopped nuts, or coconut. Use a fine-mesh sieve to get an even layer of powdered sugar or cocoa on the cake. Decorating with fresh flowers is a nice touch, but be sure you use edible blossoms; some are poisonous (see page 58).

↪ **HOW CAN I DISGUISE A COOKING DISASTER?** When a situation calls for more drastic measures than garnishing, try disguising or transforming the dish. For example, if the meat or fish is overcooked and has fallen apart, mix it with cooked rice or noodles to make a casserole. Top it with bread crumbs, a few dots of butter, and some grated cheese, place it under the broiler and watch it carefully as it browns—this will take only a few minutes—and then serve it. Just about anything (except sweets, of course) can be given this treatment. Serve it with pride and pretend it's exactly what you planned. No one will ever know. The last thing you want to do is wail about the catastrophe or apologize profusely. Your guests are hungry; they want to eat, not listen to you kvetch.

If you unmold something and it lands lopsided or crooked, use your hands to straighten it very gently. When all else fails, use a row of parsley or sliced vegetables or fruit to hide the crooked or uneven edge.

If your cake comes out of the pan in two or three large pieces, let them cool completely and then push them back together again on a cake plate and top the whole thing with frosting or whipped cream. If there is an ugly crack or sinkhole in the middle, fill it with whipped cream or frosting. For a serious sinkhole, arrange sliced fruit on top of the whipped cream—but be sure to tend to these cosmetics shortly before serving, otherwise the fruit will leak liquid and the whipped cream will turn watery. If the cake falls apart in lots of pieces, make a trifle (see page 358). If the single layer you made is not enough for the trifle, supplement it with store-bought cake.

I steer new cooks away from gelatin-based desserts that need unmolding. If you try one and it doesn't jell to the point where you can unmold it before you are ready to serve it, pour it into a small bowl, serve it with a ladle, and call it a cold sauce. If you need something to sauce, use fruit, ice cream, or store-bought pound cake.

⌇ **HELP! THIS DOESN'T TASTE RIGHT!** *Too salty?* Try adding thick slices of a peeled raw potato (or two) to the soup, stew, vegetables, or pasta sauce and cooking a few more minutes with the dish covered (you don't want any more liquid to evaporate). The potato will absorb some of the salty taste. Be sure to remove the raw potato before serving. Lemon juice, added a teaspoon at a time, cuts saltiness, too. If you have added too much salt to a tomato-based soup or sauce, try adding some unsalted or low-sodium tomato juice. To a cream-based soup, sauce, or puréed vegetable, add cream or milk, a tablespoon at a time. In the future, always season dishes with salt last—many other ingredients include high levels of sodium, and saltiness intensifies as cooking liquids evaporate.

Too acidic or vinegary? Add some fat in the form of oil or butter. To salad dressing, add olive oil; to sauces, add butter. Add only a teaspoon or tablespoon at a time and taste frequently.

Too sour? Add sweetener such as sugar, brown sugar, maple syrup, or honey, a tablespoon or so at a time. Make sure that the sour taste comes from too much acid, not from spoilage.

A little mold on cheeses, yogurt and sour cream does not mean the food is spoiled. It can be scraped or skimmed off. Taste the remaining product to make sure it hasn't spoiled.

Too sweet? Add some lemon juice or vinegar, a teaspoonful at a time. A little goes a long way. Lemon juice is best with desserts and vinegar with savory dishes.

Too bland? Try adding a few drops of hot sauces, soy sauce, or steak sauce, or a sprinkling of celery salt, salt, or pepper.

Too spicy? This is a tough one. If you've added too much hot sauce to the soup, you'll need to add more stock or broth and then probably more vegetables, etc. to dilute the heat. You can also try adding cream or milk to cream soups and then correcting the other seasonings. You can add tomato juice to tomato-based soups and sauces. Otherwise, serve something cooling along with it, such as sour cream or plain yogurt on top of the spicy soup or next to the burning chili.

HELP! THIS IS OVERDONE! As long as they are not completely dried out or burned, many overdone foods are still fine to eat. Overcooked vegetables can be mashed, puréed, or even made into soup by placing them in the blender or food processor with some canned beef or chicken broth or a little cream or milk.

Chicken that has fallen off the bone can be completely removed from the carcass and layered on a platter in slices (or pieces), with any remaining pan juices spooned over them. It also makes perfect chicken salad when mixed with scallions (or chopped red onion), pecans or walnuts, and mayonnaise.

Overcooked steaks, roasts, and chops can be sliced into thin strips and served over noodles or rice topped with a quick gravy (page 92).

You can turn overdone fish steaks into a warm salad (very trendy these days) by slicing the fish into half-inch strips and placing them on a bed of greens with some boiled potatoes and a few green beans and dressing this with a simple vinaigrette dressing (page 306).

Overcooked pasta and rice isn't salvageable. You can quickly cook up another batch of pasta, or make a quick batch of rice in the microwave or on top of the stove.

◠ **HELP! THIS IS BURNED!** It depends on what you've burned and how badly. If you burn chocolate, then you must throw it away. If you burn butter to the point where it has little brown specks, use a small spoon to skim them off. The remaining butter will taste nutty, which is fine for savory dishes but not in desserts. If you scorch milk, pour the milk into another pan, let it cool slightly, and then taste it before proceeding. If you cannot detect a burned taste, use it.

If you are making an egg-based sauce, dressing, frosting, or other dish (custard, for instance), and you overcook the eggs, they will curdle. While this is sometimes possible to salvage, the trouble isn't worth the time and effort. For the new cook, it's far better to take the time to cook these things in a double boiler. Yes, it will take more time, but the results will be much better—and more economical in the long run.

If you have burned scrambled or fried eggs to more than a medium brown, throw them out (or feed them to the dog) and start again. Ditto with pancakes. Lower the heat next time.

If you have burned the bottom of a cake or loaf of bread, use a sharp knife to scrape away the burned area. If you have to do a lot more than surface surgical repair, it's probably more expedient to slice up the part that isn't burned and make a trifle or bread crumbs. If you have burned the crumb and/or cheese topping of a casserole, use a spatula to remove the burned area. Make a new topping and reheat the casserole carefully.

If you have burned the roast, cut away the burned part, slice the rest thinly (because overcooked meat is tough), and layer it on the serving plate, or cut it into small cubes to use in a tomato-based casserole such as chili. If it's too burned to slice, it's too burned to serve.

If you burn chicken while baking or broiling, remove the meat and skin from the bones (if it's boneless, skip this step), cut away all the burned parts, cut the remaining meat into bite-sized pieces, and make a chicken casserole by mixing together a can of cream of mushroom soup, a third of a cup of white wine, and two thirds of a cup of milk. Pour the sauce over the chicken, heat, and serve over noodles, potatoes, or rice.

If you burn the bottom of a pot containing soup or stew because you haven't added enough liquid, or haven't stirred it frequently enough, carefully pour the unburned part into another pan, taking care not to scrape any of the burned part from the bottom. Add some liquid (broth, vegetable juice, wine, or water) and stir carefully until it is heated through. If you've done a heavy-duty job of scorching the pan, make sure to test the food for any burned taste. Sometimes a squeeze or two of lemon juice can mask a faint burned taste.

If you find that you are burning things, buy a timer that goes on a string around your neck to remind you when to stir or when to remove the cake or roast from the oven.

HELP! THIS IS STILL RAW! The roast is raw and the guests are hungry. Remove the meat from the oven and turn the temperature up to 500°F. Slice the roast into half-inch pieces and layer them back in the pan. Add half a cup of beef broth either from a can or made with a bouillon cube and boiling water. Cover the pan tightly with foil and cook for another 15 to 20 minutes. Check and serve or continue cooking, checking every 5 minutes.

A cooked chicken should not be pink. If you are cooking a whole bird, raise the oven temperature to 425°F, carve the legs off the chicken and place them next to it in the roasting pan. Put some butter or margarine on top of the chicken to keep it from drying out, add half a cup of water, wine, or broth to the pan, cover it tightly with foil, and return it to the oven, checking every 10 minutes.

Alternatively, you can carve the whole chicken in the kitchen and place it in the microwave set on high. Cook for 5-minute intervals until the chicken is done. If the color is unattractively pale, dot with butter or margarine and put the cut-up chicken under the broiler for 2 to 3 minutes.

If you are cooking chicken pieces on the bone, raise the oven temperature to 450°F, dot the pieces with butter or margarine, add half a cup of broth to the pan, cover with foil, and continue cooking, checking at 10-minute intervals until it's done. Alternatively, you can place the pieces on a baking sheet, dot them with butter or margarine, and broil them on high until they are no longer pink.

If you are grilling fish either under the broiler or on an outdoor grill, remember the thinner the cut, the faster it will cook. However, the thicker the cut, the juicer it will be. Fish cooks so fast that undercooked fish probably only needs a few more minutes of heat to be finished. It's better not to rush it.

HOW DO I SAVE A SAUCE? If your sauce is lumpy (for reasons other than any eggs in it have overcooked), first try whisking it vigorously. Next try straining it and processing it in a blender or food processor. If your sauce is runny and watery, you can thicken it with a little cornstarch. Here's how: In a small cup, mix together 1 tablespoon of cornstarch and 2 tablespoons of water. Bring the sauce to a simmer (a very gentle boil) and add the corn-starch paste, little by little, until the sauce begins to thicken. Serve it at once. Sauce thickened this way does not reheat well.

If your sauce is too thick, add hot water, cream, or broth, a table-spoon at a time.

If your sauce has separated so that it resembles watery tapioca, proc-ess it in a food processor or blender with an ice cube.

Instant Sauce
for Chicken and Veal

YIELD: About 2 cups

1 13-ounce can chicken broth (low-sodium, if possible) or 1 chicken bouillon cube, dissolved in 1¾ cups hot water

½ teaspoon dried herbs, such as tarragon, chervil, or marjoram

¼ cup dry vermouth, white wine, or dry sherry

2 to 3 tablespoons instant flour, such as Wondra

2 to 3 tablespoons unsalted butter (optional)

Salt to taste

Freshly ground black pepper to taste

Skim the fat off the juices remaining in the cooking pan. Place the juices and drippings (bits of cooked meat) in a 1-quart saucepan. Add the chicken broth, herbs, and vermouth. Set the pan over medium heat and bring the mixture to a simmer. Whisk in the flour, stirring continuously until the mixture thickens slightly. Continue cooking and stirring gently an additional 5 minutes to cook the flour. Off the heat, whisk in the butter, a tablespoon at a time, stirring vigorously until it melts. Season to taste and serve immediately.

VARIATION: If you want a richer-tasting sauce, use 1 bouillon cube and 2 cups of cream, proceeding as above.

Instant Sauce
for Beef, Lamb, and Pork

YIELD: About 2 cups

1 13-ounce can beef broth (low-sodium, if possible) or 1 beef bouillon cube, dissolved in 1¾ cups hot water

¾ teaspoon dried herbs, such as tarragon, chervil, or marjoram

½ cup dry red wine

2 to 3 tablespoons instant flour, such as Wondra

2 to 3 tablespoons unsalted butter (optional)

Salt to taste

Freshly ground black pepper to taste

Skim the fat off the juices remaining in the cooking pan. Place the juices and drippings (bits of cooked meat) in a 1-quart saucepan. Add the broth, herbs, and wine. Set the pan over medium heat and bring the mixture to a simmer. Whisk in the flour, stirring continuously until the mixture thickens slightly. Continue cooking and stirring gently an additional 5 minutes to cook the flour. Off the heat, whisk in the butter, a tablespoon at a time, stirring vigorously until it melts. Season to taste and serve immediately.

Instant Sauce for Fish

This is a much thinner sauce than the other two.

YIELD: About 1½ cups

2 tablespoons olive oil

1 medium onion, chopped

1 cup water

1 cup dry white wine or dry vermouth

1 fish-flavored or chicken bouillon cube

¾ teaspoon dried herbs, such as tarragon, basil, sage or a mixture of all three

1 to 2 tablespoons lemon juice

¼ cup fresh parsley, chopped

1 teaspoon capers

2 tablespoons tomato paste

Freshly ground black pepper to taste

Heat the olive oil in a medium-sized skillet set over medium heat. Sauté the onion until it is translucent. Add the water, wine, and bouillon cube. Raise the heat and stir until the mixture simmers and the bouillon cube has dissolved. Add the herbs and continue to cook until the mixture is reduced by a third. Add the lemon juice, parsley, capers, and tomato paste. Simmer 2 more minutes, stirring occasionally. Add pepper to taste. Serve immediately.

Rice—long grain, not instant or minute, to extend a meal either to feed an unexpected guest(s) or to use as filler when something else hasn't worked.

Pasta—always have extra on hand in case you overcook the original batch or an unexpected guest(s) shows up.

Egg noodles—to make an excellent casserole base.

Tomato paste—in a tube, to flavor sauces and to add zest and flavor to many savory dishes.

Sun-dried tomato paste—in a tube, to use like tomato paste for a more intense flavor.

Pesto—in either a jar or tube, great as an easy pasta sauce, for stuffing vegetables, and making the Baked Pesto Frittata on page 334.

Anchovy paste—in a tube, the perfect "secret addition" that gives life to salad dressings, fish sauces, and many pasta sauces. Use sparingly; it's strong-tasting and very salty.

Tomato sauce—several jars, for those times when you can't make your own, to add to stews and soups, and to make a quick sauce or casserole topping.

Fresh garlic or chopped garlic in oil—found in the refrigerated section of your supermarket, to add flavor to dishes and sauces.

Onions—for flavor in many dishes and sauces.

Potatoes—to stretch a meal, and to desalt soups, sauces, and stews.

Horseradish—for cold sauces and dressings.

Italian salad dressing—for marinating chicken and meat.

Bread crumbs—homemade are preferable, but store-bought can be used to top casseroles, thicken cold sauces, and mix with other ingredients to make stuffings for mushrooms and tomatoes.

Vermouth or dry white wine (for cooking)—to add in small amounts to give flavor and depth to many dishes and sauces.

Dried herbs of Provence—found in gourmet and specialty food shops, a wonderful melange of rosemary, tarragon, chervil, and other special flavors of southern France to add a deliciously authentic flavor to meats, stews, and sauces.

Wondra (instant flour)—to thicken sauces.

Cornstarch—to thicken sauces.

Chicken bouillon cubes—to add instant chicken flavor (and salt) to foods and sauces.

Fish bouillon cubes (I like Knorr's)—to add instant fish flavor (and salt) to foods and sauces.

Beef bouillon cubes—to add instant beef flavor (and salt) to foods and sauces.

Confectioners' sugar—for a base of, and to add body to, frostings and icings, and to use for decorations or to hide cosmetic flaws.

Seedless red currant jelly—heated together with a small amount of orange juice, sherry, or Madeira, to make an easy, delicious glaze for cakes and fruit tarts.

Cocoa—for frostings and decorations, and to hide flaws.

Superfine or bar sugar—to use when you need the sugar to dissolve instantly without having to reheat (ice coffee or ice tea, for example).

Brown sugar—to add sweetness and depth to both savory and sweet dishes and sauces.

Capers—to add a piquant touch to sauces, dressings, and dishes, especially fish and chicken.

Grated Parmesan cheese—to use as a topping browned under the broiler, and to add flavor to spreads and life to pasta and rice. The best kind of Parmesan cheese is imported from Italy and should be freshly grated just before using—either by you or by the shop where you buy it.

Hot sauce—such as Tabasco® Brand Pepper Sauce, to add life and zest to dishes and sauces. Use it judiciously; a little goes a long way.

Salsa—an instant appetizer to serve with chips, and great to add to hearty stews, vegetable soups, and even pasta.

Crackers and chips—to scoop up the salsa and spread with cheese.

Frozen orange juice concentrate—to enhance a sweet-and-sour sauce, and to use for mixed drinks (and, of course, to make OJ).

Ice cubes—For floating in pan juices, stocks, and soups to get the fat to coagulate faster, which makes for easier removal.

Sliced or slivered almonds—to decorate the tops of cakes, and to give casseroles, baked fish, and chicken a lovely crunchy texture. Sprinkle on top of steamed or sautéed vegetables for a delicious garnish.

Popcorn—for a great last-minute snack. Try tossing in a handful of Parmesan cheese or a dash of seasoned salt instead of butter.

Cream cheese—to make a million different kinds of spreads, to make frostings, and to thicken soups. The easiest party spread in the world is made by laying a package of cream cheese in a rimmed plate or shallow dish and adding a jar of pepper jelly on top of it. Serve on crackers.

Canned chicken broth (low-sodium, preferably)—a lifesaver to use as the liquid base for sauces, soups, and stews.

Canned beef broth (low-sodium, preferably)—a lifesaver to use as the liquid base, when you have meat or duck, or to use in hearty dishes.

Red wine or sherry vinegar—to give a perfect touch to sauces, to make great salad dressings, and to use as an ingredient in sweet-and-sour dishes.

Olive oil—a must for many Italian dishes and for quality salad dressing. Really great olive oil (extra-virgin) can be used instead of butter on French bread.

Garlic oil—a lovely fragrant way to sauté chicken or fish; a great addition to salad dressings and cold sauces.

Cooking sherry—to give flavor to sauces and stews.

Soy sauce—to add salt (and extra flavor) in a more creative way to dishes and sauces.

Seasoned salt—to perk up the flavor of foods. Don't use it in every dish or everything will taste the same.

Do You Need a Caterer?

A caterer can be a lifesaver when you need to entertain a large crowd in a manner that is completely out of your range of experience. You can hire a caterer to orchestrate the entire party—from the food to the flowers, the music to the wine, the rental plates to the tablecloths—or you can hire a caterer to take care of only a few segments of the event, such as food and service.

When you rent certain function rooms at hotels or clubs you often have no choice but to use the caterer that comes with the package, or to select a caterer from an approved list. These are also times when your menu choices may be limited and you are left with very little leeway as to what you can provide to personalize the event, such as the wine or floral arrangements. If this is the case, arrange to view a function in progress—you can peek into the room during someone else's wedding reception—and take note of the number of servers, their apparent efficiency, the attractiveness of the buffet table, and the care taken with each table. Get several references and call each one before making a final decision.

There are many other ways to take advantage of caterers. Some will deliver food to your house for you to set out on serving platters and serve yourself (not always a small feat). Some will come in just to serve and clean up—you supply the food and liquor. Some will supplement what you have made and also serve and clean up. Every caterer has rules about what goes. Some will explain that their insurance will not cover them if you provide any of the food, although this is most common when you are renting a function room, not when you are giving a party in your own house. It is my experience that the smaller the catering firm, the more flexible the arrangements can be.

Because there are so many creative ways to make use of caterers, it behooves you to spend time interviewing more than one and asking the right questions. You don't want any surprises. You must think of yourself as a consumer who is buying a rather expensive service (exactly what you are doing) and making every effort to get the most value for your hard-earned dollars. Don't worry. I am going to tell you the right questions to ask. And then I will tell you the right answers.

✎ **WHEN DO YOU NEED A CATERER?** I don't think it's a great leap of faith on my part to assume that if you are using this book for guidance, your experience is limited and you might consider yourself a novice when it comes to entertaining. So, while I don't suggest you hire a caterer every time you issue a dinner invitation, there are times that a novice (and probably even many folks with lots of experience at this game) should call for help.

If you have been elected to organize your firm's Christmas party or summer outing, think: caterer. If your daughter, sister, or niece is getting married and you have generously offered to host the wedding, think: caterer. Ditto for a bar mitzvah. Even if your daughter is getting married at home and inviting only twenty guests to the ceremony, you owe it to yourself to get some help so you can enjoy yourself. If budget is an issue, remember that the caterer doesn't have to take care of the whole event. You can hire one to supplement dishes you have made, heat up the food, serve, and clean up. You can even take care of all the cooking yourself (dishes that are made beforehand) and have hired help take care of heating, serving, and cleaning up. If you are entertaining for business (the firm outing or holiday party), all you are expected to do is make the arrangements, confirm them, and then be on hand to see that everything goes smoothly.

If there are times when money is not an issue and you want to entertain just a few guests, you might consider hiring a caterer— what a lovely extravagance! Or hire one to deliver a romantic dinner for two to your home. Most catering firms will cook for from two to two thousand people. Your job is to interview several (or as many as necessary) to find the right one for your needs.

🖙 **HOW DO YOU FIND A CATERER?** Word of mouth is the best way to find a good caterer. Naturally, you need to ask someone whose taste and finances approximately match your own. You shouldn't ask Ivana Trump for the name of her caterer unless you . . . well, use your imagination. I go to an exercise class where the dressing room is a fantastic resource for all kinds of information like that. Try your co-workers, your neighbors, your friends, the parents of your children's friends, and people such as your travel agent, hairdresser, stockbroker, and accountant. Ask the secretary in the office of a local church or synagogue. They see caterers come and go all the time and are privy to the results—both good and bad—of every event. You don't have to belong to the church or synagogue to request a list of caterers. Ask the owner of your favorite restaurant (if he or she says it caters, you may well be on to something). Ask the managers of the best butcher store, fish store, gourmet and produce shops in town. Ask the person who runs the local wine store. Keep in mind that while caterers do buy wholesale, they still frequent the same shops you do and have constant dealings with the people you are asking. When running your errands on a Saturday, end each transaction not with "Have a nice day" but "Do you know a good caterer?" Keep a list and when you see the same names being mentioned again and again, you'll know those are the ones to call first.

If you have no luck in the word-of-mouth department, turn to the Yellow Pages. If you are doing this in Manhattan or Chicago, you'd better pour yourself a drink and put your feet up. Look for ads that are tasteful and a bit understated rather than flamboyant. Skip the ads that say "We can do everything from an inaugural dinner to a Hawaiian luau complete with dancing fire-eaters." If you are thinking of throwing a clambake or barbecue, look for ads that state that the firm specializes in that kind of event. The goal is to end up with a list of four or five names to call and interview, whether you have found them by word of mouth or in the Yellow Pages. Before you make the call, write down as much pertinent information about your event as possible so that you'll be giving consistent information to each caterer. Take good notes to keep everything straight.

HOW DO YOU INTERVIEW A CATERER? You should be able to give the caterer the date or a choice of several dates, the type of occasion (wedding, dinner party, pool party), the place (you may need the caterer's help with this—many can recommend function halls or other places that can be rented for private functions), the time of day, the number of guests (actually make out the guest list, don't ballpark it), and your thoughts on the food you'd like to serve. You don't have to have a specific menu in mind; it is the caterer's job to suggest dishes and work with you to establish an appropriate menu that falls within your budget. However, you should know whether you want something down-home and casual or upscale and formal or somewhere in between. You should also know if you want a sit-down meal, a buffet, or a party with hors d'oeuvres only.

Before you call the caterer, know how much you can afford to spend. That is not to say this amount will fall within the realm of what the caterer of your dreams will charge. You need to be realistic about what a caterer costs, but there is always room for compromise—usually on your part. It means, for instance, serving chicken instead of roast beef, or paring down the guest list. Most caterers charge by the person.

Once you have the caterer on the phone, the conversation should go something like this:

YOU: Hi, this is Fred Fledgling calling to get information about your catering services. I got your name from Marie, the secretary at the Church of the Seventh Seating. I am planning a surprise thirtieth birthday party for my wife on Saturday evening March twentieth. I'm thinking about inviting twenty people.

CATERER: Would this be a buffet or sit-down dinner, or would you be serving just cocktails and dessert?

YOU: Well, I'm not exactly sure. I'm a novice at entertaining and I could use some advice. I'd like to know what the price difference between all those things would be, as well as the other pros and cons. And I'll need help with the menu. Actually, I'm going to need a lot of help since I haven't ever done anything like this before.

CATERER: Of course. That's our job, to help you with those decisions. Depending on the menu you choose, the seated dinner usually costs slightly more than the buffet, since you will need additional service help. However, you save slightly on the food costs since our staff has control over the amount of food served.

YOU: I want to make sure that there is plenty of food. I wouldn't like to run out or have things look skimpy.

CATERER: I completely agree, sir, since that wouldn't make us look very good either. At a buffet people tend to help themselves to more food than they can eat and there is a certain amount of waste that is more easily controlled when the food is served by the staff.

YOU: Okay, I understand now. What's this cocktail and dessert deal?

CATERER: Well, when your invitation says "cocktail and dessert," guests expect one and a half to two hours of substantial hors d'oeuvres with either a full bar or wine and champagne (since it's a birthday), followed by dessert and coffee. In this case I would recommend a large birthday cake, ice cream, and fresh fruit.

YOU: I see. What kinds of things would you serve beforehand?

CATERER: We have a rather extensive list of hot and cold hors d'oeuvres for you to choose from. Someone from our office would be happy to come out to meet with you either at your home or place of business. At that time she could take a look at the setup of your home. This would help us choose and plan the menu and service.

YOU: Do you also take care of rentals, such as dishes and tablecloths?

CATERER: Yes we do. We also have a complete staff including someone who can provide you with flowers.

YOU: Does that mean they come early and set everything up?

CATERER: Absolutely.

YOU: After I meet with your people and choose a menu will I have a firm price for what this will cost me?

CATERER: Yes, sir. We have a contract that spells out every detail. We require a deposit upon signing and the rest at the end of the evening. Gratuities for the staff are, of course, discretionary. We have hundreds of clients who give us repeat business.

YOU: I assume some of those clients would be willing to give you references.

CATERER: Naturally. I would be delighted to furnish you with a list of names.

YOU: Do you have some literature that you could send me?

CATERER: Certainly. Since this is a surprise, shall I send it to an address other than your home address?

The things I like best about this caterer are that he sounds professional without being pretentious. In other words, you came right out and said you were a rank amateur and he didn't make you feel like a fool. A party is an emotional exercise and you want to spend your energy (both physical and emotional) in a positive way, not battling some snotty caterer. This guy was happy to give you lots of information. He wasn't pushy and he sounded delighted to get your call, which hopefully means he will be delighted to get your business. He proved that he gives attention to detail by asking where he should send the information.

Other questions you might ask him are: How long has his company been in business, how many parties does he handle at a time (large caterers do many parties in one day, while smaller establishments are limited to one or two). You should ask him about cancellation fees,

what happens if you want to change the guest list by adding or sub-
tracting at the last minute, and if he is fully covered by insurance. If
you are having children attend, is there a special price or even a special
menu for them?

A full-service caterer will bring everything—even the birthday candles. Perhaps you aren't in the market to have your whole event catered.
Perhaps you want to do part of it yourself. You could talk to a caterer
about this or you could call a local "gourmet" shop. Here's how the
conversation should *not* go:

G.S.: Yo, the Leaky Strainer, PeeWee here.

YOU: Good morning. This is Noreen Neophyte calling from the Newly
Rich Group. I understand you furnish food for parties.

G.S.: Yeah, we do takeout.

YOU: I'm organizing a luncheon for one hundred executives in our
new office park located at the intersection of Park Place and Board-
walk.

G.S.: Hey, no problem. But could you hold for a sec, honey? I gotta
to show the exterminator where to spray.

Noreen, darling, you've called the wrong place. Let's start again
after you've asked around and called another gourmet shop: Here's how
the call ought to progress:

A.G.S.: Good afternoon, Lick Your Lips, LuLu speaking.

YOU: Good morning. This is Noreen Neophyte calling from the Newly
Rich Group. I understand you furnish food for parties.

A.G.S.: We certainly do. How may I assist you?

YOU: My boss, who is a really good cook, wants to bring in the main
course for a luncheon I'm organizing for about one hundred executives next Wednesday at noon. He needs a caterer to provide
some kind of salad and dessert.

A.G.S.: Will you need soft drinks and coffee as well?

YOU: No, we can take care of that. Can you recommend something to
go with tofu lo mein?

A.G.S.: Will that be served cold or hot?

YOU: Heavens, I have no idea.

A.G.S.: No problem. We have a nice vegetarian pasta salad that is
served cold and goes with just about everything. It sounds like your
boss may be into the veggie scene. The pasta salad is pretty sub-

stantial, and it's mainstream without being boring, if you know what I mean, just in case someone doesn't love tofu as much as your boss.

YOU: Great idea, thanks for mentioning it.

A.G.S.: We also make lovely seven-grain rolls. They're baked fresh every morning and would be a nice accompaniment to the salad and lo mein.

YOU: I'll keep that in mind. What about dessert?

A.G.S.: I'd suggest a selection of our famous home-baked cookies and nut bars and fresh fruit salad.

YOU: Gee, I was thinking of serving ice-cream sundaes.

A.G.S.: Well, that certainly is a possibility, although I hope you don't mind my mentioning that it's my experience that sundaes don't usually go over very well at executive luncheon meetings. So many people are on diets, and ice cream can be a tad messy to serve. If you offer cookies and fruit, the people who want something sweet are happy, and the people who are watching their diets are happy too.

YOU: Of course. I never considered that, since I love sundaes so much and never have to worry about my weight. How do I arrange to order the food? What about the quantity? Do you deliver?

A.G.S.: You should call me the morning of the day before with the exact number, and I'll be able to let you know how much you'll need. I always include extra so you won't get caught short. We will be happy to deliver. There is an extra charge for that. Will you be needing paper plates, cups, forks, and plastic glasses?

YOU: I'll be taking care of all that. Thank you very much.

A.G.S.: If you have any questions, or need more information, give me a call.

Obviously, this is a best-case scenario, but if you find someone even vaguely resembling this caterer, you are golden. She's polite, helpful, creative, professional, and interested in your business. She's diplomatic—steering you gently away from a potentially disastrous dessert selection without making you feel foolish. The only thing I would recommend is that you stop by the shop and get a dish of the pasta salad, a roll, and a few cookies to sample yourself. If you are satisfied, then place the order in person with the store manager and get a written receipt, which I feel is the most businesslike way of doing things.

If you are organizing a large event in a hotel or function hall it is perfectly acceptable to ask to taste the food beforehand. You would be expected to pay for this, of course, but it will give you a chance to check out not only the quality of the food but the service, the linen, the noise level, and the overall ambiance (feeling) of the place. Also look into parking. Is there a garage, valet parking, on-the-street parking? If only street parking is available, how safe is the neighborhood in the evening—if that's when your function is to be held? If someone in your party needs handicapped access, is it available?

As you can see, hiring the services of a caterer is a little more complicated than just picking up the phone. But now you have a head start, and when you find a good caterer, that person will help you along the rest of the way. If you possibly can find the time, keep notes. They will be invaluable for the next time you do this.

Other Helping Hands

Having a helping hand in the kitchen for cooking, serving, and cleaning up can go a long way to making you a guest at your own party. If you are not using a caterer for full service, the caterer may still be able to supply you with the names of some free-lance waiters, kitchen helpers, and bartenders. The local church or synagogue is a a good source too. Or you can try local college or high school kids. Obviously, these young people need more guidance than more experienced staff, but they will also cost less. If you are not good at training or delegating, it makes sense to hire the more experienced person.

When I hire teenagers or any inexperienced people, I start them at casual affairs where they are expected to do no more than empty chips into bowls and clean up paper plates and napkins. They then graduate to washing dishes and finally to heating food, dressing salads, making coffee and seeing that the right number of coffee cups are ready to go when I need them.

Make sure to talk to the person or people who are helping you before the party—a phone conversation is fine. Tell them what to wear (I don't like fussy uniforms and usually request clean black pants and white shirts and black shoes or sneakers—I supply the aprons), give them detailed instructions to your house, and ask them to arrive at least half an hour before the guests. Mention the number of guests and briefly outline the helper's responsibilities. I suggest one wait person for every fifteen people at a buffet and one for every ten at a sit-down dinner.

Make the job easier by writing the menu out on a piece of paper along with specific instructions. "From 7 to 8 we'll have cocktails in the living room. The white wine on the bottom shelf of the refrigerator should be served. Use the small wineglasses on the counter. Pass the smoked salmon with the toothpicks and little red napkins, please."

You can continue your instructions with notes such as: "While we are having drinks, stir the soup, don't let it boil. Wash the lettuce (in the bottom bin of the fridge) and spin it dry. Break it into bite-sized pieces and put it in the salad bowl. Check the roast every 15 minutes and call me when the meat thermometer reads 180." As you and your helpers get more experienced, you won't have to be so specific, but it saves time and energy during the party to be as precise as possible with instructions.

Before the help arrives, take out the plates, glasses, serving bowls, etc. so he or she or they do not have to interrupt you to locate them. Show how to operate the coffee machine, where you keep the cream and sugar, and so on. Be as clear as you can but reassure the helper(s) that you don't mind being interrupted for help or information.

When you hire a catering firm or an independent waiter, remember to tip the wait staff (if any). You don't tip the owner of the catering company.

When to Use Rentals

If hiring a caterer does fit your lifestyle or budget, don't rule out rentals. When you're hosting an event that requires more dishes than you own, or different-size dishes, or you need to supplement the china and glassware you have, turn to the Yellow Pages and look under "Rentals." The listing is often entered as "Party Rentals," and with one phone call you have access to plates, glasses, flatware, table linens, chairs, tables, trays, coffeemakers, coatracks, salad bowls, serving platters, salt and pepper shakers—you name it. Samples of everything are on display in the rental company's showroom and my experience is that the staff is extremely helpful. They will help you decide on the quantities and sizes you need.

Obviously, it costs money to rent. However, there is a time savings in cleanup, since the dishes and utensils need only to be scraped, rinsed, and stacked back in the racks in which they were delivered. You can sometimes stack the dishes first, carry them out to the driveway or backyard the morning after the party and hose them off. It's cheaper to rent than buy extra dishes if you rarely will need more than eight place settings. You can rent a place setting (china and cutlery) for as little as $2.50 a person and for another $2.00 per person you can rent a tablecloth and napkins, depending on where you live. This way you can spend time with your company rather than cleaning up or doing laundry. Sounds like a good deal to me.

Rental services deliver and pick up. There is often a small charge for this, although if your order is large enough, most throw in delivery and pickup free of charge. Be sure to count the items as you pack them up. You will be charged for any that are missing.

Children

Children play an important role at appropriate social events. Family get-togethers, holidays, birthdays, informal barbecues, and laid-back Sunday suppers are all great for kids. You, as host or hostess, know that you will be feeding children and can plan the menu accordingly. Even for these social events, children are welcome only when specifically invited.

I fully acknowledge that in a world where more often than not both parents are juggling careers and children, moms and dads don't get enough time to spend with their offspring. New parents, especially, are loath to leave newborns and young babies and may well ask if they can bring the baby when you invite them to dinner. You need to be honest with them and yourself. If you can handle the fact that the child will cause some disruption, then by all means encourage them to bring their pride and joy. But be prepared for crying, Mom and Dad springing from the table to feed Baby, more crying, Mom and Dad getting up again to walk Baby, more crying, other guests leaving the table to offer advice, more crying . . . Need I say more? If you are the type who likes everything just so and looks forward to an evening of adult conversation, for the sake of sanity and friendship, say, "I'd feel more comfortable having you and the baby at a more casual event. Why don't you come for a cookout in two weeks?" This is even more important if you have bribed your own kids to go to bed before the party starts and your other guests are paying big bucks for baby-sitters so they can log some time in a child-free zone.

Entertaining children can be a joy when you are prepared. It's not fair or realistic to expect Junior to want to eat the same things grownups do—come on, you were a kid not that long ago. Remember how much you did *not appreciate* spicy or slimy food or food you could not identify? Nor is it realistic to expect children to sit patiently and quietly at the dinner table for very long. Experience with my own three sons has taught me that children usually eat the first thing offered (unless it's yucky) and then play with everything else until dessert, at which time they are suddenly hungry again! I start kids off with fruit kabobs dipped in fruit yogurt, garlic cheese bread, or pita spread with peanut butter. This way, they have at least downed something nutritious and if they prefer to race around in the backyard (if it's daylight) or hang out in the family room while the old folks enjoy themselves at the table, I don't get bent out of shape.

Of course, your experience may be vastly different from mine. You may know little darlings who ask for seconds of black bean soup and spinach-stuffed turkey roulade and sit quietly at the table while the grown-ups discuss current events. Ha! I'm not holding my breath.

The parent(s) who shows up at a dinner party with an unexpected third party in tow in the form of a child of any age should be greeted with a look of astonishment (you won't have to fake it, believe me!) and a sputtered "Gee, I had no idea you were bringing little Bobby along." Period. That's it. You can't order them out, and you are under no obligation to enlist your own kids as playmates or baby-sitters. The guest should figure out by your barely masked displeasure that he or she goofed.

Try to make the best of the situation. If the child is old enough, install him in front of the television—unless that means vacating a room reserved for the party. Offer pencils or crayons and a pad of paper or a magazine and a deck of cards and suggest to the parent that he or she supervise an art project or game. It's not your job to create a special meal for this child, either. If the parent won't be in your way, offer him or her kitchen time to fix something simple for the child, or suggest a bowl of cereal, peanut butter and jelly or buttered toast.

Other Types of Entertaining

When you entertain, you won't always be hosting a party. Other forms of entertaining involve welcoming friends or relatives into your home for overnight or weekend visits, or hosting a meeting. Visits to sick friends and the elderly in nursing homes is a form of entertaining—you don't expect them to entertain *you*. Although I don't plan to go into great detail about any of these alternative types of entertaining, I will touch on them.

OVERNIGHT AND WEEKEND GUESTS: Most of us are not blessed with guest quarters or even a guest room. This means that overnight guests need to be housed in a child's room, den, home office, or living room with a pull-out sofa. These accommodations may be less than splendid and while no one expects you to turn into Mr. Hilton for the visit, there are some touches that will make your guests feel welcome—even if they are sharing the living room sofa with your cat.

Make the bed(s) rather than leaving a pile of sheets and blankets out. If your guest is sleeping on a pull-out sofa bed, offer to make the bed but leave the guest the option of making it after everyone else has left that part of the house.

Pick up and put away stray clutter, such as stacks of books and papers and furniture that your guest might trip over in the middle of the night. Put a night light in the hall or otherwise illuminate the way to the bathroom or down treacherous steps and stairways. Leave toothpaste, soap, and other toiletries in the bathroom where they can be located without requiring your guest to search through your drawers and cabinets. Point these out to the guest so that he or she will feel comfortable using them.

If this is a weekday, show your guest around the kitchen so that he or she can fend for himself or herself if you are not available in the morning. Set up the coffee so that all your guest needs to do is flip the switch. Leave dishes, cereal, and muffins where they are easy to find and be sure to leave your office number if you must leave before your guest awakens.

Weekend guests arrive with more time and expectations for socializing. In order to have ample time to relax and enjoy your company, organize menus and meals before the guests arrive. Going out for dinner one night is an option, while a simple supper, breakfast, and Sunday brunch should not strain your resources too much (see pages 142–145 and 167–173). Lunches can be help-yourself sandwiches, easy soups or salads, or leftovers from the night before.

You want to make your guests feel very much at home, but no one expects you to become maid, chauffeur, chief cook and bottle washer, and proprietor of a twenty-four-hour-a-day restaurant. Make your time, energy, and resources very clear to your guests before they arrive. I once invited acquaintances from another city for the weekend and offered to host a dinner party for some of their local friends. I expected one or two couples. When I was presented with a guest list with twenty names, I gulped and suggested that it would make more sense if they organized dinner at a Chinese restaurant, since I did not have the space (or budget or time) to seat twenty-four at my dining room table.

You also don't have to spend every minute entertaining your guests. If you live near public transportation, don't hesitate to give them a map so that they can go off and explore the city. You might also provide them with a guidebook and list of local attractions you think they would enjoy. On the other hand, you might like sightseeing with them. I love seeing Boston "fresh" through the eyes of a tourist.

↪ **MEETINGS AT HOME:** When you volunteer to host a meeting at your house, try to keep the head count to a number that you can accommodate. You'll need a place for each person to sit, as well as a place to hang coats (if it's snowy or wet you won't want to stuff thirty dripping coats in your closet). Will you need name tags? If so, have a hard surface available for people to fill them out and provide a marker heavy enough for other people to be able to see the writing. Set a basket nearby in which to throw away the peel-off backs of the name tags. It's your duty as host or hostess to answer the door, introduce yourself, and then, if it is a meeting of just a few people, introduce everyone. If it is a large meeting, suggest that the newly arrived guests go in and introduce themselves to the other people.

If you have handouts, try to package them together (with a stapler or paper clip) so people don't have to juggle multiple sheets of paper. Have extra paper and pens on hand for those who want to take notes. If your meeting requires some sort of audiovisual aids, make sure they are set up and functioning well before the meeting starts. You don't want to waste time fiddling with the projector, VCR, microphone, or screen during the meeting.

(Brewed) coffee and an equally decent pot of tea are the magic ingredients that will make most people happy to attend a meeting at your home. In the summer, ice coffee and ice tea are welcome substitutions. Even if you use paper cups (not Styrofoam—they're bad for the environment and nasty to drink from), a decent cup of coffee is still a treat. At evening meetings, offer decaf as well. If you have only one coffeepot, buy high-quality, freshly ground decaf beans and hardly anyone will know the difference. Don't forget the milk (or half-and-half), sugar, sugar substitute, and slices of lemon for the tea, as well as a pitcher of ice water and glasses. Don't forget spoons, napkins, and a place to dispose of used cups. Since most coffeepots hold only eight to ten cups of coffee, you might want to consider borrowing or renting a thirty-cup coffeepot for a large meeting. Plan on enough time for the coffee to brew (as long as twenty minutes). If you think many people will want tea, get two large coffeepots and use one to heat water.

If you do plan on serving something to eat, keep it simple, small, and most important, not messy and crumbly. The brownies and squares on pages 372 and 367 are particularly good for meetings since they can be cut into small pieces and do not require plates.

If you are holding a breakfast meeting and are serving muffins, bagels, and other morning fare, you'll want to have plates, knives, and spreads such as butter, cream cheese, and jam. You can either toast the bagels and muffins in the kitchen, or set the toaster out on the table in the meeting room for people to do their own.

If people eat during the meeting, try to keep the area picked up so dirty cups and crumpled napkins don't accumulate—they look unsightly, create potential for spills, and get in the way of business.

↳ **SICK VISITS:** Perhaps you haven't ever considered a visit to a sick friend or relative a form of entertainment, but when you think about entertainment in terms of offering hospitality and comfort, visiting the sick (and the bereaved) should be at the top of your list. Too many of us have grown up without learning how to do this and as a result either feel awkward and uncomfortable when we force ourselves to pay these visits, or don't make them at all.

You don't have to be an entertainer or brilliant conversationalist. Your very presence and the ability to listen can be comfort enough for someone in the hospital or recuperating at home. Last year I had surgery and a long hospitalization. I was in considerable pain and wasn't in any mood for conversation. I just wanted to know that someone I knew and liked was sitting in that chair next to my bed. Friends and family took turns and it was exactly what I needed.

Keep these rules in mind and you'll do just fine:

- Respect visiting hours (if you are going to a hospital).

- Call ahead to make sure the patient wants company.

- Ask if there is anything that you can bring, and then follow through with the offer.

- Come in quietly without a lot of hustle and bustle.

- If you do wish to bring a small gift, make it something useful like hand cream, or hard candy, or some other nonperishable item. Don't bring a bunch of loose flowers and expect the patient or nurse or attendant to run around looking for a vase. If you want to bring flowers, bring them in a vase.

- A gentle squeeze of the hand is a far better greeting than an exuberant hug.

- Don't load your coat, bag, etc. on the bed.

- If there are other visitors, say a brief hello and offer to wait in the hall until they leave or to come back at another time.

- Don't engage in loud or nonstop conversation; it's exhausting to a sick person.

- Remember that silences are fine.

- Don't ask for details about the illness or operation unless the patient seems happy and willing to offer them; listen attentively and quietly.

- Don't tell horror stories about your friends who have had the same illness or operation.

- Unless the patient asks you to stay longer (and isn't just being polite), limit your visit to ten minutes.

↬ **VISITS TO NURSING HOMES:** Residents of nursing homes delight in visitors and you certainly will brighten the day of an elderly or chronically ill person with a visit. As opposed to a sick person at home or in the hospital, most elderly people love conversation. You should remember to speak up (quite loudly in some cases), as hearing loss is an issue for many elderly people. Speak slowly and clearly and look directly at the person. Since many aged people have memory loss, you may be asked the same question over and over again. Be patient and answer it over and over, while reminding yourself that you get to leave after the visit and they cannot. Also remember that some day you'll be asking the same questions over and over.

Offer to take your friend or relative for a stroll or a wheelchair ride. If the weather is pleasant, ask if you can go outside. Your friend or relative might want to introduce you to his or her friends in the nursing home—have a chance to show you off—since visitors are a valued commodity.

There is a long list of welcome gifts that you can bring along: the usual toiletries such as powder, nice soaps, hand or body cream, shampoo, perfume, etc. Make sure to mark the box with the patient's name. A warm shawl is useful for someone in a wheelchair or bedbound. Make sure it is large enough to fit over the shoulders and be tied or gathered in front. Gifts of food are also welcome. I sometimes bring fruit compote that is easily made in the microwave oven (page 333). It's a lovely gift that people with slow-moving digestive systems always appreciate. Cookies are another nice gift, especially if they're homemade. Again, remember to label the box or container with the person's name. If your friend or relative likes to read, a book with large type is a nice present, as well as books on tape.

Your conversation and news from the outside world is a cherished form of entertainment to someone whose world has shrunk to the size of a room in a nursing home. I acknowledge that many elderly people can be very trying and a visit with them is a challenge at best, but if this is something you can find the time and energy to do, it may result in your learning that you're pretty good at entertaining in difficult situations, after all.

〜 **CONDOLENCE CALLS:** Although they are a very long stretch of the entertainment category, if, in its broadest meaning, entertainment is the act of providing hospitality, I want to include condolence calls here for the benefit of those who simply are at a loss when it comes to paying respects to someone bereaved by a death.

You don't need to worry about what to say. A simple "I'm so sorry about your loss" followed by a hug or handshake is all that is necessary. Your presence is what counts. If you go to the funeral home during calling hours (sometimes these are included in the newspaper along with the obituary, or you can call the funeral home or the family to get this information), there will be other friends and family there. This is true as well if you pay your respects to a Jewish family during the traditional week of mourning that takes place after the funeral.

While you shouldn't bring anything to the funeral home, it is nice (but not obligatory) to bring something to the person's home, usually food, the idea being to spare the person(s) in mourning of the job of food preparation. You can bring (or send) a basket of fruit, cookies, a coffee cake, or candy. Either store-bought or home-made is appropriate, although it is a nice gesture to bring the food on a dish or in a container that does not have to be returned.

If you enjoy cooking and have the time, it is a lovely gesture to bring a meal or covered dish that can be stored in the refrigerator or freezer and eaten later. Label the container and add reheating directions along with your name (this makes the job of thank-you notes much easier).

If you have had a death in your family and find yourself with the sad job of organizing an open house to receive callers, the best advice I can give you is to accept help from all who offer. Friends and family need a way to express their sympathy. Keeping busy is how many people deal with grief. Give someone the job of making sure there is always a pot of coffee available, as well as paper cups (both for hot and cold beverages), cream, sugar, and napkins. Ask someone else to arrange for a supply of soft drinks, plastic utensils, and plates. Assign someone the job of cleanup and keeping the refrigerator organized (which includes keeping a list of dishes that can be used as meals later on). Probably some of these dishes will need to be stored in the freezer—ask someone to take care of this and to make a list of what is stored where. Give someone else the job of answering the phone and provide this person with all the information he or she needs including the hours you would like company and the name of a charity to which anyone who asks can make a donation in memory of the deceased. Have someone write out directions to your home for the person answering the telephone. Try to have a guest book for people to sign—this also makes the task of writing thank-you notes easier.

About thank-you notes: Printed ones are fine. Usually they say something brief and to the point like "The family of (name of the deceased) thanks you for your kind expression of sympathy." You should add a handwritten line or two, such as "we appreciate your thoughtfulness," and then sign your name. This is a job friends and other family members can help you with.

CHAPTER FIVE

Planning the Meal

Because you have read the first four chapters of this book, you have a pretty good idea of what to expect as a host or hostess. You know how to decide on what type of party to give, how many people to invite, and how to stock your bar. You know what to do if a guest has to leave early or turns up with a two-year-old in tow. You can cope with a stain on your new carpeting and a cellular phone at the dinner table. You can whip up a quick sauce to disguise overcooked beef and won't hesitate to use take-out food in a pinch. But I have not yet addressed one huge, gigantic, and—yes!—maybe terrifying aspect of party giving: planning the meal.

In this chapter I will guide you through the chores of making a shopping list, going to the market, scheduling your time, and prepping for the ultimately pleasurable task of cooking. I even give you detailed advice about cleaning up the kitchen after you have cooked and after the party is over. In the next chapter are suggested menus. Recipes follow last but absolutely not least.

Menu Planning

You should have a pretty good idea of what the menu will be when you issue invitations, since the menu usually determines the kind of party you are having. And once you have planned the menu, it's a short leap to writing a shopping list and then setting out for the supermarket, greengrocer, butcher, baker, or gourmet specialty shop.

〜 **PLANNING THE MENU:** While it may not be crucial for someone with experience in entertaining to plan the menu down to the final crouton and stuffed olive, it is for the novice. Last-minute decisions should be things like which scarf to wear, not whether to serve roast chicken or lamb stew.

When planning the menu, you should have a clear vision of how many courses you will serve, what the courses are, what kinds of pots and pans you will need for cooking, and what kinds of dishes you will need for serving. Also think about how you will set up your dining room or eating area. For instance, you should know whether you will be serving a casserole, roast beef, or grilled fish, since the preparation and cooking times of these differ substantially from each other.

The shopping schedule will vary as well. The last thing you want to be doing is driving around town the morning of the party looking for fresh turkey because you did not realize how long it took frozen turkey to defrost in the refrigerator. As you acquire more experience, you will be able to shop, set up the house, and cook faster. Along the way you will probably find that much of your anxiety turns into anticipation of an enjoyable event.

Write the menu on a piece of paper and leave spaces between each dish to write down ingredients you will have to buy. Make notes about garnishes, serving dishes, and timing—you don't want to choose a menu that requires cooking three dishes at different oven temperatures all at the same time (unless you have three ovens). If you use menus from this book, it's an easy flip of a few pages to find the recipe. If you put together a menu using recipes from a few different books, mark the pages and list the ingredients you need from the ingredient list in the recipe. I have assembled menus that provide a good balance of flavors, textures, and colors. All three are important.

Knowing how to match the menu to the company, the season, the space, and your energy level takes some practice. There are many issues to consider, budget not being the least of them.

Who are you entertaining? Young people tend to eat more and are more open to ethnic foods (meaning hot and spicy, unusual ingredients, unconventional presentations), while older folks tend to like their chicken to look like chicken, taste like chicken, and not cause them gastric distress. Young folks don't have to worry about chewy foods (like caramel) ruining their dentures. I'm not saying there aren't plenty of adventurous seniors out there, but unless you are absolutely sure that Granny and Gramps won't be up all night thinking (not too fondly) of the jalapeño pepper stuffing that you used in the turkey, bag it.

Are your friends sophisticated world travelers who think that eating sushi or pasta with squid ink sauce is the cat's meow? Or are they less adventuresome and more comfortable with more familiar dishes, such as roast beef or spaghetti with tomato sauce?

Are your friends wildly diet conscious? Then don't serve an entrée swimming in cream sauce followed by cheesecake for dessert and then wonder why no one cleaned his plate. Might your politically sensitive friends turn down veal scallopini? Your friend who keeps kosher will certainly not be able to eat chicken in cream sauce or roast pork (see page 119).

Unless you know the company really, really well (blood relatives?), don't serve weird stuff like organs, intestines, and fish with eyeballs still in place. Also, don't serve hard-to-eat or messy things to people you've invited over for a nice dinner party. Lobster in the shell and tacos are delicious, but not at the expense of someone's silk blouse. Other things that may seem easy to eat to you can be a problem for some people: artichokes, for instance, which are eaten with your hands, or mussels still in the shell.

Check the menu carefully to avoid dishes with similar colors, flavors, ingredients, and textures: Don't serve cream of tomato soup, followed by lasagna, stuffed tomatoes, and puréed carrots. It's too much red and too many soft textures. Make the soup Italian vegetable (page 208), the vegetable Marinated Green Beans (page 325), and the second vegetable a salad, and you've got wonderful company for the lasagna.

Remember that many people are weight conscious. If you are planning to serve a "heavy" entrée like roast beef, accompany it with lots of vegetables, plus a starch made without an overload of cream or butter. This way, people who don't eat meat, or don't eat a lot of it, will still have something to fill up on. Watch the number of courses that have cheese. If you serve cheese and crackers or a cheese spread first, don't follow it up with a casserole topped with cheese and then (God forbid) cheesecake for dessert. You'll have to have a cardiologist pay a house call. If you do plan to serve a very rich dessert, consider offering fresh fruit as well.

Plan your menu with the season in mind. Don't set your heart on poached peaches in raspberry sauce and then go nuts when you discover the only peaches available in February are from Chile, cost $2 each, and are not so good. Serve peaches in July and August when they taste their best. The same goes for any ripe, seasonal local produce. August's tomatoes and sweet corn are a short-lived treat. Indulge your guests.

I think the easiest way to plan a menu is first to choose an entrée, next the dessert, then the first course and whatever you're going to serve with drinks. It's sort of like picking out a dress or suit to wear and then choosing the accessories to go along with it. I always work it out on paper so that I can play around, changing and substituting course choices and ending up with the final decision written down.

The process goes something like this: Let's say I'm going to have a dinner party for three couples (plus us). I know one of the couples quite well, and the other two only slightly. The husband of the couple I know well has a cholesterol problem and watches his fat intake very carefully. His wife hates fish and loves chocolate. Since I don't know very much about the two other couples, I'm going to play it safe and serve something fairly conservative: chicken. The easiest form of chicken for eight people is breasts. If I bake the breasts, I'll have to use a sauce to keep them moist, but I don't want to spend calories that way. I decide instead to serve boneless, skinless chicken breasts and marinate them in a low-calorie barbecue sauce and then broil them. I'll make a sauce but serve it on the side so the cholesterol watcher can pass. It's spring and asparagus is in season. I could serve asparagus as a vegetable, seasoned with lemon juice, a little olive oil (no cholesterol), and garlic, and carrots with ginger and honey. Soup would be a good first course, and one that I can make ahead. How about cream of carrot soup made without cream? Oops, I'll have to serve another vegetable—can't have carrots twice. Let's see . . . I can make red cabbage coleslaw, and a couple of days ahead. Now for dessert. I've held back on the fat and calories and everyone loves a great chocolate dessert. But what about Mr. Diet? I could make a chocolate cake and serve strawberries on the side. He could eat just the strawberries and the chocolate lovers would be happy too. Or, I could make "no guilt" chocolate mousse and save myself the trouble of preparing the berries.

As you can see, menu creating is a little bit like doing a puzzle, an exercise in fitting pieces together. Once you have a menu that works for you (don't decide this until the party is over), keep a note of it along with the names of the guests you have fed. This way you can easily repeat a good menu that worked well when you have different guests to dinner. Of course, if parts of it didn't work, note that too so you won't make the same mistake twice.

↩ SPECIAL DIETS: These days everyone seems to be on a special diet—low-fat, high-fiber, no gluten, lactose-free—or has some personal dietary approach to eating such as organic, vegetarian, or food combining. This is all well and good but can put terror in the heart of a host or hostess who doesn't share a particular dietary philosophy. Rest easy. In most cases, another person's diet is not your problem.

People who are strict vegetarians, people who don't consume alcohol (even in cooking), people who keep kosher, people who have allergies, all have the obligation of informing their host or hostess of these dietary restrictions when they accept the invitation. People who are on special liquid fasts (a phenomenon seen more and more frequently these days) should either volunteer to concoct their own "meal" or allow the host or hostess to do so with instructions. They should not expect the host or hostess to have special ingredients, such as skim milk, unless they have requested them beforehand. In no way should the host or hostess single out or purposely call attention to a person on a restricted or special diet. The rest of the company should have the same good manners.

When people accept an invitation to dinner at my house, implied in that acceptance is that they will eat what I am making unless they state upfront (when accepting the invitation) that they have some sort of dietary restrictions. I have several choices at that point: I can tailor the menu to their needs, I can make special food for them, I can invite them to bring their own, or I can forget the whole thing and take them out to lunch in a restaurant of their choice where they can select the food they want. I can also plan the meal so that they can eat at least some of it.

Let's assume you have invited a vegetarian to dinner; you can do one of two things. As part of the meal, you can serve lots of good vegetables, a big salad, and plenty of rice or pasta. The vegetarian won't starve. Or you may wish to tailor the entire menu to his or her needs. You should ask the person exactly what kind of vegetarian he or she is. There are several different kinds, from those who will eat fish and chicken, but not red meat, to those who do not eat eggs or milk or any animal products at all, like butter or cheese. This certainly limits the kinds of dishes you are probably used to making, but if you are up to the challenge, you can turn out a delicious vegetarian meal either by turning to the vegetarian menus in this book or referring to any number of vegetarian cookbooks.

It is a simple matter of menu planning to accommodate people on reduced-fat diets. You'll find several low-fat recipes here, or you can use one of the many low-fat cookbooks available.

Here are a few ways you can trim the calories off when choosing a menu: Round up and exile the usual suspects: butter, cream, high-fat cheeses, fatty meats, and fried foods. Go heavy on fresh, steamed vegetables, fish, and pasta or rice without heavy sauces. Remove the skin from chicken or turkey, and skim the fat off soups and stews. Read labels to check for "hidden" fats, and particularly saturated fats such as coconut oil and palm kernel oil. Cook food in defatted broth, stock, or wine. Serve fresh or poached fruit with frozen yogurt or sorbet for dessert. Let diners serve themselves and no one will feel deprived.

When you entertain people who keep kosher, you should keep

the following things in mind: If they are very strictly kosher they will not eat food prepared in your house or on your dishes. My ultra (*glott*) kosher friends bring their own food and I serve it to them on paper plates. When planning a menu for guests who keep kosher a little less strictly, keep the following things in mind: Do not use dairy products in any form in a meal where there is meat (including poultry). This rule isn't flexible from course to course— you can't serve vegetarian lasagna topped with cheese after a first course soup made with chicken or beef broth. Neutral foods such as fish (but not shellfish, which like pork and pork products is strictly forbidden) and eggs go with both dairy meals and meat meals. Again, it is essential to read labels to check for foods made with ingredients that are not allowed in a kosher meal. An easy way to plan a kosher meal is to make it all vegetarian (page 145).

If you are serving a meal to a guest who is diabetic and would like to make food that he or she can eat, the best thing to do is confer beforehand to get an idea of what kinds of things will be all right. Fresh fruit or a fruit dessert made without the addition of sugar is probably fine, although you should check first with the person who is going to eat it.

Fussy eaters constitute their own category of special diets. Whether you cater to these people is up to you. I have a dear friend who is funny and interesting and a great conversationalist. She would make a terrific dinner guest except she doesn't eat anything but cinnamon raisin bagels, iceberg lettuce, and chocolate chip ice cream. Since I rarely combine these foods in any dinner menu, let alone the same dinner menu, I am faced with a dilemma. It's agony (for me) to watch her play with the food I have so carefully prepared, but I love having her at the table since she adds so much to the conversation. I've settled this by inviting her only to very informal meals where I haven't killed myself whipping up fancy dishes that take hours of my time. If she doesn't want to eat the lasagna it's taken me twenty minutes to make, I somehow don't mind. If you have friends who are fussy eaters, don't make yourself crazy by preparing elaborate feasts and then being furious when they don't lick their plates. They are who they are and your efforts in the kitchen aren't going to change that. Keep the food really simple and easily identifiable, and don't let your ego be trampled if they don't finish.

When people show up at dinner and unexpectedly start making demands for special foods prepared special ways (remember *When Harry Met Sally?*), and the requests go beyond something rational such as "really well done meat versus really rare" or "sauce on the side" or "I'd like an end piece, please," I put on my nicest hostess smile and offer them a peanut butter sandwich or a bowl of cereal. They get the hint right away.

⌒ **FOOD ALLERGIES:** Some special dietary requests are perfectly legitimate: food allergies, for instance. Food allergies are no joke. People who are deathly (and I do mean deathly) allergic to foods such as fish, nuts, some fruits, and certain additives have an obligation to let their host or hostess know upon accepting an invitation that they cannot eat certain foods. Whatever the problem ingredient(s) is, it shouldn't appear on the menu or at least on the allergic guest's plate. Guests with non–life-threatening allergies can opt to avoid the foods they are sensitive to without making a big fuss. Someone who is lactose-intolerant can skip the cheese spread, for instance.

Once the deathly allergic person has made his limitations clear, you as the host or hostess have two options: You can religiously cook everything according to the allergic person's specifications, and with some menus this is not too hard, or you can suggest that the person bring his own food.

When a guest asks if there are nuts in a dish, and he is very allergic to nuts, think beyond the obvious. Nuts may not be an ingredient, but you may have used almond, walnut, hazelnut, or peanut oil in the recipe.

Scheduling Your Time

After you have planned the menu, devise a time line, or schedule, for accomplishing it. In my menus, I have figured this for you, telling you which dishes can be made ahead of time and frozen or refrigerated, and which you should make on the day of the party or at the last minute. Study the recipes and decide how you can best accomplish what needs doing. If possible, break down the cooking tasks into reasonable segments. For instance, if you are making Germaine's Fudgy Brownies (page 372), you can bake and freeze them two weeks in advance and then defrost them at room temperature the night before the party. If you are making Texas Slaw (page 306), make it the day before the party and refrigerate it. If you are planning a Christmas dinner and want to prepare Beef Tenderloin (page 280), you will have to remember to take the tenderloin from the refrigerator an hour before roasting time. And then, after the tenderloin is cooked but before you slice it, you can cook the Easy Potato Pancakes (page 317), which you have bought and frozen one or two weeks earlier, and also heat the asparagus in the microwave—asparagus you steamed until barely limp the day before and stored in the fridge already tossed with butter and arranged in a microwave-safe dish.

None of this is hard, but it does take planning. I cannot overemphasize the importance of a time line or schedule. Not only will it keep you sane, you will feel immensely satisfied as you check off each task.

Making Shopping Lists and Shopping

If two of the recipes in your menu call for eggs, add up the number of eggs. Do you need to buy more than a dozen? If more than one recipe calls for heavy cream, figure how much you need in all and then buy that much plus a cup (eight ounces) or two more in case you spill some or carelessly whip the cream to butter (it happens). On page 74 I discuss serving sizes and these should give you guidance about how much protein (meat, poultry, fish) to buy and how much vegetables and starches. Don't forget to jot down garnishes on the shopping list—lemons, parsley, cocoa powder, strawberries—and always buy a little extra. I am not advocating buying double of everything, but a little extra gives you peace of mind, which you may very well need.

When you make your list, put down the items that you will buy at the supermarket in one column, those you will get at the deli in another, and those you will buy at the cheese/gourmet shop in a third, and so on. Organization counts. Try to pick up nonperishable things ahead of time so you won't have to spend an enormous amount of time shopping on the day before, or the day of, the party. All canned, boxed, bottled, frozen, and packaged goods can be bought weeks before, and things such as cheese, eggs, and half-and-half can be bought at least a week to ten days ahead. Wait until the day of your party, however, to buy very perishable items such as fish, bread, and flowers. Chicken, beef, pork, and veal can be bought the day before, and as with dairy products, make sure to check store expiration dates! Fruits should be bought with an eye to ripeness. In other words, if you want to serve melon on Friday start checking the stores on Tuesday for one that will be ripe by Friday. If you are not sure how to do this, ask the produce clerk to select one for you. It's one of those inexorable rules of life that things like ripe melons, bananas, peaches, mangoes, and avocados are never available the day you need them. Fruits such as grapes and berries ideally should be bought the day you are going to use them. Fragile berries lose their beautiful sheen and become dull-looking after even a day or less in the refrigerator. The same is true of delicate greens such as watercress and dill. However, no one is going to yank your license to entertain if those items are bought the day before.

Preparing to Cook and Reheating Food

Once you have the groceries unpacked, the kitchen cleaned, and the recipes out, you are ready to cook. This is fun. As I said earlier, take out all the ingredients and pots and pans you will need for one dish. Measure ingredients that need measuring and put them in bowls or leave them in the measuring cups if that makes sense; chop or dice those that need chopping or dicing; scrub and peel those that need it; trim the fat from meat and check fish for bones. Be sure to use the right size pan and the correct heat. If the recipe says to stir constantly, do it. If the recipe says to strain through a sieve, don't ignore this instruction. Take your time and be as deliberate as you can.

I have designed my kitchen so that no one feels free to come into my work space. I am a loner when I cook and, once the party begins, it makes me nuts to share my work area with guests who want to chat while I work. My compromise is that they can watch from the other side of a six-foot granite island. I strongly recommend that if you are a new cook or just starting to entertain, keep company out of the kitchen so that you can pay attention to what needs to be done. You can work far more efficiently if you don't have to keep up your end of a conversation at the same time. Here are some ways to keep guests out of the kitchen:

- Have as much of the cooking as possible done ahead. This way you can be in the living room with your guests.

- Have several bowls of snack-type food, such as nuts or cheese and crackers or veggies and dip, set out in the living room for guests to help themselves.

- Serve drinks in the living room and leave a bottle of wine or seltzer there so guests can refill their own glasses. Or ask another guest to keep an eye out for people who need refills.

- If there is a door to the kitchen, keep it closed while you are working.

- Stay long enough with the guests to get the conversation rolling and then excuse yourself with as little fanfare as possible. You might turn to another guest and quietly say, "I have to finish cooking and I'd appreciate it if you would keep things rolling for me out here."

- If someone does wander in to talk or offer to help, tell the person that the way to help most is to pour another round of drinks, pass the cheese, or act as host or hostess in your temporary absence. Do not keep up your end of the conversation and that person will get the hint.

There will be times when you might appreciate offers of help to toss the salad, slice the bread, or open the wine. Choose someone who seems happy to help as opposed to happy to chat. What you want to avoid is getting everyone in on the act. This is you entertaining them, not an exercise in group cooking.

Many recipes in this book can be made ahead of time and refrigerated or frozen until you need them. There are some tricks to successfully reheating food so that it is as moist, flavorful, and attractive as if you had made it that very afternoon.

First, do not overcook the food when you originally make it. With the exception of stews and soups and other recipes with lots of liquid in them, the action of heat on food dries it out, which makes it tough and flavorless. Don't cook things like casseroles to within an inch of their lives. If a recommended cooking time is 40 minutes, stop at 35 or 40 minutes, knowing that it will need an extra 10 or 15 minutes for reheating.

Cover the food to be reheated either with foil (if it's in the oven or on top of the stove) or with plastic wrap (if it's in the microwave). This will keep the food moist. If necessary, remove the cover for the last few minutes of heating to let the top get crisp.

Add moisture in the form of butter, margarine, or broth (chicken, beef, or vegetable) to the dish prior to reheating. Keep the amounts small—about two to three tablespoons of butter or margarine—or a third to a half cup broth for a standard one-and-a-half- to two-quart casserole—and cover the dish while heating.

Heat the dish in a water bath. The steam heat of a water bath gently reheats food—especially anything that is delicate, like a sauce or pudding. This is a lot easier than it sounds. A water bath is simply a double boiler for your oven. Use a large pan (a roasting pan is good) and set the pan (which also needs to be ovenproof) of food in it. Cover the pan of food well with foil. Place both pans in a preheated medium oven (usually 350°F). Pour hot water into the larger pan until it reaches about one inch up the sides of the food pan. Check every twenty minutes and replenish the water if necessary.

You can tell if a dish is hot all the way through by sticking a small sharp knife into it. Pull it out and feel the end of the knife with your fingers. It should be hot, not warm. Another way is to use something called an instant thermometer. You insert it into the food and wait for a reading, and then remove it. Food at 180°F is hot enough to serve.

Washing Up

Dishes should be washed after the guests depart. The only exceptions are if you need the pots, pans, or dishes twice in the same evening, or you need to wash forks or spoons for another course. If you are entertaining in the kitchen, it's sometimes acceptable to wash the dishes as your guests linger around the kitchen table or help, and if you are hosting a family meal (such as Thanksgiving or Christmas), it might be traditional for family members to pitch in.

Do yourself a huge favor and make it a rule never to leave the dishes for the next morning. The sight of the mess may prevent you from ever entertaining again. The exceptions are pots and pans that need soaking. Organization is the key to a quick cleanup. Remove any leftover food from the pots and pans, put them in the sink, and fill them with hot soapy water—hot water activates the detergent. The sooner you do this the easier the cleaning will be because the food won't have a chance to dry out and stick.

As you clear the table, scrape the food into the sink (if you have a garbage disposal) or into a garbage pail lined with a heavy-duty trash bag. Toss the forks, spoons, and nonsharp knives into one of the pots filled with the hot soapy water. Place all sharp knives off to the side of the sink. Soaking sharp knives ruins the handles and putting something with a sharp edge in a sinkful of soapy water invites flesh wounds.

Rinse the dishes as you scrape each one clean. Even if you have a dishwasher you should take care to scrape off all the food. Asking your dishwasher to be a garbage disposal is a big mistake and will result in many large checks to repairmen. If you have a garbage disposal, run hot water over the dishes as you scrape them. If not, scrape first and then run hot water over them. Make it as hot as you can stand it and wear rubber gloves if your hands are sensitive. Put the dishes in the dishwasher or leave them stacked in the sink while you organize the rest of the dishes.

Don't make a practice of storing leftover food in the serving dishes. The dishes are usually half empty, which means you are taking up needless space in your refrigerator, plus it's easier to wash the serving dish now before the food dries on it—and dried food gets more stubborn when chilled. Store the leftovers in plastic containers with snap-on lids, and do it soon after serving the food so you won't have to worry about food poisoning. Foil or plastic wrap is okay if containers don't have lids, but they are no protection against refrigerator accidents later on. Did you ever try to wipe spilled cranberry sauce out of a vegetable crisper days after it spilled?

As you clear the table, put like things together for washing: flatware in the pot of hot, soapy water, glasses together, plates in the sink, serving dishes on the counter. It's easier to wash a series of the same things in a row.

If you have a dishwasher, take care not to place the glasses next to anything that can rattle around and break them. Don't jam the dishes so close together that water cannot run between them, and be careful about where you put small items that could fall through the racks into the bottom of the machine. If you have trouble with spots on your glasses, buy small containers of special cleanser that hook onto the dishwasher racks.

If you are washing by hand, clear a large space right next to the sink for the clean dishes or use a dish rack. You can buy a special rubber mat that goes under the dish rack and slants into the sink for runoff or you can place a bath towel under the dish rack to eliminate water running onto the floor. Have a large sponge for washing the dishes, a plastic-coated scrubbing pad for nonstick pans, and either a steel wool pad or steel brush for scrubbing pots and pans that are not Teflon-coated. You'll need a bottle of liquid detergent and a can of cleanser, such as Ajax or Comet, as well as several clean dishtowels.

Tackle the dishes first and let them drain while you wash the glasses and flatware. If you use really hot water, by the time you finish the dishes, they will need only minimal drying. Take care to rinse off all the soap (check by holding the dishes under a light—they should look completely grease-free). Place the washed glasses upside down on a clean dish towel. If you run out of room, stop and dry some of the dishes and put them away.

Next come pots and pans. If you have been careful to prepare the cooking dishes according to the recipe and have not burned food onto the pans, then they will be much easier to clean. Simply use lots of hot soapy water, a scrubbing pad, and a little elbow grease. For burned-on food, try one of the following things: Add two tablespoons of dish-washer detergent, fill the pot with hot water, and set it over a low flame. Let the water come to a simmer and turn off the flame. This will smell unappetizing but helps loosen burned-on food. Alternatively, dampen the burned area and sprinkle it liberally with cleanser. Let it sit for several hours (or overnight) before scrubbing the burned areas with a steel wool pad and additional cleanser. Do not be tempted to allow bits and pieces of burned food to stay on the pan. It will attract additional food and will make the pan look like hell as well. Also, don't put dishes with burned-on food in the dishwasher. The heat cycle bakes the food on so you'll never get it off.

Once you have finished washing everything, you can either let things air-dry or dry them with dish towels. If you chose to dry them, make sure you switch to a clean, dry dish towel when the one you are using gets too soggy to do the job. Put things away as you dry them rather than restacking. You may be exhausted tonight but you'll thank me tomorrow.

End the cleanup by shaking off the tablecloth or place mats or placing them in the laundry if they are too far gone. Discard the candle stubs and run the candlesticks under scalding water to get rid of any wax. Wipe down the table, counters, and sink. Scrub the top of the stove (remove the burners so you can mop up any food that dripped down inside while you were cooking). Sweep the floor if you still have some energy and rinse out the empty wine and soda bottles and place them in the recycling bin. On your way to bed, pat yourself on the back for having done a terrific job and look forward to all the nice thank-you notes you're going to get from your wildly appreciative guests.

CHAPTER SIX

Suggested Menus

Welcome to the menu section of this book. I've arranged the menu selections by level of ease, starting with the least complicated and time-consuming and moving on to the slightly more challenging, and then on to the big time. I identify these levels of difficulty as Stage 1 through Stage 8. If this is all new to you, please start from the beginning (Stage 1) and work your way through. This will save you headaches and disasters—and save me from your frantic calls and letters.

Each menu is followed by a time line, which will help you get organized in terms of setup and food preparation. This way you'll know what you can do one to two weeks ahead, what to do two days ahead, and what to do the morning of your party. Here, too, you'll find strategies to save you lots of last-minute work. Obviously, you have the freedom to play with the schedule and use your own judgment about what works best for you. Someone who has spare time the day before won't have to make brownies two weeks ahead and freeze them. But, if you want ripe avocados or melons, you had better go shopping several days ahead to give them time to ripen. I always set the table or at least lay out my dishes, linens, serving utensils, wineglasses, and the like the day before.

For your own sanity and that of your guests, don't leave everything until the last moment; you'll be exhausted, depleted, perhaps hostile, and never want to have another party.

These menus are flexible. I've tried to offer recipes that can, in many cases, be switched from one to another. This means that, if you see a menu that appeals to you but you aren't crazy about one of the courses, look through the other recipes and choose something else. I've also offered meatless entrée choices to menus where the main course wouldn't do for your vegetarian friends. Be sure to make notes in the book right next to the menu or recipe: "great," "so-so," "should have made more," "looked great in the big blue bowl," "Aunt Bella's very favorite" . . . etc. You'll never remember these fine points if you don't write them down. And they really come in useful.

How to Increase or Decrease a Recipe

The majority of the recipes in this book serve eight people. If you are feeding six, my advice is to make the full recipe and enjoy the leftovers. For four, cut the recipes in half by simply dividing the ingredients by two. This does not always work and in some cases you'll have to be creative; it will be hard to find someone who will sell you a half a tenderloin, but you could make individual filet mignons instead (page 282). Any recipe can be cut in half but whether it's worth the time and trouble is another matter. Someone who is an experienced baker can probably figure out how to make half a recipe of cake or cookies, but for most cooks, it's far less complicated to make the whole thing, or pick another recipe. For other recipes, you'll find that it's almost easier to make the whole thing (lasagna or stuffed grape leaves, for instance), using two dishes and freezing one for another time. Remember that you'll need smaller baking dishes or casseroles and that cooking times must be decreased; a two-pound pork roast will cook faster than a three- or four-pound roast will. If you are cooking for two, pick individual chops, fish steaks, or vegetarian recipes that can be divided by four, adjusting the cooking time as well. This is where an instant-read thermometer comes in handy. (Pages 83–86 in *The Kitchen Survival Guide*, my previous book, tell you how to know when things are done.)

Take care when you double or triple recipes. You don't want to pick something so time-consuming that you double and triple the work too. The buffet menus beginning on page 156 are chosen with an eye toward how easy the recipes are to increase for a crowd. It's best, in many cases, to make the standard recipe for eight several times in several pans, pots, or bowls, rather than doing it in one overwhelming batch and worrying about if it will cook all the way through before it burns on the outside.

Stage 1: Super-easy Get-togethers, Barbecues, and Potluck Suppers

The menus in this section are so informal and easy that they are practically fail-safe. Even if you do have a problem, no one will notice. I've called the first event a "Super Bowl" party—but it can just as easily be an after-the-marathon-party, a pool party, or a get-together to watch the election returns or Academy Awards. All the food is prepared and cooked beforehand, with the exception of some last-minute reheating and/or outdoor grilling (which can also be done indoors).

The mood and dress at these parties are extremely casual, and the food is not the main focus. When you invite your guests to this type of party, they may very well volunteer to bring or buy food, and your immediate response will be "YES!" The only trick will be to assign them things that will be time-saving for you. When someone asks, "What can I bring?" suggest several bags of pretzels or chips or a few six-packs of beer. Be specific. If someone asks, "What can I make?"

assign her a dip or salad or batch of brownies. Make sure there is an understanding between you and the person who offers as to the amount she is bringing. "Macaroni salad for eight" or "a dozen brownies" is far more instructive than "Oh, just bring whatever you feel like." Make sure you make a note on your menu sheet so you don't accidentally duplicate the item.

Super Bowl Party

I call this get-together a Super Bowl party, but it can be any afternoon or evening gathering of friends without the expectation of being served a meal. The main goal is to have enough to give people to put in their mouths while they root for the home team.

A get-together being the most informal version of an open house, you can expect the crowd to wander in over a period of time, and you need to be sure that snacks and drinks are served throughout the evening or afternoon. The following menu offers food that can all be made ahead of time. The sesame chicken and Buffalo chicken wings can be served hot or room temperature. The brownies can be made ahead of time and frozen.

The menu is for eight people and can be doubled, tripled, or even quadrupled.

Layered Taco Dip (page 202) with pita wedges

Korean Beef (page 278) or Nancy Belsky's Sesame Chicken (page 272)

Spicy Buffalo Chicken Wings (page 190)

Salsa (page 203) and tortilla chips

Wheat Chex Cocktail Mix (page 188)

Avery Island Hot Nuts (page 187)

Fruit Salad in a Watermelon Bowl (page 360)

Germaine's Fudgy Brownies (page 372)

Drinks: beer, soft drinks, wine

MENU VARIATIONS: If you want to add something more for the vegetarian crowd, consider Guacamole (page 204), Pronto Focaccia Appetizer (page 186), Marinated Mushrooms (page 185), or Five-Spice Shrimp (page 192).

HELPFUL HINT: If you are entertaining more than ten people, have several dishes or platters of each kind of food and position them around wherever people might be mingling.

SUPER BOWL PARTY TIME LINE

UP TO 2 WEEKS AHEAD: Bake and freeze the brownies. Allow them to defrost at room temperature the night before the party. They actually will only take 2 hours to defrost, in case for some reason you want to wait until the day of the party.

1 WEEK AHEAD: Shop for all the paper goods, soft drinks, beer, wine, chips, salsa (if you're not making your own), and all the canned goods.

3 DAYS AHEAD: Make the Avery Island hot nuts and Wheat Chex mix. Buy any fruit that needs to ripen such as melons, peaches, bananas, and pears. Buy avocados and tomatoes for the layered taco dip.

DAY BEFORE: Shop for the remaining perishables, including the pita bread. Make the salsa if you haven't bought it. Marinate and then cook the chicken, chicken wings, and/or beef (reheat before serving). Make a place either in the refrigerator or in a cooler to chill the drinks (perhaps the climate will allow you to do this outside). Check the ice.

MORNING OF: Make the layered taco dip. Cut up the fruit and arrange it either in the watermelon or on platters, cover with plastic, and store in the refrigerator or on a cool porch. Cut pita wedges. Put dips and snacks into bowls.

Down-home Cookout

Barbecues are friendly meals. No one is expecting haute cuisine served in a formal setting. The mood is relaxed and rain is the only possible disaster. But this is a cookout that you can easily move inside.

The menus are for eight people and can be doubled or halved.

Salsa (page 203) and tortilla chips

Assorted pretzels and potato chips

Marinated Flank Steak (page 276) or Cheddar-Stuffed Turkey Burgers

(page 261)

Easy Potato Salad (page 305)

Texas Slaw (page 306)

Fruit Salad in a Watermelon Bowl (page 360)

Brownie Sundae (page 374)

Drinks: lemonade, soft drinks, beer, wine

MENU VARIATIONS: Main course—Grilled Vegetable Kabobs (page 236), Curried Rice Salad (page 244), or Southwest Pasta Salad (page 235).

DOWN-HOME COOKOUT TIME LINE

UP TO 2 WEEKS AHEAD: Bake and freeze the brownies.

1 WEEK AHEAD: Shop for all the nonperishables (canned, bagged, bottled, and boxed goods and paper goods). Buy charcoal and lighter fluid or check amount of propane in your gas grill.

2 DAYS AHEAD: Shop for the vegetables (salsa, potato salad, and slaw), watermelon (store it in the refrigerator or a cool place), fruit for the fruit salad, meat, salsa ingredients, ice cream, and fudge sauce. Marinate the meat. Make the fudge sauce for the brownies.

DAY BEFORE: Make the salsa, potato salad, and slaw. Chill the drinks. Check the ice. Remove the brownies from the refrigerator, still wrapped, to defrost at room temperature.

MORNING OF: Cut up the fruit for salad and fill the watermelon. Put the salsa and snacks in bowls. Shape the turkey burgers, if serving. Make whipped cream for the sundaes.

Upscale Cookout

This menu is slightly more sophisticated than the previous one, but just as easy to make. Remember that children probably will still want something more to their taste than these dishes, so make sure to buy hot dogs or hamburger patties and buns.

Chick-pea Pesto (page 201) and pita wedges

Marinated Mushrooms (page 185)

Grilled Teriyaki Mustard Tuna Steaks (page 292)

Grilled Vegetable Kabobs (page 236)

Pesto Orzo (page 308), served cold

Garlic Cheese Bread (page 390)

Olga's Carrot Cake (page 352)

Drinks: White Wine Sangria (page 386), soft drinks, beer

MENU VARIATIONS: Main course—Marinated Flank Steak (page 276), Nancy Belsky's Sesame Chicken (page 272); dessert—Denver Chocolate Pudding (page 356).

UPSCALE COOKOUT TIME LINE

1 WEEK AHEAD: Shop for all the nonperishables, paper goods, charcoal, lighter fluid, drinks, spread, carrot cake ingredients, and bread for garlic bread. Make and freeze the garlic bread, wrapping it in heavy foil. Make and freeze the cooled unfrosted cake.

3 DAYS AHEAD: Shop for the remaining ingredients except the tuna. Make the marinated mushrooms. Order the tuna, if necessary.

DAY BEFORE: Shop for the tuna. Defrost the cake and ice it. Make the tuna and vegetable marinades; make chick-pea pesto and pesto orzo. Check the ice.

DAY OF: Cut up the vegetables and marinate the vegetables and tuna. Cut pita wedges; make the sangria. Heat the garlic bread.

Potluck Suppers

There are two ways of doing a potluck supper, and your personality will dictate which one is best for you. The first is to invite your friends to bring their favorite dish without a specific assignment. Just tell them to bring anything they want—appetizer, main course, salad, vegetable, or dessert—as long as it will feed eight to ten people. Now, when I say friends, I really do mean *friends*, because you're going to get a first-hand lesson in what is important food-wise to certain people. You could end up with ten desserts and a loaf of zucchini bread! In this case, the food becomes the entertainment and you absolutely have to be prepared to have a sense of humor about it. You also should be smart enough to prepare a main course large enough to serve everyone coming.

The second way is a little more organized: Give assignments. That doesn't mean you still can't have fun. Every year I host an event called the Great Women's Nostalgia Potluck Dinner. I invite fifteen or twenty of my friends to bring a course from their childhood. Four people bring appetizers or pickup hors d'oeuvres for eight to ten, four people bring desserts, three people bring salads or vegetables, and the rest bring main courses. I provide the drinks (wine, soft drinks, coffee, tea), bread or rolls, plus another main course, which is usually vegetarian.

It is important to be specific in some areas when you give assignments. Ask people to bring enough food in microwavable or oven-to-table serving dishes to feed the number of guests. Ask them to bring food that is easy to serve and easy to eat at a buffet-style meal. If their dishes need a condiment, like a certain kind of mustard or sauce, or to be served on crackers, ask them to bring those as well. Soup and dishes with a lot of loose sauce are not great ideas at this kind of meal, since it means providing another dish, or having the sauce run into the other dishes on the plate.

Ask that people try to bring things that are already hot or that can be served at room temperature. This will free up your oven for things that have to be heated at the last minute. Ask the people who are bringing the appetizers or predinner pickups either to come a little early so that you can be sure there will be food available when people show up, or to drop the food off earlier in the day. You might have some salsa and chips on hand, just in case.

Request that the people who have the salad and vegetable assignments bring "hearty" salads (complete with dressing) and substantial vegetable or starch dishes, such as pasta salad, to feed people who are vegetarians. If there are people who don't have the time or desire to cook, you can ask them to purchase prepared foods, wine, beer, or soft drinks.

My favorite main course dishes to make for potluck dinners are the pasta or rice casseroles that can be made with or without meat, Speedy Turkey Chili (page 255), a pasta casserole such as Four Seasons Pasta Salad (page 233), or Zucchini Lasagna (page 248). Garlic Cheese Bread (page 390) is a great and easy-to-make accompaniment to all these dishes.

The table should be set buffet style (see page 31), and please take the time to read the section about buffet dinners which is full of handy tips about coping.

Stage 2: Just Appetizers, Just Dessert, Simple Suppers

Stage 2 menus begin with cocktails before going out to dinner, or dessert after dinner out. It proceeds to two simple suppers (both with vegetarian alternatives) for four, six, or eight people. Here, with the exception of one entrée, all the food is prepared well ahead of time.

Drinks Before Going Out to Dinner

This is a nice way to practice entertaining skills without having to make the whole meal, or even set the table. Next time you make dinner plans, invite the other couple(s) to your house first for drinks and an appetizer, which you serve in the living room, den, or family room (or whatever you call the room where you entertain company). Here are three menus.

MENU 1

Smoked Salmon Pâté (page 196)
Rosemary Goat Cheese Wedges (page 194)

MENU 2

Five-Spice Shrimp (page 192)
Cheese-Stuffed Sugar Snap Peas (page 198)

MENU 3

Baked Brie (page 193)
Avery Island Hot Nuts (page 187)

Drinks: wine or Champagne Cocktails (page 387), soft drinks

HELPFUL HINTS: Any of the appetizers that require cooking can be served at room temperature, so if you are not comfortable with last-minute preparation, cook what you need up to an hour before you plan to serve it and place it on a serving plate. If you make the goat cheese wedges ahead of time, let them cool on a rack without stacking them so that they won't get soggy.

MENU 1

UP TO 3 DAYS AHEAD: Shop for all the ingredients and beverages.

DAY BEFORE: Make the smoked salmon pâté. Check the ice.

MORNING OF: Chill the beverages. Cut the pita bread and store it in a plastic bag. Take the goat cheese out of refrigerator to soften for several hours.

MENU 2

DAY BEFORE: Shop for all the ingredients. If you buy uncooked shrimp, cook and peel them. If you buy frozen, peeled shrimp, cook them. Marinate the shrimp. Check the ice.

MORNING OF: Chill the beverages. Prepare the stuffed peas and refrigerate until ready to cook.

MENU 3

UP TO 4 DAYS AHEAD: Shop for all the ingredients except the bread for the Brie. Prepare the Avery Island hot nuts. Locate a source for the kind of bread you'll need, and if necessary, reserve a loaf. Check the ice.

DAY OF: Chill the drinks. Buy the bread and make the baked brie.

Dessert After Going Out to Dinner

You don't need to go out to dinner first to invite friends over for dessert and coffee. Choose *one* of these sinfully delicious but so easy-to-make-ahead recipes and you'll get raves and requests for seconds.

White Chocolate Cheesecake (page 350) with Raspberry Sauce (page 366)

Linzer Bars (page 369)

Denver Chocolate Pudding (page 356)

Strawberries with Raspberry Sauce (page 366)

Drinks: coffee, tea, cordials

HELPFUL HINTS: It's always easier and far less messy to cut and serve desserts in the kitchen. In the case of linzer bars, place them on a pretty serving plate and allow people to help themselves (you can eat these either with a fork, or like a cookie with your fingers). Cheesecake is easier to cut if you use a sharp knife that has been rinsed with very hot water and then wiped dry. Use a spoon to scoop the Denver chocolate pudding onto plates and pass a bowl of whipped cream or ice cream separately. (Feel free to substitute frozen yogurt for the ice cream. Do not feel free to substitute fake whipped cream—it will insult your lovely-tasting dessert.)

Simple Supper 1

Now that you've tried your hand at one-course meals, welcome to the next step: three courses. Again, make-ahead is the key to your sanity and success. As you can see, the first dinner has a Tex-Mex orientation.

Guacamole (page 204) on pita wedges

Salsa (page 205) and tortilla chips

Classic Gazpacho (page 214)

Southwest Pasta Salad (page 235) or Speedy Turkey Chili (page 255)

Spicy Corn Bread (page 392)

Texas Slaw (page 306)

Strawberries with Raspberry Sauce (page 366) or Denver Chocolate Pudding (page 356)

Drinks: White Wine Sangria (page 386), beer, soft drinks, coffee, tea

SIMPLE SUPPER 1 TIME LINE

UP TO 1 WEEK AHEAD: Shop for all the nonperishables. Make and freeze the corn bread and chili. Buy unripened avocados to soften at home.

2 DAYS AHEAD: Shop for the rest of the ingredients. Make the raspberry sauce. Make or buy the salsa. Make the gazpacho.

DAY BEFORE: Make the slaw (and chili and cornbread if you haven't done so already). Move the premade frozen chili to the refrigerator to defrost. Chill the beverages. Make the sangria (keep chilled). Check the ice. Make the guacamole and the pasta salad. Set out serving dishes and utensils.

DAY OF: Make the Denver chocolate pudding and store it at room temperature. Cut pita wedges, prepare the strawberries, remove the cornbread from the freezer and allow it to defrost at room temperature, still wrapped. Place the chips in serving bowls.

Simple Supper 2

This is a perfect cool-weather menu that offers vegetables that are in season in the autumn months.

Avery Island Hot Nuts (page 187)

Roquefort Celery Boats (page 197) or Chick-pea Pesto (page 201) on sliced
French bread

Tomato Cheddar Soup (page 207) or Caesar Salad (page 222)

Picadillo (page 264) and Lemon Orzo (page 309) or Sweet-and-Sour Curried
Cabbage Rolls (page 240)

Sesame Green Beans (page 326)

Cheddar Biscuits (page 388)

Frozen Espresso Chocolate Mousse (page 346) or Cider Baked Apples (page 363)

Drinks: wine, beer, soft drinks, coffee, tea

SIMPLE SUPPER 2 TIME LINE

UP TO 1 WEEK AHEAD: Shop for all the nonperishables, as well as the soup, mousse, and picadillo or cabbage roll ingredients if you wish to make these ahead for freezing. Make the frozen mousse. If you wish, you can prepare the picadillo or the cabbage rolls in an oven-to-freezer casserole and freeze it. Make the Avery Island hot nuts.

DAY BEFORE: Shop for all the other ingredients. Make the Roquefort celery boats or chick-pea spread. Make the baked apples, but undercook them by 10 minutes so that you can reheat them if you wish to serve them warm. Refrigerate them until 2 hours before you are ready to serve or reheat them: Warm in a microwave or in a 300°F oven for 10 minutes.

If you have made the picadillo or cabbage rolls ahead, remove from the freezer the morning before and allow to defrost in the refrigerator. If you haven't already prepared the soup, picadillo, or cabbage rolls, you can do it today and refrigerate until ready to reheat in the microwave or conventional oven. Chill the wine. Check the ice.

DAY OF: Make the salad and orzo. Prepare the biscuits early in the day and reheat in the microwave just before serving. Prepare the green beans. Heat the soup just before serving.

Simple Supper 3

This vegetarian menu has an Italian theme and is suitable for any season.

Marinated Mushrooms (page 185)

Pronto Focaccia Appetizer (page 186)

Garden Salad (page 224) or Quick Italian Vegetable Soup (page 208)

Zucchini Lasagna (page 248) or Pesto Orzo (page 308), served hot

Garlic Cheese Bread (page 390)

Cider Baked Apples (page 363) or Chocolate Cassata (page 354)

Drinks: wine, coffee, tea

SIMPLE SUPPER 3 TIME LINE

UP TO 1 WEEK AHEAD: Shop for all the nonperishables and lasagna ingredients. Buy the garlic bread ingredients. Prepare and freeze it. Make and freeze the cassata and lasagna.

2 DAYS AHEAD: Buy the pasta and salad or soup ingredients. Buy the mushroom ingredients. Make the marinated mushrooms. Make or buy salad dressing.

DAY BEFORE: Buy focaccia. Check the ice. Chill the beverages. Defrost the lasagna and cassata in the refrigerator.

DAY OF: Prepare the salad or soup. Prepare the orzo pesto and place in a covered ovenproof casserole for reheating. Prepare the apples and leave at room temperature. Heat the garlic bread.

Stage 3:
Seasonal Suppers

Stage 3 menus are slightly more challenging than Stage 2 menus. The following four menus are for informal suppers that do nicely for something as simple as family or friends getting together or something a bit more festive such as a birthday celebration. I have created a menu for each season to take advantage of produce that is at its best and is also affordable because of its availability. Each dish serves eight people but can be halved or doubled.

While you can make this menu during the week, I think of this sort of cooking as "weekend entertaining," since the dishes are a little fancier than usual weekday fare in most homes. Don't worry, fancy doesn't mean difficult—I promise.

Spring Supper

Wheat Chex Cocktail Mix (page 188)

Chick-pea Pesto (page 201) with Crudités (page 206)

Curried Carrot Soup (page 210) or Caesar Salad (page 222)

Steamed Asparagus with Lemon Butter (page 322) or Lemon Mustard Sauce (page 323)

Oven-Roasted Salmon with Red Potatoes and Dill (page 294) or Sweet-and-Sour Curried Cabbage Rolls (page 240)

Cheddar Biscuits (page 388) or French bread

Strawberries Romanoff (page 364) and Lemon Bars (page 370)

Drinks: wine, coffee, tea

SPRING SUPPER TIME LINE

UP TO 1 WEEK AHEAD: Call around to find out who has fresh salmon and place an order. Shop for all the nonperishables. Make Wheat Chex mix. If serving cabbage rolls and/or soup, make them now and place them in a freezer-to-oven or microwave casserole dish. Make the lemon bars and freeze them.

DAY BEFORE: Chill the beverages. Check the ice. Shop for the rest of the ingredients. Defrost the cabbage and/or soup. Make the chickpea pesto. If you wish to serve the asparagus cold, steam them today and refrigerate. Prepare the lemon mustard sauce.

DAY OF: Buy bread or make the biscuits. Rinse and hull the strawberries and prepare dessert. Cut up the vegetables for the crudités and make the salad. Assemble the salmon and potatoes and roast just before serving. Do not cut the potatoes ahead of time; they will turn black.

Summer Supper

Five-Spice Shrimp (page 192)

Garlic Cheese Bread (page 390)

Guacamole (page 204) with pita wedges or corn chips

Steven Raichlen's Mangospacho (page 212) or Summer Salad (page 303)

Grilled Teriyaki Mustard Tuna Steaks (page 292) or Grilled Vegetable Kabobs (page 236)

Pesto Orzo (page 308), served cold

Oreo Ice-Cream Cake (page 348) or Raspberry Trifle (page 358)

Drinks: White Wine Sangria (page 386), ice coffee, Orange-Spiked Ice Tea (page 384)

SUMMER SUPPER TIME LINE

1 WEEK AHEAD: Shop for the nonperishables. Buy the garlic cheese bread ingredients, prepare the bread, and freeze it, wrapped in foil. Make and freeze the Oreo ice-cream cake. Order the tuna, if necessary.

2 DAYS AHEAD: Shop for all the other ingredients. Chill the wine. Check the ice.

DAY BEFORE: Marinate the shrimp. You can store them in a heavy-duty plastic freezer bag. Prepare the mangospacho and refrigerate it. Prepare the fish marinade. Make the trifle and guacamole. Make the pesto orzo.

DAY OF: A.M.—Assemble the kabobs, if necessary, place them on a tray, cover with plastic wrap, and refrigerate. Make the sangria, ice coffee, and tea and refrigerate. If you wish to serve the kabobs at room temperature, they can be grilled up to 4 hours ahead and left at room temperature. Heat the garlic bread.

Fall Supper

Pronto Focaccia Appetizer (page 186)

Cheese-Stuffed Sugar Snap Peas (page 198)

Tomato Cheddar Soup (page 207) or Pear and Roquefort Salad (page 220)

Perfect Roast Chicken (page 274) with Garlic Potatoes (page 314) or

Zucchini Lasagna (page 248)

Garlic Cheese Bread (page 390)

Olga's Carrot Cake (page 352) or Cider Baked Apples (page 363)

Drinks: beer or ale, cider, coffee, tea

FALL SUPPER TIME LINE

1 WEEK AHEAD: Shop for all the nonperishables. Prepare and freeze the unfrosted carrot cake. Purchase the garlic cheese bread ingredients, prepare the bread to the point just before baking, wrap in foil, and freeze. Prepare the lasagna in a freezer-to-oven baking dish.

DAY BEFORE: Shop for the remaining ingredients. Defrost the lasagna in the refrigerator. Defrost the carrot cake at room temperature, still wrapped. Prepare the cream cheese frosting and frost the cake. Wrap it lightly in plastic wrap and store at room temperature (unless your kitchen is very hot, in which case put the cake in the refrigerator). Make the cheese filling for the peas. Check the ice. Buy the chicken(s), if serving.

DAY OF: A.M.—Chill the beer, ale, or cider. Late afternoon—Prepare the chicken and potatoes. Prepare the salad and dressing or soup. Stuff the peas. Heat the garlic bread.

Winter Supper

Baked Brie (page 193)

Marinated Mushrooms (page 185)

Pesto-Stuffed Tomatoes (page 324)

Lightning Creole Chicken (page 270) with Lemon Rice (page 310) or

Zucchini Lasagna (page 248)

Spicy Corn Bread (page 392)

Garden Salad (page 224)

Mega Apple Crisp (page 362) or Frozen Espresso Chocolate Mousse (page 346)

Drinks: Hot Mulled Cider (page 380), wine, coffee, tea

WINTER SUPPER TIME LINE

1 WEEK AHEAD: Shop for all the nonperishables. If you wish to make the chicken or the lasagna ahead, buy the ingredients, make the dish, and freeze it in a freezer-to-oven casserole dish. Prepare the cornbread and freeze it in foil. Prepare the frozen espresso chocolate mousse or apple crisp and freeze it.

3 DAYS AHEAD: Shop for all the remaining ingredients except the bread for the baked Brie, if you haven't already made and frozen it. Prepare the mushrooms and refrigerate in a covered container.

DAY BEFORE: Put the frozen chicken or lasagna and cornbread in the refrigerator to defrost. Assemble the pasta and bake, if serving. Chill the wine and soft drinks. Check the ice. Prepare the pesto-stuffed tomatoes up to the point to just before baking. Refrigerate in a covered container until ready to cook. Defrost the apple crisp.

DAY OF: Prepare the salad (store the washed and dried greens in a plastic bag). Prepare the mulled cider. Prepare the lemon rice in a heatproof casserole. Make the baked Brie. Late afternoon—if you plan to warm the apple crisp, cover it loosely with foil and, just before you sit down for the meal, place it in a 225°F oven until ready to serve. Don't let it warm more than 30 minutes or it will dry out.

Stage 4:
Holiday Dinners

If you can handle the menus that came before in Stages 1 through 3, you're ready for Stage 4. These menus simply require more balancing, more planning, and more doing ahead. What better way to take the plunge than with a simplified traditional holiday dinner? For many of us these occasions are made up of friends and family who are so grateful that you have volunteered to host the meal, that they would be loath to criticize anything. This is also the kind of meal to which people typically volunteer to bring things, so chances are you won't have to prepare all the courses. Make sure that the person who volunteers knows how much to bring and can be trusted to follow through. If you have a microwave, it makes sense to ask anyone who is bringing something that needs reheating to bring it in a microwavable container or serving dish.

Every family serves holiday meals at different times. My favorite time is midafternoon, around two o'clock. This way, the guests are hungry enough to enjoy the large meal to come and will finish early enough so that the host and hostess do not face a monstrous pile of dishes at ten P.M. If there is any way you can afford it, consider hiring someone to wash the dishes. You'll have to start your search early since lots of people have discovered the joys of paying someone else to wash up. College employment offices are a good place to start. For more on this, see page 104.

Thanksgiving Dinner

Thanksgiving dinner is a perfect place to try your wings. Usually it's family and close friends who expect a certain level of chaos on Turkey Day. Forgive the following sexist assumption, but many of the male members of the guest list will be happily glued to the TV with a bowl of pretzels, while the kids wander around underfoot before dinner. A great activity for kids is a simple scavenger hunt: Have an adult hide pennies or peanuts in clearly defined on-limit areas (not the kitchen or near the hutch with the priceless crystal) or, weather and neighborhood permitting, outside is a great idea. It's helpful to remind the big kids that, as in an Easter egg hunt, they have to let the little kids find the treasures as well. You can award prizes (have lots of categories) or just let the kids keep the pennies or peanuts.

Let go of any compulsive notions I've drummed into you and allow anyone who isn't watching the game or looking for pennies to help out in the kitchen. Or, if it's easier for you and them, encourage them to relax in front of the fire or to visit among themselves.

Except for the turkey, which will feed twelve (with leftovers), the recipes here are for eight people, which means that if you are feeding twelve people, plan to make one and one half times each recipe. If you're having fewer people and don't want a lot of leftovers, get a smaller turkey. Consult the meat person at the market about size.

If you need to simplify this menu, cut out the first course and go right into the entrée.

Nuts in the shell (don't forget a nut cracker and a bowl for the shells)

Assorted melon wedges, served on toothpicks

Pretzels

Baked Brie (page 193)

Ambrosia (page 219)

Perfect Roast Turkey with Corn Bread Stuffing (page 257) or Sweet-and-Sour
Curried Cabbage Rolls (page 240)
Stove-Top Cranberry Sweet Potatoes (page 316)
Marinated Green Beans (page 325)
Cheddar Biscuits (page 388) or store-brought freeze-and-bake rolls
White Chocolate Cheesecake (page 350) or Cider Baked Apples (page 363)
and Pecan Squares (page 367)

Drinks: cold cider, wine, soft drinks, coffee, tea

THANKSGIVING DINNER TIME LINE

2–3 WEEKS AHEAD: Order the turkey. This may seem like an in-
ordinately long lead time, but I like to buy a fresh, organic turkey and
the farms tend to run out, so I make sure to place my order early. Even
if you don't insist on organic turkey, it's a good idea to order this far
in advance. The butcher gets lots of orders at this time of year.

1 WEEK AHEAD: Shop for all the nonperishables plus ingredients for
the cheesecake. Prepare the Brie up to the point to just before cooking.
Wrap it in foil and freeze. If you are serving the vegetarian entrée,
prepare and cook the cabbage rolls, baking them in a freezer-to-oven
casserole dish for only three fourths of the instructed time. Cool and
freeze them. Prepare the cheesecake or pecan squares, cool, and freeze.

2–3 DAYS AHEAD: Shop for the remaining ingredients. If you are
using a frozen turkey, place it in the refrigerator to defrost. Buy the
melons and store them at room temperature to ripen.

DAY BEFORE: Cut up the green beans, blanch, and marinate them.
Cut the melons into chunks. Store both in refrigerator. Prepare the sweet
potatoes up to point to just before cooking. Refrigerate. Chill the wine
and soft drinks. Check the ice. Buy dinner rolls (or you can use frozen
"you bake" dinner rolls). Set the table and lay out all the serving dishes
and utensils you will need. You can make the stuffing the day before.
Store it in plastic bag in the refrigerator (NOT IN THE TURKEY!!!).

Make the baked apples, cooking them only 20 minutes. Store them at room temperature, covered with foil. Make the ambrosia.

NIGHT BEFORE: Remove the cabbage rolls and cheesecake from the freezer. Since you have undoubtedly run out of room in the fridge, let them defrost overnight at room temperature, still wrapped in foil. You'll have room for them when you remove the turkey from the refrigerator the next morning.

DAY OF: Stuff and roast the turkey, removing the stuffing as soon as the turkey is cooked. (Spoon the cooked stuffing into an ovenproof dish and cover it with foil.) Or finish baking the cabbage rolls. Prepare the sweet potatoes and keep them warm on the stove top. When you remove the turkey from the oven, replace it with the stuffing. It can also be microwaved. Make the baked Brie. Finish baking the apples. The dinner rolls can be warmed in a toaster oven or microwave.

Christmas or New Year's Day Dinner

Your Christmas or New Year's dinner can be a carbon copy (atmosphere-wise) of Thanksgiving, or it can be more formal with a more sophisticated menu. If, in fact, the Thanksgiving menu is more your style, and you haven't just hosted Thanksgiving, consider it for these December and January holidays. Baked ham is a nice alternative to turkey if you prefer.

This menu is as appropriate for a mid-afternoon meal as it is for dinnertime. If children are in attendance, ask them first if they like lobster (some kids love it) before giving it to them for the first course. Or if you are feeling the need to simplify, then cut out the first course and go right into the entrée.

Smoked Salmon Pâté (page 196)

Roquefort Celery Boats (page 197)

Pronto Focaccia Appetizer (page 186)

Lobster Melon Cocktail (page 226) or Cold Cherry Soup (page 216)

Beef Tenderloin (page 280) or Cranberry Cider–Glazed Pork Roast (page 286)

Easy Potato Pancakes (page 317) or Grilled Vegetable Kabobs (page 236)

Steamed Asparagus with Lemon Butter (page 322) or Lemon Mustard Sauce

(page 323)

Chocolate Cassata (page 354) or Strawberries Romanoff (page 364) and

Chocolate Truffles (page 377)

Drinks: wine, soft drinks, coffee, tea

CHRISTMAS OR NEW YEAR'S DAY DINNER TIME LINE

1–2 WEEKS AHEAD: Check the suggested menu and decide if you wish to serve a first course. Shop for all the nonperishable ingredients plus the cassata ingredients. Find a source for (and order, if necessary) the tenderloin or pork roast. Buy the frozen hash browns for the potato pancakes and store them in the freezer. Make and freeze the cassata. Make and freeze the truffles in a tightly covered container.

2 DAYS AHEAD: Shop for all the remaining ingredients, especially the melons to make sure they are ripe.

DAY BEFORE: Defrost the cassata and truffles in the refrigerator. If you're serving a first course, make the soup or cut the melon and lobster for the salad. Make the dressing and toss them together. Store in the refrigerator. Chill the wine and soft drinks. Check the ice. Wash and cut the vegetables for the kabobs. Rinse and trim the asparagus. Store all vegetables in plastic bags in the refrigerator. Make the Roquefort celery boats. Set the table. Steam the asparagus until barely limp, toss with butter, place in a microwavable dish, and cover with plastic wrap. Make the smoked salmon pâté and refrigerate.

DAY OF: Make the strawberries Romanoff. Assemble the salmon pâté. One hour before roasting, remove the tenderloin from the refrigerator and allow it to come to room temperature. After roasting the tenderloin or pork, raise the oven temperature and cook the potato pancakes while the roast rests before cutting. Make the focaccia appetizer. Microwave the asparagus just before serving.

Easter Dinner

Unless you live in sunny Florida or California, Easter can be wonderfully springlike or just another cold, gray day. If the temperature is hovering in the fifties or lower, your guests will want something on the hearty side. Naturally, the opposite is true if you're serving your pascal feast in Phoenix. I'm including some warm- and cool-weather alternatives in this menu.

Even though this is called dinner, it can be served as the afternoon meal as well.

Five-Spice Shrimp (*page 192*)

Baked Brie (*page 193*)

Caesar Salad (*page 222*)

Steamed Asparagus with Lemon Butter (*page 322*) or Lemon Mustard Sauce (*page 323*)

Crescent rolls (*store-bought freezer-to-oven*)

Oven-Roasted Salmon with Red Potatoes and Dill (*page 294*), *served hot or cold,* or Garlicky Butterflied Leg of Lamb (*page 288*)

Pesto Orzo (*page 308*), *served hot or cold depending on the weather*

Raspberry Trifle (*page 358*) or White Chocolate Cheesecake (*page 350*) with Raspberry Sauce (*page 366*)

Drinks: wine, soft drinks, coffee, tea

1 WEEK AHEAD: Order the salmon, shop for the nonperishables and baked Brie ingredients. Make the Brie up to point to just before baking, wrap it in foil, and freeze it. If you're making white chocolate cheesecake with raspberry sauce, purchase the ingredients and make the cheesecake and the sauce. Freeze the cheesecake and refrigerate the sauce in a covered container.

DAY BEFORE: Shop for the remaining ingredients. Prepare the pesto orzo and, if you're planning to serve it hot, refrigerate it in a microwavable dish. Prepare the asparagus and lemon butter or lemon mustard sauce and refrigerate. Chill the soft drinks and wine. Check the ice. Defrost the cheesecake, or if serving the trifle, prepare it today. Set the table. Wash and dry the salad greens and store them in a plastic bag in the refrigerator. Prepare the five-spice shrimp. Defrost the Brie. If serving the salmon cold, prepare it today and refrigerate it, or prepare the lamb and marinade.

DAY OF: Bake the Brie and cook the salmon, if serving it hot. Heat the pesto orzo in the microwave, if serving it hot. Bake the crescent rolls.

Stage 5:
Buffets and Open Houses

Here is where you learn to organize and run a buffet. The menus in this stage are organized by occasion, with one menu fitting several different kinds. For instance, the luncheon buffet would be great for a bridal shower, a bar mitzvah luncheon, a birthday party, a graduation party, etc. There are two luncheon buffet menus—one for hot-weather entertaining and one for cooler weather. The recipes are for twelve people but they can be halved or doubled or even tripled.

The two supper buffet menus also keep the season in mind. These occasions are slightly more formal than daytime buffets. You might have a supper buffet as a rehearsal dinner before a wedding, to honor a birthday or anniversary, or just to get a group of friends, neighbors, or co-workers together for dinner.

The open house buffet menus are for occasions when you cannot fit all your guests in your home at once. The arrival times will be staggered, so serving a traditional meal is not feasible, which is fine since people shouldn't come to an open house expecting a meal. Instead, offer a steady stream of hot and cold food that can be eaten without a lot of effort while people are standing or walking around. You may choose to serve things requiring only fingers or a toothpick, or you can serve things with small dishes and forks. Be sure to read the section on buffets (page 31) and open houses (page 36) before you plan yours.

There are two open house buffet menus to choose from: One is a traditional cocktail party offering appetizers (both hot and cold) and the other is a dessert buffet. By the way, "cocktail" party does not mean that you're obligated to serve mixed drinks, although you may if you wish; wine (or champagne), punch, and soft drinks are completely acceptable.

These menus would be appropriate for holiday entertaining (New Year's, Christmas) or a large celebration (birthday, anniversary) or any gala gathering of a large group of people.

Luncheon Buffet: Cool Weather

Remember to assemble the food in serving dishes that can be placed either in a chafing dish or on a warming tray. A microwave is the perfect place to warm many of these dishes, so give some thought to using microwavable serving dishes as well so you don't have to spend time transferring food—which cools it off as well.

Baked Brie (page 193)

Avery Island Hot Nuts (page 187)

Layered Taco Dip (page 202) and tortilla chips

Zucchini Lasagna (page 248) or March 13 Blizzard Stew (page 262)

with white rice

Texas Slaw (page 306)

Spicy Corn Bread (page 392)

Mega Apple Crisp (page 362) or Germaine's Fudgy Brownies (page 372)

Drinks: Hot Mulled Cider (page 380), wine, beer, soft drinks, coffee, tea

LUNCHEON BUFFET: COOL WEATHER TIME LINE

1–2 WEEKS AHEAD: Decide on your entrée and then shop for all the nonperishables plus the ingredients for the baked Brie, lasagna, or stew as well as the corn bread and apple crisp or brownies. Prepare the Brie up to the point of baking, wrap it in foil, and freeze. Make the other above recipes and freeze them, storing the lasagna or stew in freezer-to-oven casseroles and the apple crisp or brownies in their baking dishes. Make the Avery Island hot nuts.

2 DAYS AHEAD: Shop for the remaining ingredients. Prepare the Texas slaw.

DAY BEFORE: Defrost all the frozen dishes in the refrigerator. Chill the wine and soft drinks. Check the ice. Set the table and set out serving dishes and utensils. Make the cider. Make the taco dip.

DAY OF: Allow the apple crisp or brownies to come to room temperature. Bake the Brie. Heat the casseroles and cider before serving.

Luncheon Buffet: Warm Weather

Keep the perishable foods refrigerated until the very last minute. You don't want your guests to remember your party by a case of food poisoning they got. Then return the perishable foods to the refrigerator right after guests have had a chance to take a second helping.

Chick-pea Pesto (page 201) with pita wedges or vegetable sticks

Pronto Focaccia Appetizer (page 186)

Marinated Mushrooms (page 185)

Curried Rice Salad (page 244) or Couscous with Currants and Pine Nuts,

(page 328), served cold

Nancy Belsky's Sesame Chicken (page 272), served cold

Sweet Corn and Tomato Salad (page 304)

Garlic Cheese Bread (page 390)

Lemon Bars (page 370)

Strawberries with Raspberry Sauce (page 366)

Drinks: White Wine Sangria (page 386), ice coffee, ice tea, soft drinks

LUNCHEON BUFFET: WARM WEATHER TIME LINE

1–2 WEEKS AHEAD: Purchase all the nonperishable ingredients plus the ingredients for the garlic cheese bread and lemon bars. Prepare the garlic cheese bread to the point to just before baking, wrap it in foil, and freeze. Prepare the lemon bars. Cool them, cut into squares, cover with plastic wrap, and freeze.

2 DAYS AHEAD: Purchase the remaining ingredients, except the strawberries. Prepare the marinated mushrooms and chick-pea pesto. Make the raspberry sauce. Refrigerate all.

DAY BEFORE: Buy the strawberries. Prepare the sesame chicken and curried rice salad or couscous. Make and chill the sangria as well as the soft drinks. Check the ice. Set the table and assemble serving pieces and utensils. Defrost the lemon bars. Cut the pita into wedges and store in a plastic bag. Prepare the ice coffee and ice tea.

DAY OF: Prepare the corn and tomato salad and refrigerate. Arrange the lemon bars on a platter. Late A.M.—Bake the garlic cheese bread and heat and cut the focaccia (if it's really warm out, serve it at room temperature). Prepare the strawberries.

Supper Buffet: Cool Weather

When fall comes people start thinking about entertaining. An informal buffet supper is a great low-stress way to entertain friends without stretching yourself thin. If "keep it simple" is your motto, you'll find yourself having as much fun as your guests.

Guacamole (page 204) with pita wedges or tortilla chips

Wheat Chex Cocktail Mix (page 188)

Hot Crab Spread (page 200) and crackers

Speedy Turkey Chili (page 255) or Armenian Chick-pea Stew (page 242)

Sesame Green Beans (page 326)

French bread or Spicy Corn Bread (page 392)

Mega Apple Crisp (page 362) or Olga's Carrot Cake (page 352)

Drinks: Hot Mulled Cider (page 380), wine, beer, soft drinks, coffee, tea

SUPPER BUFFET: COOL WEATHER TIME LINE

1–2 WEEKS AHEAD: Decide on an entrée and dessert and shop for the ingredients plus all the nonperishables. Prepare the entrée of your choice and freeze it in a freezer-to-oven casserole. Prepare the apple crisp and freeze it. Or prepare the carrot cake and freeze it, unfrosted. Prepare corn bread and freeze it.

2 DAYS AHEAD: Shop for the remaining ingredients (except French bread). Prepare the Wheat Chex mix. Defrost the entrée and dessert in the refrigerator.

DAY BEFORE: Frost the carrot cake, if serving. Make the guacamole and cut the pita into wedges. Prepare the crab spread. Chill the wine and soft drinks. Check the ice. Set the table, laying out serving pieces and utensils. Prepare the cider.

DAY OF: Buy the bread or defrost the corn bread. Defrost the apple crisp. Prepare the beans. Reheat the entrée. Keep the cider warm on a hot plate, taking care that the pitcher is impervious to heat.

Supper Buffet: Warm Weather

With the exception of the first appetizer, this menu consists of food made ahead and served cold—even the grilled shrimp. You'll be happy not to have to heat up your kitchen the day of the party, and you'll have time to relax as well.

Pronto Focaccia Appetizer (page 186)

Avery Island Hot Nuts (page 187)

Skinny Dip (page 205) and Crudités (page 206)

Steven Raichlen's Mangospacho (page 212), served in mugs or paper cups

Beef Tenderloin (page 280), served cold, with Quick Creamy Herb and
Horseradish Sauce (page 282)

Garlic Greek Shrimp (page 298) or Kasha Primavera (page 246), served cold

Cucumber Salad (page 218)

Spicy Corn Bread (page 392)

Raspberry Trifle (page 358) or assorted pickup pastries, either store-bought or a
selection of Germaine's Fudgy Brownies (page 372), Lemon Bars (page 370),
Linzer Bars (page 369), and Pecan Squares (page 367)

Drinks: White Wine Sangria (page 386), ice tea, ice coffee, soft drinks

SUPPER BUFFET:
WARM WEATHER TIME LINE

1-2 WEEKS AHEAD: Select an entrée and dessert and shop for all
the nonperishables. If baking pickup pastries, purchase the ingredients
and start baking and freezing. If getting store-bought pastries, place an
order with the bakery. Order tenderloin. Make the corn bread, cut into
squares, and freeze.

2 DAYS AHEAD: Shop for the remaining ingredients except berries
for the trifle. Prepare the cucumber salad and mangospacho and refrigerate. Make the Avery Island hot nuts. Make yogurt cheese for the skinny
dip.

DAY BEFORE: Defrost the pickup pastries or purchase berries for the
trifle and prepare it. Defrost the corn bread, still wrapped. Roast tenderloin and slice. Prepare the horseradish sauce, cover it with plastic
wrap, and refrigerate. Cook the shrimp and chill, or prepare the kasha
primavera. Check the ice, make the sangria, and chill it and the soft
drinks. Set the table, setting out serving pieces and utensils. Cut the
vegetables for the crudités, storing them in plastic bags in the refrigerator. Make the dip.

DAY OF: Arrange the pick-up pastries on a platter. Cut the focaccia
into wedges to serve at room temperature. Remove tenderloin ½ hour

before serving to come to room temperature, slice it in ½-inch slices, and place overlapping slices on a serving platter. Cover with plastic wrap until just before serving. Place the sauce in a serving bowl with a ladle. Set out the nuts.

Open House: Cocktail Buffet

A cocktail buffet is a different animal from any preconceived images of a 1950s-style cocktail party. Here people drop in, have a glass of wine or punch, something to eat, and a visit. The happier you make them, the longer they'll stick around. If the idea of mixed drinks appeals to you, I urge you to hire an experienced bartender. Actually, I recommend hired help no matter what you plan to serve, since you'll want to act as host, not beverage pourer.

Read the section on page 31 so you'll know what kinds of foods are appropriate to serve in a room where there is a good chance people will be crowded together and jostling for space—the sign of a successful party: lots of people showing up and wanting to stay for a while. You'll want to offer them nondrippy food that's easy to deliver to the mouth without danger of spills and without need of a knife to cut things. That section will also alert you to the amount of food you'll need for the number of people you're expecting.

Open house means that arrivals and departures are staggered. Trust me, if the invitation says one to five o'clock, someone will arrive on the dot of one and someone else will breathlessly show up at the stroke of five. You'll need to hit the deck running at the beginning and stay upright and smiling until the bitter end. I always wear comfortable, low-heeled, rubber-soled shoes for do's like these.

Crudités (page 206) and Skinny Dip (page 205)

Wheat Chex Cocktail Mix (page 188)

Five-Spice Shrimp (page 192)

Avery Island Hot Nuts (page 187) or store-bought assorted salted nuts

Smoked Ham or Smoked Turkey Breast (page 260)

Curried Rice Salad (page 244)

Texas Slaw (page 306)

Assorted rolls

Fruit Salad in a Watermelon Bowl (page 360)

Platters of assorted pickup pastries: Lemon Bars (page 370), Germaine's Fudgy Brownies (page 372), and Pecan Squares (page 367)

Drinks: Fruit Punch (page 381), wine, soft drinks, beer, Hot Cider Rum Punch (page 382)

OPEN HOUSE:
COCKTAIL BUFFET TIME LINE

1–2 WEEKS AHEAD: Purchase all the nonperishable ingredients, plus the ingredients for the brownies, lemon bars, and pecan squares. Make, cut into squares, and freeze them. Order the ham or turkey.

2 DAYS AHEAD: Purchase the remaining ingredients except the shrimp, rolls, and very perishable fruit. Prepare the Avery Island hot nuts and Wheat Chex mix. Prepare the dip.

DAY BEFORE: Buy the remaining ingredients. Prepare the five-spice shrimp, curried rice salad, and Texas slaw. Defrost the cookies in the refrigerator. Chill the wine and soft drinks. Check the ice. Prepare the vegetables for the crudités and store them in plastic bags in the refrigerator. Prepare the fruit punch and hot punch. Set the table, assembling serving pieces and utensils.

DAY OF: Cut and assemble the fruit bowl. If the ham or turkey is not presliced, slice it onto a serving platter and cover with plastic wrap until ready to serve. Place the pastries on platters.

Open House: Dessert Buffet

The section on page 31 explains exactly what a dessert buffet is. It's many mortals' idea of heaven on earth. A cool (or even really cold)

Sunday afternoon is a great time to hold an event like this. Midsummer, for obvious reasons, is the worst. Almost everything in the following menu can be made well ahead and kept frozen until the day before the party.

Remember, it's much easier to have most of the desserts precut into bars or squares and prettily arranged on doily-covered trays or dishes, with the extras stashed nearby in the kitchen to replenish when needed. Place a loop of tape (sticky side out) to secure the doily to the plate so it doesn't side around. Save one or two showpiece desserts to set on the table whole, to be sliced by a server (not by the guests, the dessert will look like a truck hit it).

Don't be shy about purchasing store-bought desserts to fill in, or even to be the main part of your menu. Be fussy; settle only for the freshest and nicest-looking ones (fruit tarts and the like should be served on the day they are made), and remember that most store-bought bars and squares are large enough to be cut into fourths. Use a very sharp serrated knife to do this and you'll have a neat, clean edge. If you want to add a personal touch, buy pretty fluted paper dessert cups in which to place the individual pastries.

Another nice touch is to place dishes of candy or nuts, or both, around. You can have a mix of upscale things like Jordan almonds (both candy- and chocolate-coated), Baci (a milk chocolate, hazelnut candy made by Perugina, wrapped in silver foil with a romantic fortune tucked inside), chocolate truffles (homemade or store-bought), glacéed or dried fruit, and mints as well as some down-home favorites like bridge mix (chocolate-covered raisins, peanuts, malt balls, almonds, etc.), Hershey kisses (the kind with the almonds inside are swell), or even M&M's.

Use the following menu as a guide to the number and kinds of things to serve, replacing some of the selections with others that might be more to your individual liking. Remember, even though you may love everything chocolate and high-calorie, offer those allergic or dieting the option of fruit and something light on the cream, butter, sugar, and eggs.

Count on four to five pieces of dessert (whether it be a slice of cake or a small pickup pastry) per person per hour. That may sound like a lot, but this is an open house and the cast of characters will change (hopefully) from hour to hour.

For the assorted pickup pastries, it's easier to pick four from the menu and make multiples of those recipes rather than change gears enough times to do them all.

Lemon Bars (page 370)

Linzer Bars (page 369)

Chocolate Truffles (page 377)

Germaine's Fudgy Brownies (page 372)

Pecan Squares (page 367)

Raspberry Trifle (page 358)

Chocolate Cassata (page 354)

Fruit Salad in a Watermelon Bowl (page 360) (if watermelon is out of season, use a large serving platter or punch bowl)

Drinks: Champagne Cocktails (page 387), Fruit Punch (page 381), coffee, tea, soft drinks

OPEN HOUSE: DESSERT BUFFET TIME LINE

1–2 WEEKS AHEAD: Purchase all the nonperishables, plus the ingredients for the brownies, cassata, lemon and linzer bars, and pecan squares. Prepare these desserts and freeze them.

2 DAYS AHEAD: Purchase the remaining ingredients except the berries for the trifle.

DAY BEFORE: Chill the champagne and soft drinks. Check the ice. Defrost the frozen desserts, still wrapped. Cut up the fruit for the bowl and the trifle. Set the table and assemble serving dishes and utensils.

DAY OF: Make the trifle. Cut the desserts into pickup pieces and arrange them on serving dishes. Set up the coffee.

Stage 6:
Breakfasts and Brunches

When I first started cooking I had the most trouble with breakfast. The thought of getting hot eggs and toast to arrive at the table at the same time gave me panic attacks. I excelled at lunch, and even got good at dinner long before I conquered breakfast. The following menus take the guesswork out of the first meal of the day. You'll be relaxing with your guests by the time the coffee is brewed.

Here are three breakfast scenarios for you to choose from.

Weekday Breakfast for Houseguests

Everything can be prepared or set out to be prepared the day before.

MENU 1

Grandola (page 330)
Sticky Bun Bread (page 340)
Brandied Fruit Compote (page 333)

Drinks: coffee, tea

MENU 2

Heart-Healthy Bran Muffins (page 336) with butter and jam
Orange slices

Drinks: coffee, tea

MENU 1

1–2 WEEKS AHEAD: Purchase all the nonperishables plus the ingredients for the grandola, sticky bun bread, and if you choose to make it, brandied fruit compote. Prepare the grandola and store it in a tightly covered container. Bake the sticky bun bread and freeze it in a foil pan for easy reheating in the oven. Make the compote and store in a covered container in the refrigerator.

DAY BEFORE: Purchase the fresh fruit. Set the table. Leave a pitcher of milk (for the coffee and the grandola) in the refrigerator (cover the top with plastic wrap). Evening—remove the sticky bun bread from the freezer to defrost, covered, at room temperature. Set the table.

MORNING OF: Place the sticky bun bread in the oven to warm. Set out the grandola and brandied fruit compote (with bowls). Set up the coffeemaker.

MENU 2

DAY BEFORE: Make the muffins, slice the oranges, cover them both with plastic wrap, and refrigerate. Set the table.

MORNING OF: Set up the coffee, set out the muffins, butter, jam, and oranges.

Simple Weekend Breakfast: Cool Weather

MENU 1

Walnut Currant Scones (page 342)

Bacon or breakfast sausages

Drinks: orange juice, freshly squeezed or store-bought

Buttermilk Berry Pancakes (page 344)

Strawberries with Raspberry Sauce (page 366)

Drinks: Mimosas (page 385), Hot Chocolate (page 379), coffee, tea

SIMPLE WEEKEND BREAKFAST: COOL WEATHER TIME LINE

MENU 1

DAY BEFORE: Purchase all the ingredients. If you are making fresh orange juice, squeeze it the day before. Set the table.

DAY OF: Start the coffee. While the scones are baking, cook the bacon or sausages either on the stove top or check the package for microwave directions.

MENU 2

1 WEEK AHEAD: Prepare the raspberry sauce. Store it in a tightly sealed container in the refrigerator.

DAY BEFORE: Purchase all the rest of the ingredients. Prepare the pancake batter and refrigerate overnight. Prepare the strawberries. If you are using fresh orange juice in the mimosas, squeeze it the night before. Set the table.

DAY OF: Make the hot chocolate, coffee, tea, mimosas, and pancakes.

Simple Weekend Breakfast: Warm Weather

MENU 1

Assorted fresh berries, brown sugar, and cream (or yogurt)

Walnut Currant Scones (page 242) with butter and jam

Drinks: coffee, tea

MENU 2

Tropical Papaya Boats (page 329)

Grandola (page 330)

Drinks: coffee, tea

SIMPLE WEEKEND BREAKFAST: WARM WEATHER TIME LINE

MENU 1

1–2 WEEKS AHEAD: Shop for the nonperishable items. Make the scones ahead and freeze them if you wish, or make them the day before, cool them, and store at room temperature in a plastic bag.

DAY BEFORE: Shop for the remaining ingredients. Set the table. Defrost the scones if frozen.

DAY OF: Rinse the berries and place them in a serving dish. Set up the coffee. Put out the brown sugar and cream.

1–2 WEEKS AHEAD: Shop for the nonperishable items. Make the grandola and store it in a tightly sealed container at room temperature.

DAY BEFORE: Purchase the rest of the ingredients. Set the table. Make the papaya boats.

Brunch Buffet: Warm Weather

Cool, fresh, and light are the guiding words here. People don't need a lot of heavy starches or things dripping with butter and syrup. Save the calories for dessert (but offer something light as well). This menu will keep you out of the kitchen and with your guests because everything is done ahead.

Smoked Salmon Pâté (page 196)

Bagels and cream cheese

Summer Salad (page 303)

Honey-Pecan Chicken Salad (page 232)

Cucumber Salad (page 218)

Fresh strawberries

White Chocolate Cheesecake (page 350)

Drinks: Mimosas (page 385) or Orange-Spiked Ice Tea (page 384), coffee and tea, hot or ice depending on the weather

BRUNCH BUFFET: WARM WEATHER TIME LINE

1–2 WEEKS BEFORE: Purchase all the nonperishables as well as the ingredients for the cheesecake. Prepare and freeze the cheesecake. If necessary, order the bagels.

DAY BEFORE: Purchase the remaining ingredients. Defrost the cheesecake. Prepare the chicken and cucumber salads, and the smoked salmon pâté. Set the table, assembling serving dishes and utensils. If you are squeezing your own orange juice for the mimosas, do this today. Check the ice. Make the ice tea. Scrape the cream cheese into a serving dish, cover with plastic wrap, and refrigerate.

MORNING OF: Set up the coffee. Rinse and hull the strawberries, placing them in a pretty serving bowl. Slice the tomatoes and onions, cover them with plastic, and refrigerate. Slice the bagels and place them in a basket or on a serving dish. Make the mimosas.

Brunch Buffet: Cool Weather

Here is a make-ahead menu that requires only that the entrée be reheated. Advise your guests to come hungry: They will be well fed! You can make your own pickup pastries or buy the best-quality store-bought.

Chick-pea Pesto *(page 201)* *with whole wheat pita wedges*

Five-Spice Shrimp (page 192)

Brandied Croissant Flan (page 338)

Brandied Fruit Compote (page 333) or Fruit Salad in a Watermelon Bowl

(page 360)

Lemon Bars (page 370)

Germaine's Fudgy Brownies (page 372)

Pecan Squares (page 367)

Drinks: Hot Cider Rum Punch *(page 382)*, *champagne, coffee, tea*

1–2 WEEKS AHEAD: Purchase all the nonperishables and the ingredients for the lemon bars, brownies, and pecan squares. Prepare them, cut them into pickup pieces, and freeze. Make the fruit compote.

2 DAYS AHEAD: Shop for the remaining ingredients except the shrimp and perishable fruit. Make the chick-pea pesto.

DAY BEFORE: Buy the shrimp and fruit. Assemble the flan to the point just before baking, cover, and refrigerate. Prepare the marinated shrimp and cut up the fruit. Defrost the pastries. Set the table, assembling serving dishes and utensils. Prepare the hot rum cider and refrigerate until ready to heat. Chill the champagne. Cut the pita into wedges and store them in a plastic bag.

MORNING OF: Bake the flan. Arrange the pastries on platters. Set up the coffee and tea.

Stage 7:
Fancy Dinners

Wow! You've come a long way from the neophyte who had trouble trying to decide which dip to serve with which chip. While there may have been some glitches, there were also moments of glory and giddiness when everything clicked and things went off exactly as planned. Your guests raved and gave you the ultimate compliment of asking for seconds and telling you that they'd be too nervous to cook for you. So, now you're up for more of a challenge. Good for you!

The following menus are for special-occasion dinners that require some last-minute cooking. But don't worry, you've passed the other tests with flying colors. We'll start with a Romantic Dinner for Two, then move right on to The Boss Comes to Dinner, and then you'll be ready to pull off the International Dinner for Eight.

Romantic Dinner for Two

In order for this to be romantic for the cook as well as for his or her dining companion, it's important to be super organized so that you're not racing around like a maniac. Pay careful attention to the time line and this will be a breeze.

Rosemary Goat Cheese Wedges (page 194)

Pear and Roquefort Salad (page 220)

Oven-Roasted Salmon with Red Potatoes and Dill (page 294) or Grilled Vegetable Kabobs (page 236)

Lemon Rice (page 310), served cold

Strawberries with Raspberry Sauce (page 366)

Chocolate Truffles (page 377)

Drinks: Champagne Cocktails (page 387), white wine, espresso or Irish Coffee (page 378), cordials

ROMANTIC DINNER FOR TWO
TIME LINE

1 WEEK AHEAD: Purchase the nonperishable ingredients plus the ingredients to make the chocolate truffles. Make the truffles and refrigerate them in an air-tight plastic container to protect them from other refrigerator odors. Find a source for and order the salmon.

DAY BEFORE: Purchase the remaining ingredients. Prepare the salmon or grilled vegetables up to the point to just before cooking and refrigerate. Prepare the lemon rice and raspberry sauce. Refrigerate all these dishes until ready to serve. Chill the wine or champagne. Set the table, assembling serving dishes and utensils. Wash and dry the salad greens and make the dressing.

DAY OF: Make the goat cheese wedges. Rinse and hull the strawberries. For the Irish coffee, set up the coffeemaker, assemble the ingredients, and whip the cream according to directions on page 376. Make the champagne cocktails immediately before serving.

The Boss Comes to Dinner

Some may say this is the ultimate test of entertaining skills. If you don't have a boss, substitute your future parents-in-law or your friend who just came back from a year in Paris and can't find anything tolerable to eat in this country. Try to remember that people are not expecting a four-star meal with all the trappings. They are expecting a lovely, relaxed evening with pleasant company and good-tasting, nicely presented food. You've done all these things before, only the cast of characters has upped the ante.

I suggest keeping guest list to six (at least no more than eight). This way you don't have to feed lots of people, and your guests can entertain each other while you are in the kitchen.

Avery Island Hot Nuts (page 187)

Baked Brie (page 193)

Cold Cherry Soup (page 216) or Lobster Melon Cocktail (page 226)

Beef Tenderloin (page 280) or Lemon-Artichoke Chicken Breasts (page 268)

Pesto Orzo (page 308), served hot

Marinated Green Beans (page 325)

Frozen Espresso Chocolate Mousse (page 346)

Drinks: champagne or sparkling cider, wine, coffee, tea, Irish Coffee

(page 378)

THE BOSS COMES TO DINNER
TIME LINE

◠◠

1–2 WEEKS AHEAD: Purchase all the nonperishable ingredients plus the ingredients for the mousse, nuts, and Brie. Make the mousse and freeze it. Prepare the Brie up to the point to just before baking, wrap it in foil, and freeze. Prepare the nuts and store them in a tightly covered container at room temperature. Order the tenderloin. Consult a wine expert.

2 DAYS AHEAD: Purchase the remaining ingredients except the lobster. Prepare the cold cherry soup and refrigerate it.

DAY BEFORE: Purchase the lobster and make the lobster melon cocktail and refrigerate it in a covered container. Prepare the pesto orzo and refrigerate it in a microwavable serving dish for reheating. Defrost the Brie. Prepare the beans and refrigerate them. Chill the wine, champagne, and/or cider.

DAY OF: If you're making chicken instead of beef, prepare it in the morning (or even the night before) and reheat it in the oven just before serving. Whip the cream for the Irish coffee according to directions on page 376. Remove the tenderloin from the refrigerator ½ hour before roasting. Bake the Brie so that it is warm when you're ready to serve it. Heat the pesto orzo in the microwave just before serving.

International Dinner for Eight
◠◠◠◠◠◠◠◠◠◠◠◠◠◠◠◠◠◠◠◠◠◠

I'll bet that when your guests receive this invitation they'll volunteer to bring something. Make sure to give some thought about how to work their dish into your menu. The best things to ask for are appetizers (but only if you are sure the bearer will arrive early enough), bread, rolls, a side dish, or an extra dessert. Not everyone has the same idea of what is enough for eight people but be sure to have your own appetizers and dessert on hand.

Pronto Focaccia Appetizer (page 186)

Curried Carrot Soup (page 210) or Steven Raichlen's Mangospacho (page 212)

Picadillo (page 264) or Zucchini Lasagna (page 248)

Texas Slaw (page 306)

French bread or Garlic Cheese Bread (page 390)

Chocolate Cassata (page 354) or Raspberry Trifle (page 358)

Drinks: White Wine Sangria (page 386), Irish Coffee (page 378)

INTERNATIONAL DINNER FOR EIGHT
TIME LINE

1–2 WEEKS AHEAD: Purchase all the nonperishable ingredients plus the ingredients for the picadillo, cassata, and garlic cheese bread, if serving. These can all be made ahead and frozen. Wrap the bread in foil and store the picadillo in a freezer-to-oven casserole dish. The curried carrot soup can be made ahead and frozen as well, but don't add the milk or cream until you're ready to heat it before serving.

2 DAYS AHEAD: Purchase the remaining ingredients except the shrimp. Defrost the picadillo, cassata, and soup in the refrigerator. If the soup has separated, purée it again in the blender or food processor.

DAY BEFORE: Prepare the white wine sangria and the shrimp. Set the table, assembling serving dishes and utensils. Check the ice. Make the Texas slaw and trifle, if serving.

DAY OF: A.M.—Make the mangospacho and refrigerate. Assemble the ingredients for the Irish coffee. Whip the cream according to the directions on page 376.

P.M.—Reheat the picadillo in either a Slow Cooker or in an ovenproof casserole. If you are serving the carrot soup hot, reheat it just before serving. Heat the garlic bread. Heat the focaccia just before serving.

Stage 8:
Special Entertaining

Meetings, both business and social, have their own unique challenges. The following menu addresses those. In addition to your role as host or hostess you will be serving meals to people who have certain dietary restrictions. Rather than looking at this as a pain in the neck, think of it as a challenge. Your guests will be wildly appreciative and you will see how simple it is to tailor-make a meal to fit your friends' needs.

Meetings

The most important things to remember about food for meetings (and I'm not talking luncheon meetings) are

- keep it simple; people are not expecting to be fed a meal.

- keep it easy to eat; stay away from crumbly, sticky, sloppy, drippy foods. Stick with things that can eaten with fingers in one or two bites—cookies, bars, squares, and the like.

- don't serve food that has be kept hot, cold, or frozen.

- pick things that people can help themselves to rather than you serving and cutting.

- if you serve something very rich, offer an alternative (such as grapes or strawberries) for people who do not wish to indulge.

- serve fresh, hot coffee (see page 66). If you serve decaf, buy premium, freshly ground beans.

- if you are serving pick-up pastries, count on three pieces per person. You will undoubtedly have leftovers, but this is far better than running out.

You can either purchase an assortment of fine-quality bakery items or make several dozen of two or three on the menu, then cut them into 1½-inch pieces.

Linzer Bars (page 369)

Germaine's Fudgy Brownies (page 372)

Lemon Bars (page 370)

Pecan Squares (page 367)

Fruit Salad in a Watermelon Bowl (page 360) or assorted fresh berries

Drinks: orange juice, coffee, tea, pitcher of ice water

HELPFUL HINTS: Slice some lemons or limes and add them to the pitcher of ice water. On very hot days, offer ice tea or ice coffee and add a sprig of fresh mint to the pitcher of ice tea. The best ice coffee is made by making ice cubes from very strong coffee or espresso and then adding them to cool or cold coffee.

MEETINGS TIME LINE

1–2 WEEKS AHEAD: Purchase all the nonperishable ingredients plus the ingredients for the linzer and lemon bars, brownies, and pecan squares. Prepare them, cut them, and freeze. Locate a large coffeemaker, if necessary.

2 DAYS AHEAD: Purchase the rest of the ingredients (sturdy fruit, orange juice, half-and-half or milk, lemons for tea). Wait until the next day to buy more perishable fruit and berries.

DAY BEFORE: Defrost the pickup pastries either in the refrigerator or at room temperature. Cut up the fruit (saving strawberries and other fragile fruit for the next day).

DAY OF: Arrange the pastries on a serving plate and the fruit on a platter. Set up the coffee and tea and ice water.

Visit to a Sick Friend

Yes, this is part of entertaining. Make it short and sweet. Bringing along a homemade treat will go a long way to making your friend feel well loved. If your friend is suffering from a long-term or debilitating illness, you might think of bringing a meal that can be frozen and enjoyed by the sick person and his or her family when they don't have the time and/or energy to cook. Pack the already cooked food in freezer-to-oven, disposable aluminum containers and label the containers with the contents and cooking instructions. Make sure they are containers that you don't need back—your friend probably has enough to worry about. Pick one of the following soups or hot dishes. Each can be portioned into single-serving-size plastic containers and stored in the freezer. Everything following can be frozen except where "cannot" or "don't" is noted.

SOUPS

Quick Italian Vegetable Soup (page 208)

Tomato Cheddar Soup (page 207) (pack the cheese separately in a small plastic bag to add when the soup is hot)

Curried Carrot Soup (page 210) (go easy on the seasoning)

ENTRÉES

Four Seasons Pasta Salad (page 233) (this cannot be frozen but will keep for at least 1 week in the refrigerator)

Kasha Primavera (page 246)

Zucchini Lasagna (page 248)

Armenian Chick-pea Stew (page 242)

Sweet-and-Sour Curried Cabbage Rolls (page 240)

Picadillo (page 264)

Speedy Turkey Chili (page 255)

Lightning Creole Chicken (page 270)

BAKED GOODS

Sticky Bun Bread (page 340)

Walnut Currant Scones (page 242)

Cheddar Biscuits (page 388)

Grandola (page 330) (don't freeze)

DESSERTS

Germaine's Fudgy Brownies (page 372)

Lemon Bars (page 370)

Linzer Bars (page 369)

Pecan Squares (page 376)

Olga's Carrot Cake (page 352), as a cake or muffins

CHAPTER SEVEN

Recipes

Appetizers: Pickups, Snacks, Spreads, and Dips

Couch Gorp

What else would you feed couch potatoes while they wait for dinner? Serve this with hot cider on a cold winter afternoon. Or put it in small bowls for guests to nibble on as they watch the game. For your more energetic friends, pack it up for an on-the-trail lunch treat.

PREPARATION TIME: 15 minutes

YIELD: About 1½ quarts, feeding 8

CAN BE MADE AHEAD? Yes. This will keep for several months when stored in an airtight container.

CAN BE FROZEN? No

CAN BE DOUBLED? Yes

CAN BE HALVED? Yes

1 cup dried apple slices

1 cup dried apricots

⅓ cup dried cherries

1 cup whole unblanched almonds

1 cup unsweetened, dried coconut

1 cup sunflower seeds

Cut the apple slices and apricots with scissors into ½-inch pieces and place them in a container with a snap-on lid, or in a heavy-duty freezer bag. Add the cherries, almonds, coconut, and sunflower seeds and shake to combine. Store in a cool, dry place.

Marinated Mushrooms

You can use your favorite bottled Italian dressing to make this almost instant appetizer or use the recipe for vinaigrette on page 228. To save yourself time and work, select the cleanest mushrooms you can find. You can tell a mushroom's fresh when the cap is closed around the stem and the gills (inside the underneath part of the cap) are not showing.

Marinated mushrooms also make a nice addition to a tossed salad.

PREPARATION TIME: 15 minutes

MARINATING TIME: At least 4 hours or as long as 48 hours

YIELD: Serves 8

CAN BE MADE AHEAD? Yes. Keep refrigerated.

CAN BE FROZEN? No

CAN BE DOUBLED AND TRIPLED? Yes

CAN BE HALVED? Yes

10-ounce package small, white, fresh mushrooms

½ to ⅔ cup bottled Italian salad dressing or Herb Vinaigrette (page 228)

½ cup (2½ ounces) feta cheese, finely crumbled

Brush all the visible dirt from the mushrooms. Trim the woody tip of the stem ends. Slice the mushrooms lengthwise in thirds, or in half if they are small.

Place the mushrooms in a plastic container with a tight-fitting lid. Add the dressing and feta cheese, cover, and shake back and forth gently two or three times to mix. Marinate in the refrigerator at least 4 hours, or overnight.

Serve with toothpicks or with forks on small plates.

Pronto Focaccia Appetizer

Focaccia is a round somewhat flat bread, a little thicker than thick pizza crust. It typically does not have a topping, but is made with herbs in the dough so that it has a wonderful smell and an even better taste.

You can buy freshly made focaccia in almost any Italian bakery and gourmet grocery, or you can buy foil-packed nitrogen-sealed focaccia that has a very long shelf life.

PREPARATION TIME: No time if served at room temperature; 2 minutes if served warm

HEATING TIME: 10 minutes

YIELD: Serves 8

CAN BE MADE AHEAD? Yes

CAN BE FROZEN? Yes. Thaw, tightly wrapped, at room temperature before using.

CAN BE DOUBLED? Yes. Buy 2 focaccia.

CAN BE HALVED? No

1 store-bought focaccia

2 to 3 tablespoons olive oil or garlic oil (available in gourmet shops)

2 teaspoons kosher or coarse sea salt

1 teaspoon freshly ground black pepper

If you wish to serve the focaccia as is, simply place it on a cutting board and slice it into 2-inch wedges.

To serve the focaccia warm, preheat the oven to 300°F with the rack in the upper third but not highest position. Place the focaccia on a baking sheet and brush the top with the olive oil. Sprinkle it with the salt and pepper and heat for 10 minutes. Serve immediately, cut into narrow wedges.

Avery Island Hot Nuts

All my friends joke that one day I'm going to retire to Avery Island, Louisiana, home of the famous Tabasco pepper, so that I'll never have to suffer through another Boston winter. I love being toasty warm inside and out! Until I head south I'll have to be content with the velvet fire generated by this recipe, which was adapted from one found in The Tabasco Cookbook by Paul McIlhenny and Barbara Hunter.

PREPARATION TIME: 15 minutes

COOKING TIME: About 1 hour

YIELD: 4 cups

CAN BE MADE AHEAD? Yes, most definitely, up to 1 week. Store in an airtight container at room temperature.

CAN BE FROZEN? Yes, in a heavy-duty plastic freezer bag, up to 2 months. Defrost, covered, and refresh on a baking sheet in a 250°F oven for 10 minutes

CAN BE DOUBLED? Yes

CAN BE HALVED? Yes

4 tablespoons garlic oil (available in gourmet food shops) or ½ stick (2 ounces) unsalted butter melted with 4 garlic cloves, minced

2½ teaspoons Tabasco Pepper Sauce

½ teaspoon salt

4 cups assorted unsalted nuts, such as pecans, walnuts, hazelnuts, whole unblanched almonds, macadamia nuts

Preheat the oven to 250°F with the rack in the center position. Heat the oil (or melt the butter together with the garlic) in a small skillet set over medium heat. Add the Tabasco Pepper Sauce and salt and cook for 1 minute, stirring gently.

Spread the nuts over the bottom of a roasting pan and pour on the oil or butter mixture. Stir very well to coat the nuts, then respread them in a single layer in the pan.

Bake for 1 hour, stirring every 15 minutes. Cool to room temperature before serving or storing.

Wheat Chex Cocktail Mix

I used to work in an upscale restaurant where this irresistible snack was given some fancy French name and served in Limoges dishes along with flutes of imported champagne. I've also seen it in bars in South Boston served along with mugs of beer. No matter when you serve it, make plenty—it will disappear in a twinkling.

The microwave oven method is quick, but I prefer the toasted taste from the conventional oven method.

PREPARATION TIME: 10 minutes

COOKING TIME: Microwave: 5 to 6 minutes; conventional oven: 1 hour

YIELD: About 12 cups, serves 16 to 20

CAN BE MADE AHEAD? Yes, up to 1 week. After it's completely cooled, store in an airtight container at room temperature.

CAN BE FROZEN? No

CAN BE DOUBLED AND TRIPLED? Yes, although it should be cooked in one-recipe batches in a microwave or in a very large roasting pan in the oven

CAN BE HALVED? Yes

1 stick (4 ounces) unsalted butter

1 tablespoon plus 1 teaspoon Worcestershire sauce

1½ teaspoons seasoned salt, garlic salt, or Cajun spice mix

8 cups Wheat Chex cereal

2 cups mixed unsalted nuts, such as pecans, walnuts, filberts, cashews, and peanuts

2 cups small round pretzels (not pretzel sticks)

Conventional oven method: Preheat the oven to 250°F with the rack in the center position. Select a large flat roasting pan that will hold 12 cups comfortably.

Melt the butter in a small saucepan set over medium heat. Add the Worcestershire sauce and seasoned salt and stir to combine. Mix the cereal, nuts, and pretzels in the pan, pour the butter mixture over them, and stir until all the pieces are evenly coated.

Bake for 1 hour, stirring every 15 minutes. Line several baking sheets with a double layer of paper towels. Remove the mix from the oven and spread on the prepared pans to cool. Store at room temperature in an airtight container.

Microwave method: In a small microwavable bowl, melt the butter. Stir in the Worcestershire sauce and seasoned salt. Mix well. Pour the cereal, nuts, and pretzels into a 2-gallon heavy-duty freezer bag. Add the butter mixture, seal the bag, and shake to coat well.

Pour the contents of the bag into a large microwavable bowl. Microwave, uncovered, on high for 6 minutes, stirring every 2 minutes. Remove the mix from the oven and spread on prepared pans to cool. Store at room temperature in an airtight container.

Spicy Buffalo Chicken Wings

These spicy morsels originated in the Anchor Bar in Buffalo, New York. I have taken some liberties with the original recipe; instead of frying, I broil the wings (you can also grill them on the barbecue). The traditional way to serve them is with blue cheese dressing (recipe follows) and celery sticks on the side. They are messy to eat, so serve them at informal events with lots of napkins.

If you are not into fiery food, cut the amount of Tabasco.

PREPARATION TIME: 15 minutes

MARINATING TIME: As long as 24 hours or as little as 1 hour

COOKING TIME: 15 to 20 minutes

YIELD: Serves 6 to 8

CAN BE MADE AHEAD? Yes, as long as 24 hours ahead, refrigerated, and then either served at room temperature or reheated in a 350°F oven for about 15 minutes. The blue cheese dressing can be made, and the celery cut and stored with the cut ends in water in the refrigerator, the day before.

CAN BE FROZEN? No

CAN BE DOUBLED AND TRIPLED? Yes

CAN BE HALVED? Yes

⅓ cup vegetable oil

½ cup dark brown sugar, firmly packed

¼ cup soy sauce

1 tablespoon dry mustard

3 tablespoons Tabasco Pepper Sauce (you can add more if you want them hotter, but taste them first)

3 tablespoons red wine vinegar

3 pounds chicken wings, tips removed at the joint (you can use the tips to make chicken stock)

1 bunch celery, rinsed, dried, and cut into 3 × ½-inch strips

Place everything but the wings and celery in a 2-quart mixing bowl and stir to combine. Add the wings and toss to coat them well. Cover the bowl with plastic wrap, refrigerate, and allow the wings to marinate for at least 1 hour, or as long as 24 hours.

Preheat the broiler to high with the rack in the upper third of the oven. Line a heavy-duty shallow roasting pan or baking sheet with foil. Remove the wings from the marinade (try to leave as much on as possible) and place them in a single layer in the prepared pan.

Broil the wings for 6 to 8 minutes on each side, basting once or twice with the marinade, until deep brown and crisp. Transfer them to a platter to serve hot or at room temperature.

Blue Cheese Dressing

PREPARATION TIME: 10 minutes

YIELD: Serves 6 to 8

CAN BE MADE AHEAD? Yes, up to 24 hours. Cover and chill until ready to serve.

CAN BE FROZEN? No

CAN BE DOUBLED AND TRIPLED? Yes

CAN BE HALVED? Yes

5 ounces best-quality blue cheese, crumbled

¾ cup mayonnaise

½ cup sour cream

Place all the ingredients in a food processor or blender and process until smooth.

Serve the Buffalo wings with the blue cheese dressing for dipping. The celery sticks are dipped into the dressing as well.

Five-Spice Shrimp

Most supermarkets now carry five-spice powder (look on the spice rack or where Asian ingredients are kept) or you can make your own by pulverizing the following in a blender or food processor until powdered: 60 black peppercorns, 4 whole star anise, 2 teaspoons fennel seeds, 4 1-inch pieces cinnamon bark, and 12 whole cloves. This will give you about 1½ tablespoons of powder which is more than enough for this recipe. Store the rest in a tightly sealed glass jar. Garlic oil is available in gourmet food shops.

PREPARATION TIME: 15 minutes

YIELD: Serves 8 as an appetizer

CAN BE MADE AHEAD? Yes, up to 24 hours. Store the shrimp in an airtight plastic container in the refrigerator.

CAN BE FROZEN? No

CAN BE DOUBLED? Yes

CAN BE HALVED? Yes

2 teaspoons five-spice powder

2 tablespoons sesame oil

⅓ cup garlic oil or vegetable oil

¼ cup soy sauce

¼ cup rice wine vinegar

2 pounds cooked, shelled medium or large shrimp (not extra-large or jumbo—they make for messy eating as a pickup appetizer)

Combine all the ingredients except the shrimp in a medium-sized bowl. Whisk to blend well, then toss with the shrimp. Marinate in the refrigerator for at least 4 hours and up to 24 hours. You can pass these around with toothpicks for serving or on small plates with forks.

Baked Brie

This is a show-stopping appetizer that you can serve either before dinner with drinks or as a first course. It's essential to find an Italian bakery that makes large round loaves of bread. Buy the Brie first so you'll know how large your loaf of bread has to be.

PREPARATION TIME: 15 minutes

COOKING TIME: 35 to 40 minutes

YIELD: Serves 10 to 12 as a pickup; 6 as an appetizer

CAN BE MADE AHEAD? It can be assembled up to 6 hours ahead to just before the point where you bake it; however, the bread will get stale if it's done too far ahead of time. You can either bake it 1 hour before you plan to serve it at room temperature, or serve it hot from the oven, in which case the cheese will be quite runny.

CAN BE FROZEN? No

CAN BE DOUBLED? Yes. Make 2.

CAN BE HALVED? No

2 8-ounce wheels of Brie (regular or pepper), rind on

1 large round loaf of Italian or hearty whole-grain bread at least 10 inches in diameter and 3 to 4 inches thick

¼ cup olive oil

1 tablespoon dried rosemary or 3 tablespoons fresh rosemary leaves, chopped

1 tablespoon dried thyme or 3 tablespoons fresh thyme, chopped

Preheat the oven to 325°F with the rack in the center position. Place one of the wheels of Brie on top of the loaf of bread and, using it as a guide, cut around the bread with a serrated knife. Remove the circle of crust and use your fingers to pull out enough bread so that the Brie fits inside with ½ inch of headroom above it.

(continued)

Heat the oil in a small saucepan and add the herbs. Cook over low heat for 5 minutes. Pour half the oil over the wheel of Brie in the bread, then place the second wheel on top of the first. Use your hands to gently press it down into the bread. Don't worry if it sticks up a little. Drizzle the rest of the oil on top of the Brie and bread.

Place the bread on a heavy-duty baking sheet that has been lined with heavy-duty foil. Gather the edges of the foil up and fold them around the bread, so that only the cheese is exposed. Bake for 35 to 40 minutes, or until a knife inserted in the cheese comes out hot.

Serve hot or at room temperature.

Rosemary Goat Cheese Wedges

The lovely aroma of rosemary will fill your kitchen while these cook. They take only minutes to prepare and can be served with drinks or with a salad. Use fresh rosemary if you can find it; if not, dried is fine.

PREPARATION TIME: 10 minutes

COOKING TIME: 1 to 2 minutes

YIELD: 48 wedges, serves 8 to 10

CAN BE MADE AHEAD? Yes, up to the point of cooking. Cover with plastic wrap and keep at room temperature for up to 3 hours.

CAN BE FROZEN? No

CAN BE DOUBLED AND TRIPLED? Yes. Cook in batches.

CAN BE HALVED? Yes

3 small (pocket-sized) pitas

½ stick (2 ounces) unsalted butter or margarine

2 tablespoons fresh rosemary leaves, finely chopped, or 1 teaspoon dried rosemary

6 ounces goat cheese, such as Montrachet, crumbled

Preheat the broiler to medium-high with the rack in the upper but not highest position. Use scissors to cut each pita loaf into 8 wedges. Open each wedge to form a diamond, then cut through the middle to make two triangles. Place the triangles close together on a baking sheet.

In a small pan set over low heat, melt the butter with the rosemary. Once the butter has melted completely, continue cooking over low heat for another 2 to 3 minutes, stirring to combine the flavor of the herb with the butter.

Use a pastry brush or teaspoon to paint the butter mixture over each triangle. Don't be concerned about covering every bit. Sprinkle about 2 teaspoons of goat cheese on each on top of the butter. Place the baking sheet under the broiler and don't take your eyes off it— these will be done before you know it. As soon as the cheese begins to brown, remove the baking sheet from the oven. If you find the edges are browning before the cheese—don't worry. They'll taste just fine.

Serve these while they are hot (although even at room temperature they are delicious).

Smoked Salmon Pâté

While it is tempting to buy premade spreads, you'll be amazed at how easy (and economical) it is to make your own. Be sure to buy the less salty smoked salmon as opposed to the high-salt lox. Many delis sell the end pieces of smoked salmons for a lower price than the prettier whole slices. This recipe makes four cups which is enough for ten to twelve. If you are serving fewer guests, you can cut it in half.

If you can find it, you can substitute smoked bluefish or trout for the salmon. You won't need to add salt since the fish is already salty.

PREPARATION TIME: 15 minutes

YIELD: Serves 10 to 12

CAN BE MADE AHEAD? Yes, up to 4 days. Cover tightly and refrigerate until ready to serve.

CAN BE FROZEN? Yes, up to 3 months. Store in a tightly covered plastic container and defrost in the refrigerator.

CAN BE DOUBLED AND TRIPLED? Yes. Make it in batches.

CAN BE HALVED? Yes

1 pound smoked salmon (or smoked bluefish or smoked trout—skin removed), cut into 1-inch pieces

8 ounces cream cheese, at room temperature

½ stick (2 ounces) unsalted butter, softened

¼ cup minced onion

¼ cup minced fresh dill

½ teaspoon Worcestershire sauce

1 tablespoon lemon juice

Place the salmon, cream cheese, and butter in a food processor. Process until smooth, then add the remaining ingredients and pulse on and off until the mixture is smooth. Use a rubber spatula to scrape the pâté into a 4-cup serving dish, cover with plastic, and refrigerate until ready to serve. To serve, spread on French bread rounds or crackers.

Roquefort Celery Boats

Here's a quick-to-prepare pickup appetizer that's a crowd pleaser. If you can't find Roquefort cheese, you can substitute blue or Stilton cheese.

PREPARATION TIME: 20 minutes

YIELD: 40 boats, serves 8 to 10

CAN BE MADE AHEAD? Yes, up to 8 hours. Cover tightly with plastic wrap and refrigerate until ready to serve.

CAN BE FROZEN? No

CAN BE DOUBLED AND TRIPLED? Yes

CAN BE HALVED? Yes

10 long celery stalks, approximately 10 to 12 inches in length

¾ pound (12 ounces) Roquefort cheese or any other blue-veined cheese

8 ounces cream cheese

⅓ cup heavy cream

Paprika

Wash the celery and cut off the thick root end so that you have stalks 8 to 10 inches long. Dry the stalks and set aside while you prepare the filling.

Place the Roquefort and cream cheese in a food processor. Process, slowly adding enough cream to make the mixture smooth and spreadable, but not runny. Scrape the mixture into a heavy-duty plastic freezer bag and secure the opening. Cut ⅓ inch off one of the bottom corners: You now have a pastry bag. Squeeze the filling down toward the open corner and gently and slowly squeeze a line of filling down the center of each celery stalk, filling the depression.

Use a sharp knife to cut the stalks into 2-inch sections. Dust them with paprika before you arrange them on a platter.

Cheese-Stuffed
Sugar Snap Peas

The more traditional way to make this popular pickup appetizer is to use snow peas, but I prefer the texture and flavor of sugar snap peas—and their rigidity makes them easier to stuff. If you don't care for the taste of goat cheese you can use any flavored cream cheese that tickles your fancy.

PREPARATION TIME: 20 to 30 minutes

YIELD: About 40 appetizers, serves 8 to 10

CAN BE MADE AHEAD? Yes, up to 8 hours. Arrange the stuffed peas in one layer on a platter and cover tightly with plastic wrap. Store in the refrigerator until ready to serve.

CAN BE FROZEN? No

CAN BE DOUBLED AND TRIPLED? Yes

CAN BE HALVED? Yes

½ pound (8 ounces) goat cheese, plain, herbed, or peppered

¼ pound (4 ounces) whipped cream cheese

3 to 4 tablespoons heavy cream

1 pound (approximately 40) sugar snap peas, rinsed and dried

Combine the two cheeses in a food processor. Process, adding the cream 1 tablespoon at a time, until the mixture is smooth and completely blended and of a spreadable consistency.

Pull the tough string off the peas and then use the tip of a small sharp knife to slip open the top side of each one.

Scoop the filling into a 1-quart heavy-duty plastic freezer bag. Seal the top. Use a pair of scissors to snip ¼ inch off one of the bottom corners. (You've just created a pastry bag!) Carefully squeeze the filling down toward the hole, then press the opening into the top of the slit in the pea. Squeeze the filling into the opening—just enough so that it fills but doesn't overflow. This may take a little practice, but you'll get it. Place the filled snap peas in a single layer on a platter, cover with plastic wrap, and chill until ready to serve.

NOTE: If you can't find snap peas, you can substitute small, tender zucchini. Select 8 to 10 that are no more than 6 inches in length. Wash them well, then cut them lengthwise. Use the tip of a teaspoon to scoop out the seeds (you'll be forming a trench of sorts). Apply the filling as above, then cut each piece into 1½-inch sections.

Hot Crab Spread

This tasty preparation is served warm, spread on crackers or pita triangles. You can bake it in either a pie plate or any shallow 3-cup ovenproof dish. Be sure to buy real crabmeat, not the imitation kind.

PREPARATION TIME: 15 minutes

COOKING TIME: 15 minutes

YIELD: 3 cups, serves 8 to 10

CAN BE MADE AHEAD? Yes, 24 hours, up to just before cooking. Cover with plastic wrap and refrigerate until ready to cook. Add the almonds just before cooking.

CAN BE FROZEN? No

CAN BE DOUBLED? Yes. Make it in 2 pie plates or dishes.

CAN BE HALVED? Yes

2 7½-ounce cans lump crabmeat

2 8-ounce packages cream cheese, softened

1 small onion, finely chopped

⅓ cup mayonnaise

1 tablespoon lemon juice

½ teaspoon salt

2 drops Tabasco Pepper Sauce

⅓ cup sliced almonds

Preheat the oven to 375°F. Empty the cans of crabmeat into a strainer and drain off the liquid. Carefully pick through the meat to remove bits of shell and cartilage. Use your fingers or a fork to flake the crabmeat. Place all the ingredients except the almonds in a bowl and mix, using a fork or rubber spatula.

Spoon the mixture into a 9-inch pie plate and sprinkle with the almonds. Bake for 25 to 30 minutes, or until lightly browned. Serve warm.

Chick-pea Pesto

Serve this as a dip with crudités or with triangles of pita bread. If serving with pita, use scissors to cut the pita. You can cut it several hours ahead of time and store it in a plastic bag at room temperature.

PREPARATION TIME: 10 minutes

YIELD: 2 cups, serves 8

CAN BE MADE AHEAD? Yes, up to 2 days. Store in a covered container in the refrigerator.

CAN BE FROZEN? Yes

CAN BE DOUBLED? Yes

CAN BE HALVED? No

1 19-ounce can chick-peas, drained

⅓ cup commercially prepared pesto

1 garlic clove, minced

1 small sweet onion, such as Vidalia or Spanish, cut into chunks

½ teaspoon salt

¼ teaspoon freshly ground black pepper

Place the chick-peas, pesto, garlic, onion, salt, and pepper in a food processor or blender and process until smooth.

NOTES: To serve this as a sandwich spread, cut open one side of a pita pocket and spread it with 2 to 4 tablespoons of the chick-pea mixture, according to the size of the pocket. Add chopped tomatoes and alfalfa sprouts.

For picnics, take the pita pockets, chick-pea spread, tomatoes, and alfalfa sprouts in separate containers and let everyone make his or her own.

Layered Taco Dip

If you like the taste of tacos, then try this new take on an old favorite. This layered spread consists of an herbed cream cheese base, covered with black beans, then a layer of salsa, and finally a topping of grated cheese accented with chopped scallions.

Use hot or mild salsa depending on your taste, or you can even make your own (page 203).

PREPARATION TIME: 15 minutes

YIELD: Serves 8

CAN BE MADE AHEAD? Yes, up to 6 hours. Cover airtight with plastic wrap and refrigerate until ready to serve.

CAN BE FROZEN? No

CAN BE DOUBLED AND TRIPLED? Yes

CAN BE HALVED? No

1 8-ounce package cream cheese, softened

⅓ cup chopped scallions (both white and green parts)

2 tablespoons chopped fresh coriander

1 garlic clove, minced

1 10-ounce can black beans, drained

1 8-ounce container salsa (mild or hot, as you prefer), drained, or 1 cup Salsa (page 203)

½ cup (2 ounces) grated Cheddar cheese or Monterey Jack cheese

Tortilla chips, for accompaniment

Place the cream cheese, half the scallions, the coriander, and garlic in a 1½-quart mixing bowl. Mix well with a rubber spatula or spoon to combine all the ingredients. Spread the mixture onto the bottom of a 9-inch pie plate. Top with the black beans.

Spread the salsa over the beans. Top with the cheese and garnish with the remaining scallions. Serve with the tortilla chips.

Salsa

There are more brands of salsa in the supermarket than stars in the sky. It gets so confusing to pick one brand over another. The solution is to make your own! Use vine-ripe or plum tomatoes if you can get them, or canned tomatoes if you can't. Don't use the pale red baseballs that masquerade as tomatoes when it's not summertime.

PREPARATION TIME: 15 minutes

YIELD: Serves 8

CAN BE MADE AHEAD? Yes, up to 1 week. Store in a covered container in the refrigerator.

CAN BE FROZEN? No

CAN BE DOUBLED AND TRIPLED? Yes

CAN BE HALVED? Yes

4 large ripe tomatoes or 8 plum tomatoes, chopped (about 4 cups), or 2 16-ounce cans chopped tomatoes (if you can't find chopped, whole are fine—you'll have to chop them yourself)

1 medium red onion, coarsely chopped

1 6-ounce jar roasted sweet red peppers, drained and coarsely chopped

1 large garlic clove, minced

⅓ cup chopped fresh coriander

2 tablespoons red wine vinegar, plus additional to taste

3 tablespoons olive oil

½ teaspoon salt, plus additional to taste

5 to 7 drops Tabasco Pepper Sauce

Place all the ingredients except the Tabasco Pepper Sauce in a food processor or blender. Process or blend in a pulsing motion until the mixture is just combined but not smooth. By hand, stir in additional salt or vinegar to taste, as well as the optional Tabasco Pepper Sauce. Serve at room temperature or chill until serving time. Pass with a basket of tortilla chips or pita triangles or vegetable crudités.

Guacamole

There is nothing quite as addictive as homemade guacamole—especially when it's made with vine-ripe tomatoes that appear in farmers' markets in the summer. While only those lucky enough to live in California will find homegrown avocados, other guacamole aficionados will have to scour the grocery stores well in advance to have nice ripe specimens to mash.

PREPARATION TIME: 15 minutes

YIELD: Serves 6 to 8

CAN BE MADE AHEAD? Yes, up to 4 hours, then it starts to turn an unappetizing color.

CAN BE FROZEN? No

CAN BE DOUBLED? Yes. Make it in 2 batches.

CAN BE HALVED? Yes

2 to 3 garlic cloves, chopped

3 large ripe avocados, halved, peeled, pitted, and cut into chunks

Juice and finely grated rind of 2 limes

2 large ripe tomatoes (remove the seeds if you wish; I don't bother), coarsely chopped

1 medium red onion, peeled and coarsely chopped

¼ cup chopped fresh coriander

½ teaspoon salt

4 to 6 drops Tabasco Pepper Sauce

Place the garlic, avocado, lime juice and rind, tomato, and onion in a medium-sized shallow bowl. Using a fork or potato masher, mash the ingredients until they're blended, but not smooth. Using a spoon, gently stir in the coriander, salt, and Tabasco Pepper Sauce until they're well distributed. If you wish to make the dish hotter, add more Tabasco Pepper Sauce, a drop at a time.

Serve with tortilla chips, cut-up vegetables, or pita triangles.

Skinny Dip

The trick to this I-can't-believe-it's-not-fattening dip is "yogurt cheese," which is easily made by allowing the liquid from yogurt to drip through a cheesecloth-lined strainer. You are left with a thick, creamy cheese that is similar to sour cream, or even cream cheese, depending on how long you strain the yogurt. Strain the cheese at least 24 hours (or as much as 48 hours) before you plan to use it.

RESTING TIME: At least 8 hours or up to 12 hours

YIELD: Serves 8

CAN BE MADE AHEAD? Yes, up to 1 week. Store in a covered container in the refrigerator.

CAN BE FROZEN? No

CAN BE DOUBLED? Yes

CAN BE HALVED? Yes

16 ounces plain nonfat yogurt

8 ounces low-fat ricotta cheese

$\frac{1}{2}$ cup fresh dill, minced

1 small onion, minced

$\frac{1}{3}$ cup freshly grated Parmesan cheese

1$\frac{1}{2}$ teaspoons salt

$\frac{1}{2}$ teaspoon freshly ground black pepper

At least 8 hours ahead, line a 2$\frac{1}{2}$- to 3-cup fine-mesh strainer with a piece of cheesecloth and set it over a mixing bowl. Pour the yogurt into the strainer, cover the top of the strainer and bowl with plastic wrap, and place it in the refrigerator. The next day discard the liquid in the bowl.

In a mixing bowl, whisk the ricotta until smooth. Stir in the yogurt and the remaining ingredients. Refrigerate, covered, for at least 1 hour, for the flavors to meld.

Crudités

Crudités is a fancy French name for what your mother called raw carrot and celery sticks. The list now includes all manner of grown-up vegetables that you never would have eaten as a kid, and the vegetables are served with any of the preceding dips. When you pick your vegetables, be fussy; look for those that are really fresh and the most appetizing. Stay away from the precut, packaged vegetables found in the produce section. Cut your own; you'll save a ton of money and you'll be giving your guests top-quality food.

PREPARATION TIME: 20 to 30 minutes

YIELD: If you are serving only crudités and dip, count on 5 to 6 pieces per person per hour.

CAN BE MADE AHEAD? Yes. You can cut up the vegetables up to 4 hours ahead and store them in plastic bags with several ice cubes tossed in to keep them crisp.

CAN BE FROZEN? Are you kidding?

CAN BE DOUBLED AND TRIPLED? Yes

CAN BE HALVED? Yes

The following make good dippers:

Carrot sticks • Celery sticks • Zucchini sticks • Red and green bell peppers, cored, seeded, and sliced into ½-inch strips

Cherry tomatoes

Belgian endive, stem cut off and leaves separated

Mushrooms, well rinsed and patted dry (if they're large, cut them in half—don't store them with an ice cube, as they absorb water)

Radishes

Daikon (Japanese radish), thinly sliced

Jícama Sticks

Cauliflower and broccoli florets

Sweet onions, cut into ½-inch rings

First Course: Soups

Tomato Cheddar Soup

This recipe comes from a very special restaurant in Keene, New Hampshire, called Henry David's. I imagine that Thoreau himself would have relished a bowl or mug of this warming treat on a cold winter's night at Walden Pond.

The chef says that the recipe is "embarrassingly simple." I say hooray for simple (and thank God for Campbell's). See if you can find some really good sharp, well-aged Vermont Cheddar—it makes a big difference.

PREPARATION TIME: 10 minutes

COOKING TIME: 10 to 15 minutes

YIELD: Serves 6 to 8 (6 if served in mugs)

CAN BE MADE AHEAD? No

CAN BE FROZEN? No

CAN BE DOUBLED? Yes

CAN BE HALVED? Yes

12 ounces (3 cups) best-quality Cheddar cheese, grated

2 10¾-ounce cans condensed cream of tomato soup

2½ cups light cream

Divide the grated cheese among 6 to 8 mugs or soup bowls. Place the condensed soup and the cream in a 2-quart saucepan set over medium heat and cook, stirring continuously with a wire whisk and scraping the bottom to prevent scorching, until the soup is very hot, just about to a simmer (tiny bubbles will appear around the edge of the pan). Then pour or ladle the hot soup into the bowls or mugs and serve immediately.

Quick Italian Vegetable Soup

Just like Grandma used to make (if you did, in fact, have an Italian grandma), this soup is chock-full of pasta, chick-peas, and vegetables. If you want to make this taste extra special, top it with freshly grated Parmesan cheese; I like Reggiano the best. Delightful!

PREPARATION TIME: 20 minutes

COOKING TIME: 35 minutes

YIELD: Serves 10 to 12

CAN BE MADE AHEAD? Yes. Cover and refrigerate until ready to reheat.

CAN BE FROZEN? Yes. Use a plastic container with a tight lid or a heavy-duty plastic freezer bag.

CAN BE DOUBLED? Yes

CAN BE HALVED? Yes

3 tablespoons olive oil

2 onions, coarsely chopped

2 celery stalks, coarsely chopped

2 garlic cloves, finely chopped

2 carrots, sliced into ¼-inch-thick pieces

1 green bell pepper, seeded and coarsely chopped

2 teaspoons dried basil or ⅓ cup tightly packed fresh
   basil leaves, chopped

1 teaspoon dried oregano

1 46-ounce can chicken broth

1 28-ounce can whole tomatoes, undrained and quartered

1 19-ounce can chick-peas, drained

1 cup uncooked pasta, such as small shells or bow ties

¼ cup fresh parsley, chopped

Parmesan cheese, for garnish

Heat the oil over medium-high heat in a 6-quart heavy-bottomed soup pot. Add the onion, celery, and garlic and sauté for 4 to 5 minutes, or until the onion is transparent. Add the carrots, green pepper, basil, and oregano and continue sautéing for 4 to 5 more minutes, or until onion just starts to turn golden brown.

Add the chicken broth, tomatoes, and chick-peas. Cook over medium heat for 15 minutes. Add the pasta and simmer until the pasta is tender (check cooking time on pasta package). Add the parsley and serve garnished with Parmesan cheese.

Curried Carrot Soup

This velvety smooth, delicately flavored vegetarian soup has such a beautiful color and such a seductive aroma. Your guests will think it's sinfully rich; however, the creamy consistency comes from the puréed vegetables—not from cream. This soup freezes beautifully, so plan on making it well ahead of time.

PREPARATION TIME: 30 minutes

COOKING TIME: 30 minutes

YIELD: Serves 8

CAN BE MADE AHEAD? Yes, up to 2 days. Store in a covered container in the refrigerator.

CAN BE FROZEN? Yes, up to 3 months. If the soup separates upon defrosting, process in a food processor or blender until smooth.

CAN BE DOUBLE AND TRIPLED? Yes

CAN BE HALVED? Yes

8 large carrots, peeled and sliced

1 large Spanish onion, peeled and diced

2 large Idaho potatoes, peeled and sliced

6 cups canned vegetable broth or 6 cups water and
   3 vegetable bouillon cubes

⅓ cup dark brown sugar, firmly packed

1 teaspoon powdered ginger

2 to 3 teaspoons curry powder

½ teaspoon white pepper

1 to 2 teaspoons salt, to taste

Plain yogurt and unsweetened shredded coconut, toasted
   (see the Note), for garnish

Place the vegetables and broth in a large stockpot set over medium heat. Cover and bring to a simmer, cooking for 30 minutes until the vegetables are very soft. Add the sugar and seasonings except the salt and cook an additional 5 minutes.

Cool slightly, then purée the soup, both solids and liquid, in 2-cup batches in a food processor or blender. Return the purée to the souppot, heat to a simmer over low heat, stirring often, and add the salt to taste. Serve hot or cold garnished with a dollop of yogurt and sprinkled with toasted shredded coconut.

NOTE: To toast coconut, preheat the oven to 350°F with the rack in the center position. Cover a baking sheet with foil and spread the coconut over it in one layer. Bake for 10 to 15 minutes, or until the coconut just starts to color. Stir and cook for 1 to 2 additional minutes. Do not allow it to burn. This can be done up to 3 days ahead of time. When it's completely cool, store in a covered container at room temperature.

Steven Raichlen's Mangospacho

My very good friend and Florida food maven Steven Raichlen knows what's good. In his book *Miami Spice*, this unusually delicious take on an old classic stands right out. You may have to scout out several markets to find ripe mangoes. A better bet is to buy them a week ahead and let them ripen at room temperature. If they become really soft, stick them in the refrigerator until you're ready to make the soup.

PREPARATION TIME: 20 minutes

YIELD: Serves 8

CAN BE MADE AHEAD? Yes, up to 24 hours. Cover and refrigerate.

CAN BE FROZEN? No

CAN BE DOUBLED? Yes

CAN BE HALVED? Yes

4 to 5 large ripe mangoes, peeled and finely diced (to make 8 cups)

2 tablespoons fresh gingerroot, finely chopped

½ cup rice wine vinegar

½ cup corn oil

About 2 cups water

2 tablespoons sugar

1 teaspoon salt

1 teaspoon freshly ground black pepper

1 medium (½ cup) red onion, finely diced

2 cucumbers, peeled, seeded, and finely chopped

½ cup fresh coriander, finely chopped

½ cup finely chopped chives

Combine half the cut-up mango, the gingerroot, vinegar, oil, water, sugar, salt, and pepper in a blender or food processor and purée until smooth. Transfer the mixture to a large container and stir in the remaining mango and the rest of the ingredients (this gives the soup its chunky/smooth texture). You may wish to add more vinegar or salt and pepper at this point; taste and see. Refrigerate for at least 1 hour before serving in individual soup bowls.

Classic Gazpacho

If you're hankering for a more familiar version, here it is. If you can't find in-season tomatoes, used the canned ones. I like to use V-8 juice, but if you prefer the taste of tomato juice, go for it. The spicy V-8 will knock the socks off your more timid guests, so serve it only to people you know well. Roasted red peppers come in jars and are found in the condiment section of the supermarket.

PREPARATION TIME: 20 minutes

YIELD: Serves 8

CAN BE MADE AHEAD? Yes, up to 3 days. Store in a covered container in the refrigerator.

CAN BE FROZEN? No

CAN BE DOUBLED? Yes

CAN BE HALVED? Yes

3 large red-ripe tomatoes, cores removed and cut into 2-inch pieces, or
   1 16-ounce can chopped tomatoes, drained

1 green bell pepper, core removed, seeded, and cut into 2-inch pieces

1 cup roasted red bell peppers

1 large Spanish onion, peeled and chopped

2 large garlic cloves, chopped

1 large cucumber, peeled and cut into 2-inch cubes

4 cups tomato juice or V-8 juice

⅓ cup red wine vinegar

⅓ cup olive oil

3 to 4 tablespoons soy sauce

6 to 8 drops Tabasco Pepper Sauce (optional)

Place the tomatoes, both kinds of peppers, onion, garlic, and cucumber in a food processor or blender. Pulse on and off until the mixture is just combined and the vegetables are in small pieces, but not puréed.

Add the tomato juice and blend or process for an additional 10 seconds, just to blend.

Place this mixture in a bowl and stir in the remaining ingredients, using the soy sauce as the salt source, adding more or less as you wish. Add the Tabasco Pepper Sauce, if desired. Chill for at least 2 hours before serving.

Cold Cherry Soup

This is one of the very first soups (right after chicken soup) I learned how to make. It remains an unexpectedly novel and refreshing way to begin a summer meal (although I must admit I love it so much I sometimes make it for the first course at Thanksgiving dinner). The only thing that has changed from the original recipe is the addition of the garnish of dried cherries soaked in liqueur.

If you can find fresh tart red cherries and are willing to pit them, you will have a truly marvelous soup. Tart cherries are also available canned and frozen. If you use these, reserve the juice and substitute it for an equal amount of the water. Make sure to check for pits!

PREPARATION TIME: 15 minutes

COOKING TIME: 40 minutes

YIELD: Serves 6

CAN BE MADE AHEAD? Yes. It must be made at least 6 hours (or as long as 24 hours) ahead. Store in a covered container in the refrigerator.

CAN BE FROZEN? No

CAN BE DOUBLED AND TRIPLED? Yes

CAN BE HALVED? Yes

⅔ cup dried cherries

½ cup cherry liqueur, or cherry or cranberry juice

4 cups tart red cherries (fresh, frozen, or canned), pitted

3½ cups (if you have used canned or frozen cherries, substitute the juice for an equal amount of the water) plus 2 tablespoons water

1 3-inch cinnamon stick

2 whole cloves

¼ cup sugar

1 tablespoon cornstarch

Sour cream or plain yogurt, for garnish

Place the dried cherries and the liqueur in a small microwavable bowl, cover with plastic wrap, and microwave on high for 2 minutes. Do not remove the plastic wrap. Set aside to cool. Or place the cherries and liqueur in a small saucepan set over medium heat. Cook, stirring constantly, until the mixture boils. Reduce the heat and cook for 1 minute. Cover the pan and set aside to cool.

Combine the cherries, juice (if any), the 3½ cups water, cinnamon stick, cloves, and sugar in a 3-quart saucepan set over medium heat. Cook, uncovered, stirring occasionally, until the mixture comes to a boil. Reduce the heat and simmer for 30 minutes (unless you are using canned cherries, in which case simmer only 10 minutes).

In a small bowl, mix the cornstarch with the 2 tablespoons of water to make a paste. Add this to the cherry mixture and cook until it becomes clear and has thickened slightly. Remove the cinnamon stick and cloves and use a slotted spoon to remove about 2 cups of the cherries. Set them aside and purée the rest of the soup. Add the reserved cherries to the soup.

Empty the dried cherries into a small strainer set over the pot of soup. Use a spoon to drain any excess liquid into the soup. Reserve the cherries for garnish. Chill the soup very well.

Serve in chilled bowls, garnished with a dollop of sour cream and some of the dried cherries.

First Course: Salads

Cucumber Salad

Fresh dill is the key to this light, refreshing dish. You may substitute all yogurt in place of the sour cream.

PREPARATION TIME: 15 minutes

YIELD: Serves 8

CAN BE MADE AHEAD? Yes, up to 3 days. Store tightly covered in the refrigerator.

CAN BE FROZEN? No

CAN BE DOUBLE AND TRIPLED? Yes

CAN BE HALVED? Yes

4 medium cucumbers, peeled and sliced ¼ inch thick

1 cup sour cream

1 cup plain yogurt

½ cup fresh dill, finely chopped

½ teaspoon salt

Freshly ground black pepper

4 scallions, finely chopped (both green and white parts), for garnish

Place the cucumbers in a bowl. Mix together the sour cream and yogurt in a bowl. Add the dill and salt and stir until well mixed. Add the sour cream mixture to the cucumbers, season with the pepper, and garnish with the chopped scallion. Serve well chilled.

Ambrosia

This classic Southern dish somehow made its way up north, where it was served at every Thanksgiving meal when I was growing up. I make it with thick-skinned navel oranges because they are seedless. No matter what kind of oranges you use, don't forget to cut away the white part (called the pith), because it's bitter.

PREPARATION TIME: 30 minutes

YIELD: Serves 8

CAN BE MADE AHEAD? Yes, up to 6 hours. Refrigerate covered with plastic wrap.

CAN BE FROZEN? No

CAN BE DOUBLED? Yes

CAN BE HALVED? Yes

4 large ripe bananas, sliced

Juice and rind of 1 lemon

4 large navel oranges, peeled, pith and seeds removed, and sliced

2 cups fresh or canned pineapple, cut into 1-inch pieces

½ cup confectioners' sugar

2½ cups sweetened shredded coconut

½ cup slivered almonds

In a bowl, toss the banana slices with the lemon juice and rind. In a glass serving bowl, alternately layer the oranges, bananas, and pineapple, sprinkling each layer with sugar and coconut, reserving some for the top. Sprinkle the top with the almonds as well. Cover the bowl with plastic wrap and refrigerate for at least 1 hour or up to 6 hours. Serve directly from the bowl or arrange on salad plates before serving.

Pear and Roquefort Salad

The sweetness of the pears perfectly counterbalances the salty tang of the cheese in this winter salad. Walnuts lend a subtle crunch.

If you buy raw nuts in a health food store, remember to toast them first by spreading them out on a heavy baking sheet and placing them in a 300°F oven for 10 to 12 minutes. Keep an eye on them and when you begin to smell the aroma of toasted nuts, you'll know they are done. Cool them before using or storing in a plastic bag in the freezer.

This recipe gives the option of a low-fat version of the dressing, using yogurt instead of mayonnaise.

PREPARATION TIME: 20 minutes

YIELD: Serves 4 to 6

CAN BE MADE AHEAD? Yes. The greens can be washed and dried the day before. Store in a plastic bag in the refrigerator and shred just before assembling the salad. The dressing can be made the day before and stored in the refrigerator.

CAN BE FROZEN? No

CAN BE DOUBLED AND TRIPLED? Yes

CAN BE HALVED? Yes

½ cup Roquefort cheese, crumbled

½ cup mayonnaise or plain yogurt (regular or low-fat)

1 tablespoon red wine vinegar or balsamic vinegar

1 bunch of watercress, thick stems removed, washed and spun-dry

1 head of Boston lettuce, washed, spun-dry, and torn in bite-sized pieces

2 large ripe Anjou, Comice, or Bartlett pears, cored, sliced lengthwise into ¼-inch wedges, and tossed with the juice of 1 lemon

2 scallions, chopped (both white and green parts)

3 celery stalks, sliced on the diagonal into ¼-inch pieces

⅔ cup walnuts, in large pieces

In a small bowl, mix together the cheese, mayonnaise (or yogurt), and vinegar. Just before serving, arrange both watercress and lettuce on individual salad plates. Top with a layer of pear slices, then sprinkle with scallions, celery, and walnuts. Drizzle the dressing over the salads and serve immediately.

Caesar Salad

Crunchy romaine lettuce, freshly grated Parmesan cheese, the zip of black pepper, and the subtle hint of anchovies make this classic salad a hands-down winner. Real Caesar salad dressing is a homemade egg-based emulsion. If you get eggs from a reputable, clean market (I like the kind my health food store carries), and you use only eggs with clean, intact shells, you don't have to be overly concerned with using them raw. You can, of course, substitute bottled Caesar salad dressing if you wish.

The other signature ingredient of this salad is croutons: bite-sized pieces of toast that get tossed in along with the dressing and grated cheese. You can buy them, but the homemade kind is so simple to make—and tastes so much better.

PREPARATION TIME: 20 minutes

YIELD: Serves 8

CAN BE MADE AHEAD? You can wash and carefully dry the lettuce the day before. Store it in a plastic bag in the refrigerator. The dressing can be made the day before. Store it in a tightly covered container and refrigerate until ready to toss the salad. The croutons can be made the day before. Store them, uncovered, at room temperature.

CAN BE FROZEN? No

CAN BE DOUBLED? Yes, and tripled, etc. etc.

CAN BE HALVED? Yes

8 slices French bread, 1 inch thick (if the slices are very wide, cut them in half)

2 tablespoons plus 1 cup olive oil

Salt and freshly ground black pepper, for the croutons

2 garlic cloves, peeled and mashed with the side of a large knife

2 teaspoons Dijon mustard

¼ cup lemon juice

1 large egg

4 to 5 anchovy fillets, drained of their oil and patted dry,
or 1½ tablespoons anchovy paste

½ to 1 teaspoon freshly ground black pepper

2 heads of romaine, leaves separated, rinsed, spun-dry, and cut
into 1½-inch pieces

1 cup (about 8 ounces) freshly grated Parmesan cheese

Preheat the broiler with the rack in the upper but not highest position. Brush both sides of the bread slices with the 2 tablespoons of olive oil and sprinkle with salt and pepper. Place the bread on a baking sheet and broil for 2 to 3 minutes, or until just golden brown; turn and repeat with the other side. Place the slices on a cake rack to cool.

Add the garlic to the 1 cup of olive oil in a spouted measuring cup, stir, and let sit for several minutes. Place the mustard, lemon juice, and egg in a food processor or blender. Process or blend for 20 seconds. With the machine running, add the garlic oil very slowly, one drop at a time, until the mixture begins to thicken. Dribble in the remaining garlic oil, then add the anchovies and finally the pepper. Taste the dressing. If it is too tart, add more oil; if it tastes too bland, add more lemon juice or anchovy.

Put the romaine in a large bowl. Toss with half the dressing to start, adding more only to moisten all the leaves. Sprinkle the salad with the cheese and then top it with the croutons, leaving them whole, or breaking them in smaller pieces if you wish. Toss the salad once more to distribute the cheese and croutons and serve immediately.

Garden Salad

Somewhere in the crush of trendy appetizers the art of making a simple, yet perfectly balanced salad has been lost to time. The secret lies in using fresh vegetables that are in season, and being stingy with the dressing. If you are making this in February, don't choose those rock-hard, flavorless tomatoes that show up in the winter, but cherry tomatoes, which always seem to have a pleasing taste. Take care to wash the vegetables (especially lettuce, spinach, and early asparagus which always are very sandy) carefully in lots of cold water, then pat or spin-dry.

Use an assortment of greens: red leaf and Bibb lettuce, radicchio, endive, watercress, and spinach. Many stores now sell cut-up assorted salad greens for quite a hefty price, but if you're pressed for time this convenience is a godsend. Some folks like to combine all the ingredients in one bowl, toss with the dressing, and serve at the table. Others prefer to compose the salad on individual plates in the kitchen and pass the dressing separately. The choice is yours. If you are under a time constraint (a roast cooking in the oven) and need to keep careful control over the timing of the first course, I would combine the two philosophies and toss and plate it in the kitchen.

PREPARATION TIME: 20 minutes

YIELD: Serves 8

CAN BE MADE AHEAD? Yes, up to 6 hours. The lettuce can be washed and stored in a plastic bag in the refrigerator. The vegetables except the tomatoes can be cut up and stored in ice water—drain and pat them well before assembling the salad. The dressing can be made several days ahead.

CAN BE FROZEN? No

CAN BE DOUBLED? Yes

CAN BE HALVED? Yes

8 cups greens, such as red leaf lettuce, Bibb lettuce, romaine, spinach, endive, watercress, well rinsed, patted or spun-dry, and cut into bite-sized pieces

3 ripe flavorful tomatoes, cut in half then into ½-inch slices, or 1 pint cherry tomatoes, halved

1 large or 2 medium cucumbers, peeled, cut in half lengthwise, and thinly sliced

2 large carrots, peeled and shredded

1 recipe Herb Vinaigrette (page 228)

The following is a list of optional additions, but I wouldn't get carried away and add them all—choose no more than two or three: sliced mushrooms, marinated mushrooms, thinly sliced red onion, small florets of broccoli and/or cauliflower, sprouts, olives, canned chick-peas (well drained), diced celery, strips of red and/or green bell pepper, roasted bell peppers, marinated artichoke hearts, cubes of cheese, crumbled blue cheese, grated cheese, or croutons.

Select a bowl large enough to accommodate all the salad fixings but that will leave you room to toss the salad. Add the prepared vegetables, lettuce first, then heavier things last. Just before serving, add just enough dressing to moisten; ⅓ cup is more than enough for a salad such as this. Dribble the dressing over the top of the salad and then use large serving utensils to toss it until all the vegetables are moistened. You also have these options: Serve the salad in the bowl, tossed but not dressed, and allow the guests to serve themselves and add their own dressing from a pitcher that you pass separately (in this case it's best to make extra dressing); serve the tossed salad on individual plates, either dressed or with the dressing passed separately.

If you wish, you can have a pepper grinder available so your guests can sprinkle some on their salad.

Lobster Melon Cocktail

This unusual (and extravagant) seafood cocktail makes a stunning presentation. If you cannot find (or justify the expense of) fresh lobster meat, you can substitute crabmeat or smoked scallops. There is a gadget called a melon baller that is available in kitchenware stores.

Select your melons a few days ahead of time to give them a chance to ripen and turn sweet. Keep them at room temperature until the ends give slightly when pushed with your fingers and they smell sweet and fragrant, then refrigerate them until ready to use.

PREPARATION TIME: 25 minutes

YIELD: Serves 6

CAN BE MADE AHEAD? Yes. The melon balls can be prepared and kept refrigerated, covered up to 6 hours ahead of time, and the dressing can be mixed the day before.

CAN BE FROZEN? No

CAN BE DOUBLED AND TRIPLED? Yes

CAN BE HALVED? Yes

1 cup mayonnaise

Juice and grated rind of 1 lime

1½ teaspoons curry powder

1½ pounds fresh lobster meat or crabmeat (picked over to remove cartilage) or smoked scallops

3 to 4 cups assorted melon balls, such as cantaloupe, honeydew, Persian, casaba

Fresh mint leaves, for garnish

Make the dressing by mixing together in a small bowl the mayonnaise, lime juice and rind, and curry powder. Set aside.

Cut the lobster meat into 1½-inch pieces (removing the dark vein that runs down the back of the tail). Place it in a mixing bowl. Add the melon balls and stir gently, trying not to squash the melon, just until mixed.

Divide the melon mixture among 6 plates or very large wineglasses. Use a tablespoon to add about a dollop of dressing to the top of each. Garnish with a mint leaf and serve immediately.

Herb Vinaigrette

Anyone can open a bottle of salad dressing, but when you see how easy it is to make vinaigrette in just a few minutes, you'll be converted. You have the option of using dried or fresh herbs. If you prefer your dressing without herbs, omit them.

PREPARATION TIME: 10 minutes

YIELD: About ¾ cup

CAN BE MADE AHEAD? Yes, up to 1 week. Store in a covered jar in the refrigerator.

CAN BE FROZEN? No

CAN BE DOUBLED? Yes

CAN BE HALVED? No

⅓ cup olive oil

3 to 4 tablespoons red wine vinegar or balsamic vinegar

2 tablespoons Dijon mustard

½ teaspoon dried thyme or 1 tablespoon fresh thyme

½ teaspoon dried tarragon or 2 teaspoons fresh tarragon

½ teaspoon dried chervil or 2 teaspoons fresh chervil

½ to 1 teaspoon salt

½ teaspoon freshly ground black pepper

Place all ingredients in a food processor or blender and process or blend until emulsified. Add additional salt and vinegar to taste. You can also make this by placing the ingredients in a bowl and whisking vigorously.

You will need to shake this dressing just before using, so it's best to store it in a tightly sealed bottle or jar in the refrigerator. If it becomes cloudy (that's the olive oil), run the bottle or jar under hot water for a few minutes.

Main Course: Salads

Citrus Shrimp Salad

This makes a marvelous summer main course, but it is perfect for a light all-weather appetizer as well. You can use already cooked shrimp or prepare your own (see the Note).

PREPARATION TIME: 25 minutes

COOKING TIME: 10 minutes for the orzo; 5 minutes for the shrimp if you cook it yourself

YIELD: Serves 4 as a main course; 6 to 8 as an appetizer

CAN BE MADE AHEAD? Yes. This must be made at least 4 hours (and up to 24 hours) ahead so that the ingredients can chill. Store in a covered container in the refrigerator until ready to serve.

CAN BE FROZEN? No

CAN BE DOUBLED? Yes

CAN BE HALVED? Yes

1 pound orzo (rice-shaped pasta), cooked according to package instructions, drained, and rinsed

⅔ cup mayonnaise

Juice and finely grated rind of 1 orange

Juice and finely grated rind of 1 lime

Juice and finely grated rind of 1 lemon

½ cup Italian parsley, finely chopped

1½ pounds cooked large (20 to 24 to a pound) shrimp (see the Note)

(continued)

Place the orzo in a large mixing bowl and set aside.

In a small bowl, mix together the mayonnaise, citrus rinds and juices, and parsley. Add the shrimp to the orzo and add the mayonnaise mixture, tossing until the ingredients are blended. Refrigerate until ready to serve.

NOTE: You can buy shelled, cooked shrimp (make sure that they look moist and plump and have no fishy or iodine smell) or you can buy frozen, shelled shrimp and cook them (without defrosting first) for 5 to 6 minutes in a large pot of rapidly boiling water, until they turn pink. Drain well and rinse with cold water.

Spinach Chick-pea Salad

This jazzed-up version of Greek salad has all the traditional ingredients: feta cheese, red onion, and olives, and some new additions: chick-peas and spinach. This makes a substantial luncheon or hot-weather supper entrée—all you need is a loaf of crusty bread and you're in business. Really good olives make this a memorable salad. Look for the oil-cured black olives suggested in this recipe; they are available in the deli section of your market.

PREPARATION TIME: 20 to 30 minutes

YIELD: Serves 8 as an entrée; 10 as a side dish

CAN BE MADE AHEAD? Yes. You can rinse and dry the spinach and prepare the dressing up to 6 hours ahead. Store the spinach in a plastic bag in the refrigerator. The dressing can be left at room temperature for up to 8 hours.

CAN BE FROZEN? No

CAN BE DOUBLED? Yes

CAN BE HALVED? Yes

1 19-ounce can chick-peas, drained

1 tablespoon dried dill or ½ cup fresh dill, chopped, plus additional fresh for garnish

½ teaspoon salt

½ teaspoon freshly ground black pepper

2 pounds fresh spinach, thoroughly washed, well dried, and torn into bite-sized pieces

8 ounces feta cheese, rinsed and crumbled

1 medium red onion, thinly sliced

1 generous cup oil-cured black olives

1 pint cherry tomatoes, halved

1 large cucumber, peeled and sliced

⅓ cup red wine vinegar or balsamic vinegar

½ cup olive oil

1 tablespoon Dijon mustard

½ teaspoon salt

Toss the drained chick-peas with the dill, salt, and pepper. Set aside. Combine the spinach, cheese, red onion, olives, tomatoes, and cucumber in a large serving bowl.

Make dressing by whisking together the vinegar, olive oil, mustard, and salt. Add the chick-peas to the vegetables in the bowl, then toss with the dressing. Garnish with fresh dill.

Honey-Pecan Chicken Salad

This dish is available at almost every fancy take-out store. You'll be delighted when you see not only how easy it is to make, but how much less the homemade will cost you. Remember that if you buy raw pecans, you should toast them to bring out the flavor. Spread them on a heavy baking sheet and place it in a 300°F oven for 7 to 10 minutes, or until you can just smell them. Cool before using or storing in a plastic bag in the freezer.

PREPARATION TIME: 15 minutes

COOKING TIME: 15 minutes

YIELD: Serves 8

CAN BE MADE AHEAD? Yes, the night before. Cover and refrigerate until ready to serve.

CAN BE FROZEN? No

CAN BE DOUBLED AND TRIPLED? Yes

CAN BE HALVED? Yes

½ cup mayonnaise or 4 tablespoons plain yogurt and 4 tablespoons sour cream

1 tablespoon lime juice

1 tablespoon honey

1 tablespoon Dijon mustard

3 pounds skinless and boneless chicken breasts, simmered in water for 15 minutes, or until cooked through

1 cup pecan halves

2 cups seedless grapes (purple, red, or green), cut in half lengthwise

2 tablespoons chopped fresh tarragon or 1½ teaspoons dried tarragon

1 bunch of watercress, washed, thick stems removed, and torn into bite-sized pieces

1 tablespoon fresh chives, for garnish

Mix together the mayonnaise, lime juice, honey, and mustard in a large mixing bowl. Cut the chicken in bite-sized pieces and add to the mayonnaise mixture. Add the pecans, grapes, and tarragon and stir until well mixed.

Mound the salad in the center of a large shallow serving bowl or platter. Surround with the watercress and garnish with the chives.

Four Seasons Pasta Salad

An easy-to-prepare crowd pleaser. You'll never buy takeout again! While this recipe calls for bow tie noodles, you can pretty much substitute most noodles of other shapes such as orzo (rice-shaped) or ziti (tubes). You can even use vegetable-flavored pastas such as tomato, basil, or spinach. Make sure not to overcook the noodles—you don't want them to become mushy.

PREPARATION TIME: 30 minutes

YIELD: Serves 12 to 14

COOKING TIME: According to package directions

CAN BE MADE AHEAD? Yes. Keep covered and refrigerated for up to 2 days.

CAN BE FROZEN? No

CAN BE DOUBLED AND TRIPLED? Yes, but watch out, it makes a lot already!

CAN BE HALVED? Yes

(continued)

1 12-ounce package pasta bow ties

1 small red onion, cut in half and thinly sliced

1 7½-ounce jar roasted sweet red peppers, drained

4 fresh Italian plum tomatoes, cut into ¼-inch slices

2 cups small broccoli florets, blanched for 3 minutes in boiling water
  and drained

½ cup fresh basil or flat Italian parsley, coarsely chopped

1 8-ounce can sliced, pitted black olives, drained

6 to 8 anchovies, drained and chopped

⅓ cup pesto

½ cup Italian salad dressing

⅔ cup coarsely grated provolone cheese

Cook the pasta according to the package directions. Drain, rinse with
cold water, and drain again.

Place the pasta in a large serving bowl. Add the onion, peppers,
tomatoes, broccoli, basil, olives, and anchovies. Toss to combine.

In a small bowl, whisk together the pesto and Italian salad dressing.
Pour this mixture over the pasta salad. Garnish with the provolone
cheese. Serve hot or chilled.

Southwest Pasta Salad

Red peppers and spinach noodles give a festive air to this dish that is seasoned with familiar flavors of the Southwest: salsa, coriander, and cumin. Even though it's called "salad" you can serve it hot as well as cold. Take care not to overcook the noodles—you don't want them to become mushy.

PREPARATION TIME: 20 minutes

COOKING TIME: 6 to 8 minutes to cook the pasta

YIELD: Serves 8 to 10

CAN BE MADE AHEAD? Yes, up to 48 hours. Refrigerate in a covered container.

CAN BE FROZEN? No

CAN BE DOUBLED? Yes

CAN BE HALVED? Yes

1 cup roasted sweet red peppers, drained and cut into strips

1 28-ounce can chopped tomatoes and juice

1 cup mayonnaise (regular or reduced-fat)

1 12-ounce jar mild, medium, or hot salsa (depending on your taste)

⅓ cup fresh coriander leaves, chopped

20 pitted black olives, sliced

1 teaspoon ground cumin

1 8-ounce package shredded Monterey Jack cheese

2 pounds spinach pasta (noodle shapes or spaghetti), cooked until just tender and well drained

4 to 8 dashes Tabasco Pepper Sauce (optional)

Stir together all the ingredients except the pasta and Tabasco Pepper Sauce in a large mixing bowl. Add the pasta and toss. Season, if desired, with Tabasco Pepper Sauce. Serve hot or cold.

Main Course: Vegetarian Dishes

Grilled Vegetable Kabobs

You can make these either in the oven under the broiler or on the grill. Inexpensive wooden skewers are available in gourmet shops and even in hardware stores. Make sure to soak them in water for several minutes before using them.

I like to put the onions on the ends of the skewers since they take the longest to cook. This position gives them the best exposure to the heat. Served with rice, lentils, or beans, this makes a perfect vegetarian entrée.

PREPARATION TIME: 15 minutes

MARINATING TIME: 30 minutes

GRILLING TIME: 8 to 10 minutes

YIELD: Serves 8

CAN BE MADE AHEAD? Kabobs can be assembled up to 4 hours ahead. Cover with plastic wrap and refrigerate until ready to cook.

CAN BE FROZEN? No

CAN BE DOUBLED AND TRIPLED? Yes

CAN BE HALVED? Yes

2 large zucchini, cut crosswise into ½-inch slices

2 large summer squash, cut crosswise into ½-inch-thick slices

2 red bell peppers, seeded and cut into 1½-inch pieces

2 green bell peppers, seeded and cut into 1½-inch pieces

2 large red onions, cut from the top into thick wedges (leave the sections joined)

12 white mushrooms, wiped clean of dirt and stems trimmed

½ cup olive oil

Juice of 1 lemon

2 teaspoons dried oregano or 2 tablespoons fresh oregano, chopped

2 tablespoons soy sauce

1 tablespoon Dijon mustard

½ teaspoon freshly ground black pepper

Thread the vegetables on skewers. If you use wooden skewers, soak them in water for a few minutes. Place the vegetable kabobs in a shallow baking dish.

Mix together the olive oil, lemon juice, oregano, soy sauce, mustard, and pepper and pour evenly over the kabobs. Marinate for 30 minutes, turning occasionally to coat evenly with the marinade.

Arrange the kabobs on an outdoor grill and grill for 4 to 5 minutes on each side, basting once or twice with the marinade, until the vegetables are softened and beginning to brown. Or place them in one layer on a rimmed baking sheet in the upper third of the oven with the broiler set on high, following the cooking directions above. Serve warm or at room temperature.

Oven-Roasted Vegetables with Couscous

Try these wonderful crisp and crackling-tasting oven-roasted vegetables. Served hot, they are a perfect accompaniment to meat, fish, or fowl. They can be the base of a vegetarian feast when paired with couscous (or rice, beans, or lentils). You can even serve them cold as part of a salad.

PREPARATION TIME: 25 minutes

BAKING TIME: 50 to 60 minutes

YIELD: Serves 8

CAN BE MADE AHEAD? Only if you plan to use them cold in a salad. They do not reheat well.

CAN BE FROZEN? No

CAN BE DOUBLED? Yes. Use a pan large enough so that the vegetables can be spread in a single layer.

CAN BE HALVED? Yes

8 unpeeled garlic cloves, mashed with the flat side of a heavy knife

½ to ⅔ cup olive oil

2 turnips, peeled and sliced into ½-inch slices

3 parsnips, peeled and sliced into ½-inch slices

10 red potatoes, washed and sliced in half

1 large fennel bulb, leaves and stems removed, rinsed, dried, and sliced lengthwise into ¾-inch pieces, leaving the bulb attached at the root end

1 large Spanish onion, peeled and cut into ½-inch slices

4 beets, peeled and quartered

2 tablespoons fresh tarragon, chopped, or 1 teaspoon dried tarragon

2 tablespoons fresh rosemary leaves or 1 teaspoon dried rosemary

2 tablespoons fresh thyme leaves or 1 teaspoon dried thyme

⅓ cup fresh basil leaves, chopped, or 1 teaspoon dried basil

4 cups cooked couscous

The night before (or as long as 2 days before), place the garlic in a small, lidded container. Add the olive oil, cover the container, and leave at room temperature for at least 12 hours, until you are ready to cook the vegetables.

Preheat the oven to 350°F with the rack in the upper third.

Place the turnips, parsnips, potatoes, fennel, and onion in a large mixing bowl. (Save the beets to add later, as they might stain the other vegetables.) Remove the garlic from the oil and discard it. Pour half the oil over the vegetables and stir until well coated. Mix in the herbs.

Drizzle 1 to 2 tablespoons of the remaining oil over the bottom of a large shallow baking pan. Spread the vegetables in a single layer in the pan, leaving room around the edges for the beets. Add the beets around the edges of the pan. Drizzle the beets with the remaining oil.

Cover the pan with foil and roast at 350°F for 30 minutes, or until the potatoes are slightly tender when pierced with a fork. Remove the foil and roast another 20 to 30 minutes, or until the vegetables are tender when pierced with a fork and crisp and slightly golden on the edges.

Place the vegetables in the center of a large shallow serving dish and surround with the couscous. Serve warm.

Sweet-and-Sour Curried Cabbage Rolls

Your vegetarian friends will delight in the combination of tastes and textures in this dish. These cabbage rolls make a great appetizer (served at room temperature) as well as a hearty main course. Be sure to use unsweetened coconut, which is available in health food stores and many supermarkets. Mango chutney is available in the condiment section of supermarkets.

Don't forget to place the cabbage in the freezer the night before so that the leaves will be wilted upon defrosting. This makes the cabbage easy to work with.

PREPARATION TIME: 30 minutes

COOKING TIME: 50 minutes

YIELD: Serves 8

CAN BE MADE AHEAD? Yes, up to 3 days. Store in a covered microwavable dish in the refrigerator.

CAN BE FROZEN? Yes, up to 2 months. Defrost and heat in a microwave.

CAN BE DOUBLED? Yes. Use 2 cabbages.

CAN BE HALVED? It's easier to make a full recipe and freeze half to serve another time.

1 medium onion, finely diced (about 1 cup)

3 cups cooked brown rice

1½ cups golden raisins

½ cup unsweetened flaked coconut

1 cup lightly toasted cashews, broken in half (see the Note)

1½ teaspoons curry powder

1½ teaspoons salt (unless you have salted the rice cooking water)

1 teaspoon freshly ground black pepper

1 large head of green cabbage (approximately 3 pounds), frozen overnight then thawed at room temperature

1 28-ounce can tomato purée

1½ cups vegetable stock (either canned or made with vegetable bouillon cubes)

⅔ cup mango chutney

2 tablespoons red wine vinegar

3 tablespoons dark brown sugar, firmly packed

Preheat the oven to 375°F with the rack in the center position. Combine the onion, rice, raisins, coconut, cashews, curry powder, salt, and pepper in a large bowl.

Separate the thawed cabbage leaves and lay them on a work surface. You want leaves that are approximately 4- to 5-inches square, so you may want to cut the very largest leaves in half, or overlap the smaller leaves.

Place a generous mound (about 2 tablespoons) of filling in the center of each leaf. Roll it into a neat bundle, tucking the ends underneath. Set the rolls, seam side down, close together in an 13 × 11 × 3-inch (or similar-sized) baking dish. You can layer the rolls as many as three deep.

In a small bowl, combine the tomato purée, stock, chutney, vinegar, and brown sugar. Pour this mixture over the cabbage rolls. Place the dish in the preheated oven and bake for 40 minutes.

NOTE: To toast cashews, preheat the oven to 350°F. Spread the cashews on an ungreased baking sheet and toast them for 6 to 8 minutes, or until they're a very light golden brown.

Armenian Chick-pea Stew

Looking for a change from chili? Consider this quick-cooking, robust vegetarian alternative which is a cross between stew and hearty soup. I like to serve this with a crusty loaf of bread and a mellow red wine, such as a cabernet. This soup makes for great leftovers (if there is any left over).

PREPARATION TIME: 15 minutes

COOKING TIME: 35 minutes

YIELD: Serves 8

CAN BE MADE AHEAD? Yes. Store in a covered container in the refrigerator. Add more vegetable broth upon reheating if the mixture is very thick.

CAN BE FROZEN? Yes

CAN BE DOUBLED? Yes

CAN BE HALVED? Yes

¼ cup olive oil

3 garlic cloves, minced

1 large Spanish onion, diced

1 large zucchini, cut into 1-inch pieces

2 red bell peppers, cored, seeded, and cut into ½-inch strips

1 pint cherry tomatoes, halved

1 cup vegetable broth (canned or made from a bouillon cube or powder)

3 cups canned tomato chunks, drained

2 19-ounce cans chick-peas, rinsed and drained

1 teaspoon ground cumin

½ teaspoon paprika or ground sweet red pepper

1½ teaspoons salt

1 teaspoon freshly ground black pepper

Heat the oil in a large soup pot placed over medium heat. Add the garlic, onion, and zucchini and cook for 5 minutes, until the onion is translucent. Don't let the garlic brown; it will get bitter.

Add the remaining ingredients. Allow the mixture to come to a gentle simmer, cover, and cook for 25 minutes, or until the stew is slightly thickened and the vegetables are tender. Add more salt and pepper as needed. Serve in large soup bowls or mugs.

Curried Rice Salad

Both long grain white rice and the nuttier-tasting brown rice lend themselves to this cold salad. Don't use instant rice, however, because it is gummy and bland. The addition of fruits and nuts make the rice salad hearty and nutritious enough for a main course. To make it even heartier, you can add 2 cups diced chicken or tofu.

PREPARATION TIME: 20 minutes, plus time to prepare the rice

YIELD: Serves 8 to 10

CAN BE MADE AHEAD? Yes, up to 24 hours. Cover and refrigerate until ready to serve.

CAN BE FROZEN? No

CAN BE DOUBLED AND TRIPLED? Yes

CAN BE HALVED? Yes

1 cup mayonnaise (regular or reduced-fat)

2 teaspoons curry powder

$\frac{1}{4}$ cup soy sauce

2 Granny Smith apples, peeled and coarsely chopped

Juice and rind of 1 lemon

3 cups cooked white or brown rice (about 1 cup uncooked rice, prepared according to package directions), cooled

1 16-ounce can pineapple chunks, drained, or 1$\frac{1}{4}$ cups fresh pineapple, cut into $\frac{1}{2}$-inch pieces

$\frac{1}{2}$ cup golden raisins

1 cup slivered almonds

1 16-ounce can mandarin orange sections, drained, or fresh clementine or seedless tangerine sections, for garnish

In a small bowl, mix together the mayonnaise, curry powder, and soy sauce. Set aside.

Place the chopped apple in a large serving bowl and add the lemon juice and rind, tossing to coat. Add the rice, pineapple, raisins, and almonds and mix well.

Toss the rice mixture with the dressing. Garnish with the oranges. Either serve immediately or cover and refrigerate until ready to serve.

Kasha Primavera

Kasha is buckwheat groats, a flavorful, nutty-tasting grain that when combined with pasta makes a fantastic vegetarian entrée or a perfect side dish with meat, fish, or fowl. This substantial dish needs only an accompanying salad or soup to make a hearty meal. You can serve it hot or cold.

PREPARATION: 25 minutes

COOKING TIME: About 15 minutes

YIELD: Serves 10 to 12

CAN BE MADE AHEAD? No

CAN BE FROZEN? No

CAN BE DOUBLED? Yes

CAN BE HALVED? Yes

2 cups chicken or vegetable broth or 1 chicken or vegetable
   bouillon cube dissolved in 2 cups boiling water

½ stick (2 ounces) unsalted butter or margarine

½ teaspoon white pepper

1 medium onion, chopped

1 egg, beaten

1 cup coarse kasha

4 cups bow tie noodles, uncooked

1 cup fresh snow peas, ends trimmed and strings removed

2 cups broccoli florets, cut into bite-sized pieces

½ pint (1 cup) cherry tomatoes, halved

1 yellow bell pepper, seeded and cut into strips

Place the broth, 3 tablespoons of the butter, and white pepper in a 1½-quart saucepan and set over medium heat. Bring to a boil, then lower the heat and allow the broth to simmer gently.

Heat the remaining tablespoon of butter in a large lidded skillet or frying pan set over medium heat. Add the onion and cook for 5 to 7 minutes, or until it is translucent. Transfer the onion to a bowl and set aside.

Place the egg and kasha in the skillet and, stirring constantly, cook the mixture for 2 to 3 minutes, until the kernels separate. Add the broth mixture, lower the heat to medium, cover, and simmer for 8 to 10 minutes, or until the kasha is tender and the liquid has evaporated. Remove the skillet from the heat, mix in the onion, and set aside.

Cook the noodles according to the package directions, drain, and add them to the kasha.

Add 1 inch of water to a medium-sized lidded saucepan. Bring the water to a boil, add the snow peas and broccoli, and cover. Cook for 2 minutes, drain, and run under cold water for a few seconds.

Add the cooked broccoli, snow peas, tomatoes, and yellow pepper strips to the kasha mixture. Serve warm or cold.

Zucchini Lasagna

Here is the perfect make-ahead vegetarian entrée. You can substitute steamed broccoli florets for the zucchini, or even steamed spinach if you carefully press out all the water after cooking. No-boil lasagna noodles make this a no-fuss, no-muss job.

PREPARATION TIME: 25 minutes

BAKING TIME: 30 minutes

YIELD: Serves 8

CAN BE MADE AHEAD? Yes, up to 12 hours. Assemble, cover with plastic wrap, and refrigerate until ready to bake.

CAN BE FROZEN? Yes, after cooking. Cool first and wrap in foil or plastic.

CAN BE DOUBLED? Yes. Use 2 pans.

CAN BE HALVED? Yes

1 32-ounce jar spaghetti sauce

1 8-ounce package no-boil lasagna noodles

2 large eggs, beaten

1 15-ounce carton ricotta cheese or small-curd cottage cheese

4 cups grated zucchini (about 1 pound)

1 10-ounce package white mushrooms, sliced

1 8-ounce package shredded mozzarella cheese

½ cup grated Parmesan cheese

Preheat the oven to 350°F with the rack in the center position. Spray a 13 × 9-inch baking pan with nonstick vegetable spray.

Spread 2 to 3 tablespoons of the spaghetti sauce over the bottom of the pan, followed by a layer of noodles. Spread one third of the sauce over the noodles.

Mix together the eggs and ricotta cheese. Spread one half of the egg and cheese mixture over the sauce.

Mix together the zucchini and mushrooms. Spread one half of the zucchini mixture over the ricotta mixture.

Sprinkle one half of the mozzarella over the zucchini mixture. Add another layer of noodles and repeat the layers, using one third of the sauce and the remaining ricotta mixture, the remaining zucchini mixture, and the remaining mozzarella cheese.

Top with the remaining noodles and the remaining sauce. Sprinkle with the Parmesan cheese and bake for 30 minutes, or until the cheese is golden and the edges are bubbly. Cool 10 minutes, cut into squares, and serve hot.

Three Cheese Pasta Bake

Think of this rich and creamy casserole as an unlayered lasagna. It's a perfect meatless entrée for a midwinter get-together, or serve it along with a light fish or chicken dish.

Herbed goat cheese is available in the imported or fancy cheese section of the supermarket. It comes in a log or disk shape, and is coated on the outside with fresh or dried herbs. For a variation, you can use half goat cheese and half Brie.

PREPARATION TIME: 20 minutes

COOKING TIME: 40 minutes

YIELD: 8 to 10 servings as an entrée; 12 to 14 as a side dish

CAN BE MADE AHEAD? Yes, mix the ingredients up to 24 hours ahead and store in the prepared baking dish, covered with plastic or foil, in the refrigerator. Bake just before serving.

CAN BE FROZEN? Yes, up to 2 months. Bake and cool first.

CAN BE DOUBLED? Yes

CAN BE HALVED? Yes

(continued)

1 pound (16 ounces) whole or skim milk ricotta

1 pound (16 ounces) herbed goat cheese

½ cup heavy cream

8 sun-dried tomatoes, packed in oil, drained and cut into thirds

1 tablespoon bottled capers, drained

1 teaspoon freshly ground black pepper

½ to 1 teaspoon salt (optional)

2 pounds ziti, cooked 2 minutes less than package directions, drained

⅔ cup freshly grated Parmesan cheese

½ cup plain or seasoned bread crumbs

Preheat the oven to 350°F with the rack in the center position. Generously butter a 12-cup casserole dish.

In a large bowl mix together the ricotta, goat cheese, heavy cream, sun-dried tomatoes, capers, and pepper. Taste before adding the optional salt. Mix in the ziti and spoon the mixture into the prepared dish.

Mix together the grated cheese and bread crumbs and sprinkle on top of the casserole. Bake uncovered for 40 minutes.

Tex-Mex Lasagna

No-boil lasagna noodles make this dish no-fail. Make extra—your guests will be back for seconds! This is a great dish for a buffet table because it's tasty even when it's been out of the oven for a while. (And it makes a great snack cold!) No-boil noodles are readily available in the supermarket.

PREPARATION TIME: 20 minutes

COOKING TIME: 30 minutes

YIELD: 8 servings

CAN BE MADE AHEAD? Yes, up to 12 hours. Assemble to the point just before baking. Cover with plastic wrap and refrigerate until ready to bake.

CAN BE FROZEN? Yes, after cooking, for up to 2 months.

CAN BE DOUBLED? Yes

CAN BE HALVED? No

2 8-ounce packages no-boil lasagna noodles (you will probably have some noodles left over)

1 32-ounce jar mild or medium salsa

1 15-ounce carton ricotta cheese

1 16-ounce package shredded Monterey Jack or Cheddar cheese

Preheat the oven to 350°F with the rack in the center position. Spray an ovenproof 9 × 13-inch baking dish with nonstick vegetable spray. Soak the noodles according to package directions.

Spread a thin layer of salsa over the bottom of the prepared pan and cover the salsa with a single layer of noodles. Spread the noodles with one third of the ricotta, one third of the remaining salsa, and one third of the grated cheese. Add another layer of noodles, then spread with half of the remaining salsa, and half the remaining cheese. Add one more layer of noodles, then top with the remaining salsa and cheese.

Bake for 30 minutes, or until the top is golden brown and the sauce is bubbling.

Thai Noodles

Here is a favorite dish of almost everyone who likes pasta with a little spice. Health food stores or Asian markets will carry most, if not all, of the ingredients. This recipe can be a vegetarian dish if you wish— just leave out the chicken.

PREPARATION TIME: 30 minutes

YIELD: Serves 8 as a side dish; 4 as a main course

CAN BE MADE AHEAD? Yes, up to 24 hours. Store in a tightly covered container in the refrigerator.

CAN BE FROZEN? No

CAN BE DOUBLED? Yes

CAN BE HALVED? Yes

4½ cups flat, cooked Asian noodles (14-ounce package fresh noodles)

⅓ cup water

⅓ cup fish sauce (available in Asian food stores)

⅓ cup freshly squeezed lime juice

⅓ cup oyster sauce (available in Asian food stores)

⅓ cup sesame seeds, toasted (see the Note)

5 tablespoons chopped fresh coriander

6 tablespoons chopped scallions

6 drops Tabasco Pepper Sauce

1 5-ounce can sliced water chestnuts, drained

1 5-ounce can sliced bamboo shoots, drained

2 cups cooked chicken (optional)

1 head of Chinese cabbage (also called bok choy) (about 4 cups), shredded

Cook the noodles according to the package directions, rinse with cold water, and drain thoroughly. Place the noodles in a large bowl and set aside.

In a small saucepan, mix together the water, fish sauce, lime juice, and oyster sauce and bring to a boil over medium-high heat. Remove from the heat. Add the toasted sesame seeds, 2 tablespoons of the coriander, 2 tablespoons of the scallions, and Tabasco Pepper Sauce.

Add the water chestnuts and bamboo shoots to the noodles. If desired, add the cooked chicken.

Stir the fish sauce mixture briskly and pour over the noodle mixture. Cover and refrigerate the salad until you are ready to serve.

Line a large shallow serving dish with the shredded cabbage. Add the noodle mixture in the center of the bed of cabbage and garnish with the remaining coriander and scallions.

NOTE: To toast sesame seeds, place a heavy skillet over high heat. Add the sesame seeds and shake the skillet back and forth vigorously so that they are in constant motion. (Alternatively, you can use a wooden or metal spoon to stir the seeds.) As soon as some of the seeds start to turn a golden brown, lower the heat and cook them for 1 to 2 minutes more, until they are all toasted.

Immediately scrape the sesame seeds into another container to cool (not a plastic bag; it'll melt). You can do this as much as a week ahead. Store the cooled sesame seeds in a plastic container or plastic bag in the freezer.

Herbed Pasta Gratin

Herbs and cheeses of Italy flavor this quick-to-prepare casserole. Place it on a buffet table accompanied by a big salad and watch it disappear. It will feed a hungry crowd on a frosty night.

PREPARATION TIME: 15 minutes

COOKING TIME: 40 minutes, plus time to cook the pasta

YIELD: 10 servings

CAN BE MADE AHEAD? Yes, up to 48 hours. Store in the refrigerator in an ovenproof or microwavable dish.

CAN BE FROZEN? Yes, up to 2 months.

CAN BE DOUBLED? Yes

CAN BE HALVED? Yes

1 ½ pounds medium-sized shells, cooked 2 minutes less than package directions, drained

1 pound baked ham or smoked turkey, cut in ½-inch pieces (about 3 cups)

2 cups heavy cream

1 8-ounce package shredded mozzarella cheese

2 teaspoons dried basil or 2 tablespoons fresh basil, chopped

1 teaspoon dried oregano or 1 tablespoon fresh oregano leaves

1 10-ounce package frozen pearl onions

1 10-ounce package frozen peas

⅔ cup freshly grated Parmesan cheese

Preheat the oven to 350°F with the rack in the center position. Generously butter a large (12-cup) ovenproof casserole dish.

In a large bowl toss together all the ingredients except the Parmesan cheese. Spoon the mixture into the prepared dish and sprinkle generously with the cheese.

Bake in the preheated oven for 40 minutes.

Main Course:
Turkey and Chicken

Speedy Turkey Chili

Ground turkey, which is readily available in the meat section of your supermarket, makes for a tasty, yet extremely low-fat version of this classic dish. Using a microwave makes the dish even speedier. Fresh coriander gives this chili its wonderfully authentic flavor.

Even though this dish will be ready after 30 minutes of cooking, you can leave it, covered, simmering on the stove top for up to 1 hour. Just remember to stir it once in a while, adding liquid, such as tomato juice or chicken broth, if it gets too thick.

PREPARATION TIME: 20 minutes

COOKING TIME: 10 to 12 minutes in a microwave, then 30 minutes on the stove top

YIELD: Serves 10 to 12

CAN BE MADE AHEAD? Yes, up to 3 days. Store in the refrigerator in a microwavable dish for quick reheating.

CAN BE FROZEN? Yes, up to 3 months.

CAN BE DOUBLED? Yes. Microwave in 2 batches and use a large pot for the stove-top cooking. Increase stove-top cooking time to 1 hour.

CAN BE HALVED? Yes

(continued)

2 tablespoons vegetable oil

2 large green bell peppers, seeded and chopped into ½-inch pieces

2 large red bell peppers, seeded and chopped into ½-inch pieces

1 large onion, coarsely chopped

3 pounds ground turkey

2 16-ounce jars mild salsa

2 30-ounce cans red kidney beans, well drained

2 to 3 tablespoons mild chili powder

3 tablespoons dark brown sugar, firmly packed

½ cup fresh Italian parsley, coarsely chopped

⅓ cup fresh coriander leaves, coarsely chopped

2 teaspoons salt (to be added at the very end of the cooking time)

7 to 8 drops Tabasco Pepper Sauce (add at end)

Sour cream or plain yogurt, for garnish (optional)

Grated Cheddar cheese, for garnish (optional)

Place the oil and chopped vegetables in a large covered microwavable dish and microwave on high for 3 to 5 minutes, or until the vegetables begin to wilt. (Or you can heat the oil in a large skillet and sauté the vegetables over medium heat for 15 minutes, turning frequently.) Transfer the vegetables to a large heat-proof casserole or deep saucepan.

Break the turkey into pieces and place it in the dish (or skillet) in which you cooked the vegetables (no need to wash it first). Microwave on high for 8 to 10 minutes, stopping halfway through the cooking time to stir the turkey to break it up. (Or sauté the turkey in the skillet, stirring occasionally till it loses its pink color.)

Add the cooked turkey and any juices to the casserole, then add the remaining ingredients except the salt and Tabasco Pepper Sauce.

Set the casserole over medium heat and cook, uncovered, stirring often, until the mixture starts to simmer. Lower the heat so that the chili barely simmers and cook, uncovered, for at least 30 minutes or up to 1 hour, stirring occasionally. Add the salt and Tabasco Pepper Sauce to taste before serving.

Serve in individual soup bowls or on plates, garnished with sour cream (or plain yogurt) and a sprinkling of Cheddar cheese, if desired.

Perfect Roast Turkey with Corn Bread Stuffing

So, you're making your first Thanksgiving or Christmas turkey! Relax—it's in the bag—the oven cooking bag, that is. Look in the foil/plastic wrap aisle of your grocery store for the turkey-size bags.

Using an oven cooking bag means your turkey will turn golden brown and remain moist and tender. It also means all those lovely gravy-making juices will stay nicely contained in the bag and not get burned all over the roasting pan. Speaking of the pan, if you choose to use a disposable pan (a great idea if dirty dishes are not your favorite thing), use two (one stacked inside the other) or place the pan on a heavy-duty baking sheet.

For your first turkey foray you might feel more comfortable buying one that has one of those little gizmos that pop out when the turkey is done. Fine with me, but remember, a fresh turkey will be far more delectable in both the flavor and texture department than one that was previously frozen. Use a meat thermometer instead, to tell when it's perfectly roasted.

PREPARATION TIME: 30 minutes

COOKING TIME: Approximately 20 minutes per pound

YIELD: Serves 12, with additional leftovers

CAN BE MADE AHEAD? No, not unless you're planning to serve it cold or reheated the next day.

CAN BE FROZEN? Yes. Leftover cooked turkey meat can be frozen and used in stews and soups.

CAN BE DOUBLED? Select a larger turkey.

CAN BE HALVED? Use a boned, rolled turkey breast instead, and make stove-top stuffing.

(continued)

2 bags Pepperidge Farm Corn Bread Stuffing Mix

1 12- to 15-pound (preferably fresh) turkey

1 turkey-size oven cooking bag

2 tablespoons vegetable shortening

1 teaspoon salt

2 13-ounce cans chicken broth

1 to 2 tablespoons instant flour, such as Wondra, for the gravy

Select a roasting pan large enough to hold the turkey comfortably (see the headnote). Preheat the oven to 425°F with the rack in the lower third.

Prepare the stuffing according to the package directions. Remove the plastic bag of giblets from the neck cavity of the turkey (cover them with water and boil them up for your dog or cat if you wish). Place the turkey in the sink and rinse it inside and out with cold water. Pat the outside dry with a paper towel.

Place the stuffing loosely in the cavity. Use cotton string to tie the turkey's legs together at the ends. Place the turkey in the bag and coat the breast and tops of the legs with the shortening. Sprinkle with the salt. Add the chicken broth and secure the bag with the tie provided. Use scissors to cut 5 or 6 small slits in the top of the bag. Insert a meat thermometer (not an instant-read thermometer) into the thickest part of the breast.

Place the turkey in the oven so that you can read the thermometer without moving the pan, close the oven door, and immediately lower the heat to 350°F. Roast the turkey for 20 minutes per pound, or until the thermometer reads 170°F. Remove the pan from the oven and allow the turkey to rest for 15 minutes. If you have a heat-proof platter, place it in the turned-off oven to warm. Sharpen the carving knife.

Cut open the cooking bag and use a bulb baster or ladle to transfer the pan juices to a small saucepan. Using a large spoon, remove as much fat as possible—most will have risen to the top, making it fairly easy to skim off. You can also drop 4 or 5 ice cubes into the juices, which will help solidify the fat, making it even easier to remove.

Open the cavity and use a long-handled serving spoon to transfer all the stuffing to a heat-proof serving dish. Cover the dish with foil and place it in the turned-off oven to stay warm while you carve the turkey.

It's easier to carve a turkey when it's on a board. If you don't feel comfortable about transferring it, start carving the breast while the turkey is still in the roasting pan. Use your carving knife to slice the breast meat into thin slices. Lay them, overlapping, on one end of the platter. Push one point of the serving fork into the joint of the drumstick, separating the bones slightly so you can slip the point of the knife in, and loosen, then finally cut through and remove the drumstick. Repeat with the other side, and then with the wings. At this point you can, if you wish, lift the turkey onto a cutting board and continue cutting the dark meat, which you should assemble at the other end of the platter. (By your organizing the platter this way your guests won't have to poke through all the pieces to find the slices of their choice.) Place a large piece of foil over the platter to keep the turkey warm while you finish the gravy.

Skim any remaining fat from the juices and season the juices to taste with salt, if necessary. Place the pan over high heat and bring the juices to a simmer. Add the flour, 1 tablespoon at a time, whisking constantly, until the gravy just starts to thicken. You don't want it any thicker than heavy cream. Pour the gravy into a small pitcher (or sauceboat), place the pitcher on a small saucer, and pass with a ladle.

Smoked Ham or
Smoked Turkey Breast

When I am entertaining a crowd and want to serve something very special that will appeal to everyone without my having to slave away in the kitchen for hours (or even minutes), I order either a smoked turkey or smoked ham from Harrington's in Richmond, Vermont (802-434-3411). You may have your own resource for world-class smoked foods; if not, I suggest you try Harrington's. They have never disappointed me. The people who handle their mail-order department are wonderfully knowledgeable and can give you good advice as to sizes and amounts.

You can order a fully cooked, glazed, presliced ham that is served at room temperature (no cooking!). Or you can order a boneless smoked turkey breast which is a novel, yet nonthreatening alternative to traditional fare. The turkey is shipped frozen, so give yourself enough time to allow it to defrost in the refrigerator prior to serving it at room temperature. This usually takes 24 to 48 hours. All you need to serve it is a thin, sharp carving knife. You want to slice the pieces very thin and serve them with grainy mustard and some really good bread.

The beauty of having your main course delivered by the mailman is that you don't have to spend one minute worrying about it—just enjoy.

PREPARATION TIME: 10 to 15 minutes to arrange the meat on a platter

YIELD: Plan on 4 to 6 ounces of ham or turkey per person, so a 2½-pound boneless smoked turkey breast or ham would be enough for 6 people.

CAN BE MADE AHEAD? Yes. The meat can be layered in overlapping pieces on a serving platter up to 3 hours ahead. Cover airtight with plastic wrap and refrigerate until serving.

CAN BE FROZEN? Leftovers can be frozen, wrapped airtight in plastic wrap, for up to 3 months.

CAN BE DOUBLED AND TRIPLED? Yes. You'll have to order several hams or turkey breasts.

CAN BE HALVED? Yes. Buy a smaller ham or turkey breast.

After defrosting, arrange the pieces of ham or turkey in overlapping layers on a serving platter along with grainy mustard, mayonnaise, rolls and bread.

Cheddar-Stuffed Turkey Burgers

This low-fat, high-flavor alternative to traditional hamburgers makes a nice change for a cookout menu. Make sure the grill is well oiled as there is little fat in ground turkey, which can make the burgers stick.

PREPARATION TIME: 20 minutes

COOKING TIME: 12 to 15 minutes

YIELD: Serves 8

CAN BE MADE AHEAD? Yes. The burgers can be formed up to 4 hours ahead, but need to be cooked just before serving. Cover tightly with plastic wrap and refrigerate until ready to cook.

CAN BE FROZEN? No

CAN BE DOUBLED? Yes

CAN BE HALVED? Yes

3 pounds ground turkey

2 egg whites

3 tablespoons Worcestershire sauce

1 8-ounce stick Cheddar cheese (regular or low-fat), cut into 8 slices

To grill the burgers: Preheat the grill and brush the rack with vegetable oil. Mix the turkey together with the egg whites and Worcestershire sauce and divide the mixture into 8 equal parts. Form patties, tucking one slice of cheese inside each and enclosing it completely with the turkey. Grill the patties for 4 minutes and then carefully turn them over and cook another 4 to 5 minutes. The burgers should be nicely browned on the outside and no longer pink in the center. Cooking time will depend on how thick you made the patties. To test, cut into a burger to make sure it is no longer pink in the center.

To broil the burgers: Preheat the oven broiler to high with the rack in the upper third but not the highest postion. Place the burgers on an oiled sheet of foil on a heavy baking sheet. Broil for 4 minutes, then turn the burgers, broiling the other side for an additional 4 minutes. Cut into the center to make sure the meat is cooked all the way through and not pink.

March 13 Blizzard Stew

Four feet of snow, drifts up to eight feet, hurricane winds, no power, and a houseful of company. It's amazing what you can pull together to serve to company from ingredients lurking on your shelves and in the back of the freezer. This was so successful (despite the fact that the first time I made it I got so carried away with the habanero peppers that we needed fire extinguishers to quell the blaze) that I wrote down the recipe by candlelight.

The first version was made on a camp stove, but trust me, this Slow Cooker version is much, much easier. A Slow Cooker is a terrific tool (and a fairly inexpensive one) for the busy person who loves to entertain and get food cooked in advance without having to hover over it every minute. If you do buy a Slow Cooker, get the largest size you can find. Mine holds four quarts.

This recipe calls for black beans and other ingredients that can be purchased in many supermarkets, gourmet stores, and stores that sell Spanish or South American foodstuffs. If you have the time, it's best (although not absolutely necessary) to soak the beans for 12 hours (or overnight) before using them. Change the water several times. This technique eliminates most of the gassy ramifications so often associated with beans.

PREPARATION TIME: 30 minutes

COOKING TIME: 24 hours

YIELD: Serves 10

CAN BE MADE AHEAD? Yes. Must be made ahead and cooked in a Slow Cooker for 24 hours.

CAN BE FROZEN? Yes. Freeze it in a microwavable or oven-proof casserole.

CAN BE DOUBLED? Yes, although you will need 2 Slow Cookers.

CAN BE HALVED? It's easier to make the full recipe and freeze half for another time.

3 cups black beans, well rinsed and soaked overnight if possible (see the headnote)

1 smoked turkey breast (about 3 pounds), unsliced, or 3 small whole, boneless smoked chickens or 3 pounds smoked ham in one large piece

1 large onion, chopped

1 1-inch piece gingerroot, peeled and chopped

8 garlic cloves, peeled and left whole

½ cup fresh coriander, rinsed and chopped

⅓ cup dark brown sugar

¼ cup Dijon mustard

1 tablespoon ground sweet chiles or 1 teaspoon paprika

1 dried smoked habanero pepper, chopped, or 2 to 3 canned chiles (hot or mild, depending on your taste), chopped

1 can of beer

5 cups water

Place all the ingredients in a Slow Cooker. cover, and cook on high (if you have this setting) for 2 hours, then turn to low or regular and cook for 24 hours. If the liquid seems to be running low, add a bit more beer or wine. At the end of the cooking time, skim off any visible fat and slice any meat that remains in large pieces. Serve over plain white rice.

Picadillo

This homey chicken stew is a real crowd pleaser. Spanish in origin, it goes particularly well served over Lemon Orzo (page 309), a side dish made of rice-shaped pasta.

PREPARATION TIME: 20 minutes

COOKING TIME: 20 to 30 minutes

YIELD: Serves 8

CAN BE MADE AHEAD? Yes, up to 3 days. Store in a covered container in the refrigerator.

CAN BE FROZEN? Yes, up to 2 months. Store in a microwavable casserole and defrost and heat in a microwave.

CAN BE DOUBLED? Yes

CAN BE HALVED? Yes

3 pounds boneless, skinless chicken breasts

2 teaspoons salt

2 teaspoons freshly ground black pepper

3 teaspoons ground cumin

3 tablespoons olive oil or vegetable oil

4 garlic cloves, peeled and minced

1 large onion, peeled and diced

1 large red bell pepper, halved, seeded, and diced

3 large ripe tomatoes, diced, or 1 16-ounce can chopped tomatoes, drained

20 pimiento-stuffed green olives, finely sliced

½ cup golden raisins

¼ cup bottled capers, drained

1 cup canned chicken broth

3 tablespoons tomato paste

4 cups cooked long grain white rice

Slice the chicken into 1-inch pieces and place it in a bowl with the salt, pepper, and cumin. Stir to combine.

Heat the oil in a large skillet or heavy-bottomed pot set over medium heat. Cook the garlic, onion, and red pepper for 3 to 4 minutes, stirring occasionally. Do not let the garlic brown.

Stir in the tomato and chicken. Cook for 3 to 4 minutes, or until the chicken begins to lose its translucent look. Add the remaining ingredients and reduce the heat so that the mixture is at a slow simmer. Continue stirring every few minutes for 20 minutes. Serve over rice.

Chicken Teriyaki

You can serve this versatile dish as a pickup appetizer for an informal party, as part of a cold salad, or as a hot entrée. You can even serve it as the main course of a barbecue. This recipe calls for chicken legs and thighs. You can substitute boneless chicken (either dark or white meat) if you don't want to serve finger food.

PREPARATION TIME: 25 minutes

MARINATING TIME: 1 hour

BAKING TIME: 30 minutes

YIELD: Serves 8 to 10 as an appetizer

CAN BE MADE AHEAD? Yes, up to 24 hours before cooking. Store in a tightly sealed container in the refrigerator. After cooking, store for 3 days in a covered container in the refrigerator.

CAN BE FROZEN? No

CAN BE DOUBLED? Yes

CAN BE HALVED? Yes

5 pounds chicken legs, drumsticks and thighs separated

½ cup dry sherry

½ cup soy sauce

4 garlic cloves, finely chopped

1 2-inch piece fresh gingerroot, peeled and finely chopped

1 tablespoon sesame oil

1 scallion, finely chopped

Use a small sharp knife to remove the skin from the chicken and set the chicken aside in a large bowl.

Mix together the sherry, soy sauce, garlic, ginger, sesame oil, and scallion and pour over the chicken pieces. Cover the bowl with plastic wrap and refrigerate for at least 1 hour, or up to 24 hours.

Preheat the oven to 400°F with the rack in the top position. Remove the chicken pieces from the marinade with tongs or a fork and arrange them in a single layer in a large low-sided baking pan. Reserve the marinade, refrigerated, for basting.

Bake the chicken pieces for 15 minutes. Remove from the oven and drizzle the reserved marinade over each piece of chicken. Lower the heat to 350°F and return the chicken to the oven for 15 minutes. Check for doneness by slitting one piece as far as the bone. The meat should be white, not pink, and the juices should run clear. Serve hot or warm.

Lemon-Artichoke Chicken Breasts

This elegantly simple dish has complex, yet subtle flavors. If you are lucky, you'll find lemons without many seeds; if not, you'll have to spend some time poking them out after you've sliced them. I find the easiest way to slice lemons paper-thin is to use a very sharp serrated knife (or the thinnest slicing disk of a food processor).

This is a dish that goes well with Pesto Orzo (page 308) or on a bed of herb- or vegetable-flavored pasta, which is available in most supermarkets and specialty food stores.

PREPARATION TIME: 20 minutes

COOKING TIME: 1 hour

YIELD: Serves 8

CAN BE MADE AHEAD? Partially. The chicken can be browned up to 24 hours ahead. Refrigerate, covered with plastic wrap, until ready to complete the dish.

CAN BE FROZEN? No

CAN BE DOUBLED? Yes

CAN BE HALVED? Yes

4 whole, boneless chicken breasts, skin on and cut in half, or 8 half breasts

½ cup unbleached all-purpose flour

1 teaspoon salt

1 teaspoon freshly ground black pepper

½ teaspoon paprika

½ stick (2 ounces) unsalted butter

1 large Spanish onion, finely chopped (about 1½ cups)

1 cup dry white wine or chicken broth (canned or made from
  a bouillon cube or powder)

2 10-ounce packages frozen artichoke hearts, defrosted

1 teaspoon dried thyme or 1 tablespoon fresh thyme, chopped

2 lemons, very thinly sliced and seeds removed

1½ cups chicken broth (canned or made from a bouillon cube
  or powder)

Rinse the chicken breasts in cold water and use paper towels to pat
them dry. Stir the flour, salt, pepper, and paprika together in a mixing
bowl. Dip each piece of chicken, skin side down, into the flour, making
sure the skin is well coated. Knock off the excess flour. Repeat with the
other side.

Melt the butter in a large skillet set over medium heat. Cook the
onion for 5 minutes, stirring frequently. Push the onion to the side of
the skillet and add the chicken, four pieces at a time, skin side down.
Cook until the skin turns golden brown (about 15 minutes), turn the
chicken over, and cook another 5 minutes. Remove the chicken and
continue with the remaining four pieces, adding more butter if necessary. The onion will turn a deep brown; this is fine.

Transfer the chicken and onion to a platter or bowl. Add the wine
to the skillet. Turn the heat to high and use a wooden or metal spoon
to scrape the browned bits from the sides and bottom of the skillet into
the simmering broth. (If you are using a nonstick pan, use a plastic or
wooden spoon.) This technique is called "deglazing," and it adds the
substantial flavor of cooked bits of vegetables and chicken to what will
become the sauce.

When you have finished scraping the cooked bits from the sides of
the skillet, lower the heat to a simmer, add all the chicken, skin side
up, the artichoke hearts, and the thyme. Stir to combine. Place the thin
lemon slices over the tops of the chicken breasts and gently pour in
the 1½ cups of chicken broth. Cover the skillet (if you don't have a
lid, you can use a large cookie sheet or foil) and simmer for an additional 30 minutes.

To serve, place one piece of chicken and several artichokes on each
plate, then spoon a little sauce along with some lemon slices over the
chicken.

Lightning Creole Chicken

Quicker than lightning and redolent with the flavors of the bayou, this adaptation of a New Orleans classic will warm your guests. This dish makes a great buffet entrée because it can be kept in a Slow Cooker, chafing dish, or on a warming tray for several hours without a problem.

PREPARATION TIME: 20 minutes

COOKING TIME: 40 minutes

YIELD: Serves 8

CAN BE MADE AHEAD? Yes, up to 24 hours. Store in a microwavable covered dish in the refrigerator.

CAN BE FROZEN? Yes, up to 2 months without the rice. Freeze in a microwavable container, defrost, and heat in a microwave.

CAN BE DOUBLED? Yes

CAN BE HALVED? Yes

¼ cup vegetable oil

4 celery stalks (plus leaves), diced

1 large Spanish onion, diced

2 garlic cloves, minced

1 large green bell pepper, cored, seeded, and cubed

1 large red bell pepper, cored, seeded, and cubed

1 16-ounce jar tomato sauce

2 16-ounce cans chopped tomatoes, drained

¼ cup Worcestershire sauce

1 teaspoon salt (plus more, if desired, at the end of the cooking time)

4 to 6 drops Tabasco Pepper Sauce

1 teaspoon freshly ground black pepper

4 pounds boneless, skinless chicken breasts cut into 1-inch strips (you can buy it this way in the supermarket or cut it up yourself at home)

4 cups cooked long grain white rice

8 tablespoons bacon bits, for garnish

Heat the oil in a large skillet or in a soup pot. Cook the celery, onion, garlic, and red and green peppers over medium heat, stirring frequently, until the vegetables soften, about 8 minutes. Don't let the garlic brown or it will turn bitter.

Add the tomato sauce, tomatoes, Worcestershire sauce, and seasonings and stir to combine. When the mixture begins to simmer, add the chicken and stir to cover with the sauce. Continue to simmer, uncovered, stirring occasionally, for 30 minutes.

Serve over white rice, garnishing each serving with a generous sprinkling of bacon bits.

Nancy Belsky's
Sesame Chicken

$\sim\!\!\sim\!\!\sim\!\!\sim\!\!\sim\!\!\sim\!\!\sim\!\!\sim\!\!\sim\!\!\sim\!\!\sim\!\!\sim\!\!\sim$

My smart and beautiful friend Nancy knows that no matter which of her tasty creations she serves for dinner this is my favorite—especially when it's done on the barbecue. Not only is it wonderful hot, but it makes a perfect cold dish as well as a terrific addition to a salad. Nancy suggests serving it cold with Dijon mustard.

Nancy also suggests buying the very good toasted sesame oil found in most health food stores. "Lite" (or low-sodium) tamari sauce can be found there as well.

PREPARATION TIME: 20 minutes

MARINATING TIME: As little as 1 hour or as long as overnight

COOKING TIME: 4 minutes

YIELD: Serves 8

CAN BE MADE AHEAD? Yes, up to 2 days, then served cold (see the headnote). Cover and refrigerate until ready to serve.

CAN BE FROZEN? No

CAN BE DOUBLED? Yes

CAN BE HALVED? Yes

4 whole boneless, skinless chicken breasts

¼ cup toasted sesame oil

2 tablespoons "lite" (low-sodium) tamari sauce or soy sauce

2 cups sesame seeds

Cut the chicken into 2 × ½-inch strips and place the pieces in a plastic container with a snap-on lid or other covered container. Mix together the sesame oil and tamari sauce and pour it over the chicken. Stir or shake to combine well. Refrigerate for at least 1 hour, or as long as overnight.

Spread the sesame seeds in a shallow pan. Roll each strip of chicken in the seeds, pressing gently with your fingers to coat each piece completely. Light a charcoal or gas-fired grill and place the chicken on the grill. Cook the chicken for 2 to 3 minutes on each side.

These can also be done on a foil-covered baking sheet under a broiler set on high heat, with the rack in the upper third of the oven.

CARVING A ROAST CHICKEN

After you practice a few times in the kitchen, then you can carve at the table.

You will need a platter large enough to hold the chicken and a serving plate on which to place the carved meat. Rinse the serving plate with hot water or place it in a 200°F oven to heat it. You'll also need a long-pronged fork and a sharp carving knife.

Position the chicken so that the legs face you. Place the fork on one side of the breast to hold the chicken steady, and cut through the skin between the opposite leg and the body. Use the knife to push the leg away from the body, exposing the leg joint. Cut through the joint and place the leg on the serving plate. If you wish, you can cut through the leg, separating the thigh and the drumstick.

Repeat with the opposite leg, then use the knife to cut a slit along the top of the breastbone. On a slant, cut thin slices of white meat, layering them on the serving platter (which keeps them warm and moist). Repeat with the other side. (Keeping the white and dark meat separated on the platter makes serving the chicken easier—people don't have to go searching around for the kind they want.)

Perfect Roast Chicken

There is a no-fail solution for the quest for a perfect, moist, tender, flavorful, beautifully browned chicken. It's called the Reynolds® Oven Cooking Bag and you'll find this terrific product in your grocery store right next to aluminum foil and plastic wrap. The chicken cooks inside the bag, which means it remains juicy and moist, yet through some sort of space-age magic the skin browns as lovely and crisp as can be. The best news is that there is no messy pan to scrub when you're finished—hey, did I promise perfect, or not?

PREPARATION TIME: 20 minutes

COOKING TIME: Approximately 1½ hours

YIELD: Serves 8

CAN BE MADE AHEAD? Not unless you plan to serve it cold

CAN BE FROZEN? No

CAN BE DOUBLED? Yes. You'll have to cook 2 chickens.

CAN BE HALVED? Use a 5- to 6-pound roasting chicken.

1 large capon (approximately 8 pounds) or 2 large
    roasting chickens (approximately 5 pounds each)

1 tablespoon unbleached all-purpose flour

1 large size (20 × 14-inch) oven cooking bag

2 large onions, peeled and thickly sliced

2 celery stalks, cut into several pieces

2 carrots, peeled and thickly sliced

1 to 2 tablespoons solid vegetable shortening

½ teaspoon paprika

2 teaspoons salt

1 teaspoon freshly ground black pepper

Preheat the oven to 325°F with the rack in the lower third but not the lowest position. Select a baking dish large enough to hold the chicken(s) comfortably. Shake the flour into the bag to lightly coat the sides.

Remove the giblets from the chicken's cavity. Rinse the chicken and cavity with cold water and pat dry.

Place half the vegetables inside the baking bag and the other half inside the chicken's cavity. Spread a layer of shortening over the breast and legs of the chicken, then sprinkle with paprika, salt, and pepper.

Place the chicken, breast side up, into the bag on top of the vegetables. Close the bag with the tie provided, place it in the baking dish, and insert an ovenproof meat thermometer into the thickest part of the breast. (If you use an instant-read thermometer, you'll take a reading from the same area after 1¼ hours cooking time.)

Use scissors to cut six ½-inch slits in the top of the bag. When the thermometer reads 180°F, the chicken is done. Let the chicken sit in the bag on the counter for 15 minutes, then slit open the bag and remove the chicken to a cutting surface. Pour the cooking juices into a glass bowl (a 4-cup glass measure is good for this). Let the liquid sit while you carve the chicken, then use a soup spoon to skim off the fat that has risen to the top. Add salt, if necessary. Pass the juice in a small pitcher or pour it over the carved chicken on the serving plate.

If this is an informal dinner you may want to serve the cooked vegetables along with the chicken. Or you can reserve them for another time, since they will be overcooked and not very attractive (although they will taste delicious).

Main Course:
Beef, Pork, and Lamb

Marinated Flank Steak

Marinated, grilled, or broiled, flank steak is one of the tastiest, most tender cuts of beef imaginable. It really is almost impossible to ruin, because cooked until well done it's still flavorful and tender. It's great hot off the grill or at room temperature mixed with vegetables and grains to make a salad. It's also fantastic spread with grainy mustard in sandwiches.

A long marinade (up to 2 days) gives the meat its great flavor, although even a short period of time (2 to 3 hours) makes a difference. Either make your own marinade or use bottled Italian salad dressing.

PREPARATION TIME: 10 minutes

MARINATING TIME: As short as 2 hours or up to 24 hours

COOKING TIME: 18 to 20 minutes

YIELD: Serves 3 to 4

CAN BE MADE AHEAD? Yes, up to the day before, if you want to serve the meat at room temperature or cold.

CAN BE FROZEN? No

CAN BE DOUBLED AND TRIPLED? Most flank steaks weigh about 2 pounds. Larger ones are available. If you wish to serve more than 3 to 4 people, and you can't find a large steak, you will have to prepare 2 or 3 steaks. This is not difficult, since they cook quickly. You can even cook two at the same time.

CAN BE HALVED? No

1 2-pound flank steak

1 small bottle Italian salad dressing or all of the following:

   ¼ cup soy sauce

   3 tablespoons dark brown sugar, firmly packed

   2 tablespoons red wine vinegar

   2 garlic cloves, crushed

   ¾ cup vegetable oil

As many as 24 hours or as few as 2 hours before you plan to cook the steak, place it on a clean work surface and use a sharp knife to score several ½-inch-deep crisscrosses on the surface of both sides. This keeps the meat from curling up when it cooks and allows the marinade to penetrate.

Place either the bottled dressing or all the other ingredients in a heavy-duty plastic freezer bag or a shallow tightly covered container. Add the meat and shake the bag or container to mix the ingredients. Store in the refrigerator until ready to cook.

To cook, preheat a gas or charcoal grill, or set the broiler on high with the rack in the upper position in the oven. Grill or broil the meat for 6 to 8 minutes on each side, basting once or twice with the marinade. When the meat has cooked the specified time, test it; it should be pink inside. Let the meat rest for 10 minutes before cutting it into thin slices the short way, across the grain.

Korean Beef

Look in the butcher's case for precut sirloin strips (sometimes called "stir fry"). A sweet and pungent marinade gives the beef a hearty flavor and tender texture that will bring your guests back for second helpings. If you have any leftovers, try them in a sandwich.

PREPARATION TIME: 15 minutes

MARINATING TIME: At least 1 hour or up to 24 hours, in a tightly covered container in the refrigerator

BROILING TIME: 5 minutes

YIELD: Serves 8

CAN BE MADE AHEAD? Yes. Up to 1 hour, it can be served at room temperature; up to 24 hours and refrigerated, served cold.

CAN BE FROZEN? No

CAN BE DOUBLED AND TRIPLED? Yes. Cook in batches.

CAN BE HALVED? Yes

2 pounds boneless sirloin strips

⅓ cup dark brown sugar, firmly packed

3 tablespoons honey

¼ cup sesame oil

½ cup soy sauce

1 2-inch piece fresh gingerroot, peeled and minced

½ teaspoon freshly ground black pepper

3 scallions, chopped (both green and white parts)

2 garlic cloves, peeled and finely chopped

½ cup sesame seeds, toasted (see the Note)

2 tablespoons unbleached all-purpose flour

½ cup water

If you have a whole piece of meat, cut it into thin strips approximately 1 inch wide and 3 inches long. It is easier to cut if the meat is slightly frozen. Set aside.

Mix together the sugar, honey, oil, soy sauce, ginger, pepper, scallions, garlic, sesame seeds, flour, and water in a large bowl or container with a cover. Add the strips of meat and marinate in the refrigerator for at least 1 hour, or up to 24 hours.

Preheat the broiler with the rack in the highest position. Remove the meat from the marinade with a fork or slotted spoon and spread it in a single layer on a foil-covered shallow baking pan. Broil for 5 minutes, turning once, until the meat is cooked through and just starting to brown. (The strips of meat may also be threaded on skewers if desired. Soak wooden skewers in water for a few minutes so they won't burn.) Serve hot or warm.

NOTE: To toast sesame seeds, select a heavy skillet and set it over high heat. Add the sesame seeds and shake the skillet back and forth vigorously so that they are in constant motion. Alternatively, you can use a wooden or metal spoon to stir the sesame seeds. As soon as some of the seeds start to turn golden brown, lower the heat and cook for 1 to 2 minutes more, until they are all toasted. Immediately scrape the sesame seeds into another container to cool.

You can do this as much as week ahead. Store the cooled sesame seeds in a plastic container or plastic bag in the freezer.

Beef Tenderloin

You will be amazed at how easy it is to make this classic dish. A lot of its flavor and character comes from the fact that it should be served rare; much of this is lost if it's overcooked. A meat or instant-read thermometer is an essential tool that will guarantee success.

The best place to buy tenderloin is a butcher shop or a grocery store where you can talk to the butcher. Tell the butcher you want a whole tenderloin, trimmed and tied—essentially ready to roast. Note the weight so you'll know how many people you'll be able to serve: A whole, trimmed tenderloin can weigh between 4 and 6 pounds. A 5-pound roast will yield 8 servings, without a lot left over. Ask to have any trimmings ground up so that you can make the world's best hamburger—or, if you're so inclined, steak tartare.

A recipe for a tangy horseradish cream sauce to serve with the beef follows on page 282.

PREPARATION TIME: 10 minutes

COOKING TIME: 25 to 30 minutes

YIELD: Serves 8

CAN BE MADE AHEAD? Only if you wish to serve it cold. A tenderloin should "rest" for 15 to 20 minutes after it comes out of the oven. It does not have to be served piping hot.

CAN BE FROZEN? No

CAN BE DOUBLED? Make 2.

CAN BE HALVED? It's easier to prepare individual filet mignons. See the headnote on page 282.

1 5- to 6-pound whole tenderloin, trimmed and tied

2 tablespoons olive oil

2 teaspoons kosher (coarse) salt

½ teaspoon freshly ground black pepper

6 to 7 whole sprigs of fresh rosemary or 2 teaspoons dried rosemary

One half hour before you plan to roast it, remove the tenderloin from the refrigerator to let it come to room temperature. Place it in a shallow heavy-duty roasting pan. Rub the olive oil over the meat, sprinkle on the salt and pepper, and if you have sprigs of rosemary, lay them down the length of the meat. If you have dried rosemary, sprinkle it on top of the meat. Insert a meat thermometer into the center of one end of the roast.

Preheat the oven to 500°F with the rack in the center position. (If you have a kitchen or oven fan, this is a good time to use it.) Place the roast in the oven and set a timer for 10 minutes. At the end of this time, reduce the oven heat to 350°F and reset the timer for 30 minutes. Do not open the oven door—you don't want to lose any heat.

When the timer goes off again, check the thermometer. For rare, you want to take the roast out of the oven when the dial reads 120° to 125°F. If you want medium-rare, let the roast stay in the oven for another 5 to 7 minutes, or until the dial reads 130°F. Don't let it go above 130°F because the meat will continue to cook after you remove it from the oven. If you have an ovenproof serving dish, place it in the turned-off oven to warm while the meat rests.

Let the roast sit in the pan for 15 to 20 minutes before cutting it into ½-inch slices and layering them on the warmed platter. Serve with the Quick Creamy Herb and Horseradish Sauce on page 282.

Quick Creamy Herb and Horseradish Sauce

Besides using this sauce as an accompaniment for beef tenderloin as an entrée, try spreading it on black bread to make a terrific tenderloin sandwich (if there are any leftovers).

PREPARATION TIME: 10 minutes

YIELD: 1½ cups

CAN BE MADE AHEAD? Yes, up to 2 days. Cover and refrigerate until serving.

CAN BE FROZEN? No

CAN BE DOUBLED AND TRIPLED? Yes

CAN BE HALVED? Yes

1 5.2-ounce package Boursin cheese with garlic and herbs, at room temperature

1 8-ounce container sour cream

2 to 3 tablespoons plain horseradish

Mix the softened cheese together with the sour cream until smooth (you can do this by hand or in a food processor or blender). Add the horseradish to taste. Serve with hot or cold tenderloin.

Pan-Seared Tournedos

(To Make Tenderloin for Two or Four People)

A whole tenderloin serves 8 people (or 6, with delicious leftovers). If you want to serve the same cut of meat but for fewer people, you have the option of buying either filets mignons, which are small steaks cut from the end of the tenderloin, or tournedos, which are thicker steaks cut from the center of the tenderloin. These are cooked in a pan on top of the stove at the last minute and served hot. My advice is to practice first before you try them out on company.

PREPARATION TIME: 5 minutes

COOKING TIME: 6 to 8 minutes

YIELD: Serves 2 or 4

CAN BE MADE AHEAD? No

CAN BE FROZEN? No

CAN BE DOUBLED? Yes. Roast a whole tenderloin.

CAN BE HALVED? Yes

2 or 4 tournedos or filets mignons (6 to 8 ounces each),
    not more than 1½ inches thick

Salt

Freshly ground black pepper

1 to 2 tablespoons unsalted butter

⅓ to ½ cup canned beef broth

2 tablespoons Madeira (optional)

Take the meat out of the refrigerator one half hour before cooking. Pat the meat dry and sprinkle it lightly with salt and pepper. Place a large heavy pan over high heat and melt the butter, swirling to allow it to coat the bottom of the pan. When the butter is sizzling (but not browned), add the meat and cook over high heat for 3 to 4 minutes. Turn the meat and cook it another 2 minutes for very rare, 3 minutes for medium-rare, and 4 minutes for not-very-rare.

Remove the meat to a heated platter or dinner plates. Add the broth and the optional Madeira to the pan and cook over high heat, stirring in the pan drippings and juices. When the liquid has reduced to ⅓ to ¼ cup, pour it over the meat and serve immediately.

Citrus Pork Chops

This is made on the stove top in one or two large skillets. Even though it is cooked right before serving, the recipe is simple to assemble and takes only a few minutes to prepare. The tartness of the citrus rind and juices is offset by the sweetness of the golden raisins.

PREPARATION TIME: 20 minutes

COOKING TIME: 15 minutes

YIELD: Serves 8

CAN BE MADE AHEAD? No, although you can grate the rinds and mix them together with the juices the day before. Refrigerate until ready to use.

CAN BE FROZEN? No

CAN BE DOUBLED? Only if you have extra skillets.

CAN BE HALVED? Yes

8 ½-inch-thick pork chops

Salt

Freshly ground black pepper

2 tablespoons vegetable oil

2 large garlic cloves, peeled and minced

Rind and juice of 2 large oranges plus enough additional
    juice to equal 1 cup liquid

Rind and juice of 2 lemons

⅓ cup dark brown sugar, firmly packed

¾ cup golden raisins

If you have a skillet large enough to hold the pork chops in one layer, then use it; if not, divide the ingredients among two skillets. Use a paper towel to dry the pork chops and then sprinkle them with salt and pepper. Heat the oil in a large skillet and sauté the pork chops, turning them once, until they are golden. Add the garlic, orange and lemon juices and rind, sugar, and raisins and place a lid or baking sheet over the skillet. Cook over medium heat, covered, for 15 minutes, then remove the cover and cook an additional 5 minutes. Serve immediately, spooning the juices from the skillet over the meat.

Cranberry Cider–Glazed Pork Roast

~~~~~~~~~~~~~~~~~~~~~~~~~~~~~~~~~~~~~~

Cranberries in two forms lend a light tartness to this roast. You can serve this hot from the oven or slice it and serve it cold as a buffet or lunch dish. Dried cranberries are available in gourmet specialty shops, or you can substitute golden raisins. This dish goes particularly well with Lemon Orzo (page 309).

PREPARATION TIME: 20 minutes

COOKING TIME: 5 minutes for the glaze; 60 minutes for the roast

YIELD: Serves 8

CAN BE MADE AHEAD? Yes, if you want to serve it cold. Roast it the day before (or at least 4 hours). Cool slightly before slicing and then refrigerate, wrapped well in plastic wrap. Collect the juices in a bowl and refrigerate. Remove the fat from the top before serving on the side.

CAN BE FROZEN? No

CAN BE DOUBLED? Yes. Use 2 roasts.

CAN BE HALVED? Yes. Use a 2-pound roast and reduce the cooking time to 30 minutes.

2 teaspoons cornstarch

¼ teaspoon cinnamon

½ teaspoon salt

1 cup apple cider

1 16-ounce can whole cranberry sauce

½ cup dried cranberries

4-pound boneless pork loin roast

Preheat the oven to 325°F with the rack in the center position. In a small saucepan, combine the cornstarch, cinnamon, and salt. Whisk in the apple cider and cranberry sauce. Place the pan over medium heat and continue whisking until the mixture thickens. Stir in the dried cranberries and remove the pan from the heat.

Place the pork in a shallow roasting pan and spoon ½ cup of the cranberry cider mixture over the top. Insert a meat thermometer in the thickest part of the roast and cook for 45 minutes to 1 hour, basting occasionally with the reserved cranberry cider mixture, until the thermometer registers 160°F. Let the roast rest for 10 minutes before slicing it. Spoon the pan juices and cranberries over the meat before serving.

Garlicky Butterflied Leg of Lamb

~~~~~~

If you like to "get in there" with the ingredients, this is the recipe for you. Your home (and hands) will be perfumed with the heavenly aromas of the south of France when you prepare this very special dish.

Buy this cut of meat in a high-quality meat market where you can ask the butcher to prepare it according to the recipe. "Butterflied" means the meat will be cut to form a rough, flat rectangle that will have varying thicknesses. This means that some parts of the meat will be cooked more than others. I find, though, that this isn't a problem since when you have eight people to dinner, some will want their meat rare, others will want it well done, and others will be delighted with what is in between.

PREPARATION TIME: 30 minutes

MARINATING TIME: 24 hours

COOKING TIME: 30 to 40 minutes

YIELD: Serves 8 to 10

CAN BE MADE AHEAD? Only if you plan to serve it cold.

CAN BE FROZEN? No

CAN BE DOUBLED? You will have to buy 2 legs of lamb, which, unless you have two ovens, will be very hard to cook at the same time. I suggest either serving this dish cold or picking something else.

CAN BE HALVED? Yes. Buy a half lamb leg.

15 garlic cloves, peeled and cut into quarters the long way
   to form slivers

1 leg of lamb, boned and butterflied (5 to 6 pounds after boning)

1 cup olive oil

¼ cup red wine vinegar or balsamic vinegar

2 tablespoons Dijon mustard

¼ cup soy sauce

¼ cup dark brown sugar

2 teaspoons dried thyme

2 teaspoons dried rosemary

2 teaspoons dried basil

Twenty-four hours before you plan to cook the lamb, prepare the garlic slivers. Use a small sharp knife to cut ½-inch slits in the surface of both sides of the lamb. Insert a sliver of garlic into each slit, pushing it in so that it is no longer visible. Continue doing this until you have inserted the garlic over the entire surface of the lamb. You won't be able to do this in the thinner parts, but that's fine, the garlic will penetrate all over.

Mix the remaining ingredients together in a small bowl. Place the lamb in a shallow pan (or plastic container with a snap-on lid). Add the marinade and turn the meat over several times to coat. Cover the container tightly and refrigerate for 24 hours, turning the meat over once or twice during that time.

To cook: Remove the lamb from the refrigerator 30 minutes before cooking. Preheat the broiler to high with the rack in the upper third of the oven. Place the lamb in a shallow heavy-duty roasting pan or in a slotted broiler pan with a drip pan underneath. Reinsert any garlic that has slipped out of the lamb. Broil the lamb 18 to 20 minutes on each side, cutting into the center to check for doneness. The lamb should be served with the outside well browned and the interior of the thickest parts very pink. Let the lamb rest for 15 minutes before cutting it into 1-inch-thick slices on the bias across the grain.

Main Course: Fish and Shellfish

Thai Halibut Steaks

This elegantly simple (and low-calorie) dish with its Asian touches lends itself to all kinds of menus. It can be served hot or cold. Try to find halibut steaks very close to the same weight and thickness so they cook the same length of time. If you cannot find halibut, you can substitute salmon steaks.

Lemongrass is available in Asian produce markets and in many health food stores that sell produce. Look for fresh gingerroot in the produce department of your grocery store. Peel it with a sharp paring knife or vegetable peeler.

PREPARATION TIME: 25 minutes

COOKING TIME: 15 to 20 minutes

YIELD: Serves 8

CAN BE MADE AHEAD? Yes. The halibut can be poached up to 24 hours ahead of time and served cold. Cover airtight and refrigerate until ready to serve.

CAN BE FROZEN? No

CAN BE DOUBLED AND TRIPLED? Yes. Use a very large skillet, cook in several batches, and keep the cooked fish warm in a covered dish in a 125°F oven.

CAN BE HALVED? Yes

1 2-inch piece of gingerroot, peeled and cut into 1-inch matchstick slivers

2 garlic cloves, minced

2 stalks of lemongrass, root end trimmed, cut lengthwise into quarters

1 lemon, thinly sliced and seeded

¼ cup chopped fresh coriander or 1 teaspoon dried coriander

⅓ cup soy sauce

1 cup dry white wine

1 cup water

8 halibut steaks, each approximately 1 inch thick and weighing approximately 8 ounces

Place all the ingredients except the fish in a skillet large enough to hold the 8 steaks in one layer (or divide them between two smaller skillets). Set over medium heat and bring to a simmer, stirring to combine the ingredients. Simmer for 10 minutes.

Add the halibut, cover the skillet, and allowing the liquid to gently simmer, gently cook for 5 to 7 minutes on each side until the fish flakes easily and is done in the center. Test for this by inserting a small knife into the fish and looking to see that it is white and not translucent in the center.

Remove the fish to a serving platter or to dinner plates. Increase the heat under the cooking liquid and boil until it reduces by a third. There will be about 1½ cups of liquid to pour over the fish along with the ginger and lemon slices.

Grilled Teriyaki Mustard Tuna Steaks

The trick to perfect tuna is to cook it quickly over high heat so that the outside is browned and the inside remains slightly pink. While an outdoor grill is the best place, you can also pan-sear it on the stove top (instructions for both follow). The brown sugar–soy sauce marinade adds a pungent sweet and salty flavor to the delicate tuna taste.

You can substitute swordfish in this recipe. If you do, make sure that it, unlike the tuna, is cooked all the way through. Check by inserting the tip of a knife into the thickest part of the steak. The flesh should be white throughout without any translucency.

PREPARATION TIME: 20 minutes

COOKING TIME: Approximately 9 to 12 minutes

YIELD: Serves 8

CAN BE MADE AHEAD? Yes. The fish must be marinated in the refrigerator for at least 1 hour or up to 4 hours.

CAN BE FROZEN? No

CAN BE DOUBLED? Yes

CAN BE HALVED? Yes

⅓ cup soy sauce

⅓ cup orange juice

2 tablespoons red wine vinegar

3 tablespoons mild sesame oil

⅓ cup dark brown sugar, firmly packed

¼ cup Dijon mustard

1 teaspoon ground ginger

8 6- to 8-ounce tuna or swordfish steaks, 1½ inches thick

Mix together all the ingredients except the fish in a shallow dish large enough to hold the fish in one layer. Use two dishes if necessary. Place the fish steaks in the dish, turning to coat both sides. Cover airtight with plastic wrap and refrigerate at least 1 hour, or up to 4 hours. Turn the fish over once halfway through the marinating time.

To grill: Preheat a gas grill or light a charcoal fire. Brush the rack with vegetable oil. Grill the fish 3 to 4 minutes on a side for rare tuna, or 5 to 6 minutes on a side for well-done tuna (and for swordfish). Baste both sides of the fish with the marinade several times during the grilling.

To pan-sear: Unless you have two large pans, you will have to do this in two batches. Warm heat-proof dinner plates in the oven to keep the cooked fish warm while you prepare the rest. Place a large nonstick pan over high heat. When drops of water sizzle on the surface of the pan, add the steaks, 3 or 4 at a time, and cook 2 to 3 minutes on each side for rare tuna, and 4 minutes for well-done tuna (and for swordfish). Remove the cooked fish to the warm plates and continue with the rest.

Oven-Roasted Salmon with Red Potatoes and Dill

The only tricky thing about roasting salmon is making sure it doesn't dry out while cooking in the high heat that ensures a flavorful and tender dish. The oven cooking bag allows the fish to brown, yet keeps in the moisture and flavor—and speeds cleanup, since there is no messy baking dish to wash. Look for oven cooking bags in your grocery store next to the foil and plastic wrap.

This dish does not call for salt since capers are quite salty. Served cold, it makes a perfect summertime luncheon dish or entrée.

PREPARATION TIME: 20 to 30 minutes

COOKING TIME: 20 minutes

YIELD: Serves 8

CAN BE MADE AHEAD? Yes. You can assemble the dish up to 6 hours ahead to the point to just before roasting. Place the baking dish in the refrigerator until ready to cook. Or, if you plan to serve the salmon cold, it can be prepared up to 24 hours ahead of time and held in the refrigerator in a covered container—or even in the cooking bag—until serving.

CAN BE FROZEN? No

CAN BE DOUBLED? Yes. Use several bags and several baking dishes.

CAN BE HALVED? Yes

1 large-size (20 × 14-inch) oven cooking bag.

16 red-skinned potatoes, scrubbed and very thinly sliced

8 6- to 8-ounce salmon fillets, all approximately the same thickness and size

1 large red bell pepper, seeded and diced

½ cup chopped fresh dill

2 tablespoons capers, drained

1 stick (4 ounces) unsalted butter, cut into 8 pieces

Preheat the oven to 450°F with the rack in the center position. Select a baking dish large enough to hot salmon in one layer. Lay the oven cooking bag in the dish and scatter the potatoes over the bottom of the bag. Place the salmon on top of the potatoes and scatter on the diced pepper, dill, and capers, covering all the fillets.

Place a pat of butter on top of each fillet. Seal the bag with the plastic tie provided and use scissors to cut six ½-inch slits in the top of the bag.

Roast the salmon in the preheated oven for 20 minutes. Remove the baking dish from the oven and allow the fillets to stay in the bag an additional 5 minutes. Cut open the bag and discard it. To serve, place a fillet on a plate and surround it with some of potato slices, pepper, and capers, then spoon a little of the cooking liquid over the top.

Sole Puttanesca

You can substitute any thin white fish for the sole in this recipe. A simple sun-dried tomato sauce is spread on the fillets, which are then rolled and baked with a zesty tomato sauce flavored with capers, black olives, and dried red pepper. The fish and sauce are served over linguine.

Sun-dried tomato paste is available in gourmet specialty shops.

PREPARATION TIME: 40 minutes

COOKING TIME: 20 minutes

YIELD: Serves 8

CAN BE MADE AHEAD? Yes. The fish can be spread with the filling, rolled, and refrigerated, covered with plastic wrap, up to 6 hours before cooking. The tomato sauce can be prepared the night before. Heat it to a simmer before adding it to the fish.

CAN BE FROZEN? Yes. The dish can be assembled to the point to just before baking, covered tightly with plastic wrap, and frozen for up to 1 month. Defrost for 12 hours in the refrigerator and then bake (it will still be partially frozen), covered with foil, in a 375°F oven for 40 minutes.

CAN BE DOUBLED? Yes

CAN BE HALVED? Yes

4 tablespoons sun-dried tomato paste

¾ cup mayonnaise

3 drops Tabasco Pepper Sauce

4 pounds sole fillets (or other white fish fillets, such as flounder or cod), all approximately the same size

2 28-ounce cans plum tomatoes, drained and coarsely chopped

2 tablespoons capers

2 tablespoons anchovy paste

10 oil-packed sun-dried tomatoes, cut in quarters, plus 2 tablespoons
    packing oil

1 cup oil-cured pitted black olives, cut in half

2 teaspoons red pepper flakes

2 teaspoons dried basil

1½ pounds cooked linguine

1 teaspoon salt, if needed

Preheat the oven to 375°F with the rack in the upper third but not highest position. Select a baking dish large enough to hold all the sole in one layer (when rolled) plus the sauce. In a small bowl, mix together the sun-dried tomato paste, mayonnaise, and Tabasco Pepper Sauce. Use a spoon to evenly coat one side of each fillet with about 1½ tablespoons of the mixture. Roll the fillets, starting from one short end, and place them, seam side down, next to each other in the baking dish.

Place all the other ingredients except the salt in a pan set over medium heat. Stir to combine, adding salt, if necessary. Pour the hot sauce over the fillets. Bake for 20 minutes, or until the sauce is bubbling and the fish cuts easily (try cutting into one roll with a butter knife—it should give no resistance).

To serve, place some linguine on a plate, top it with sauce, and place a fillet on the side.

Garlic Greek Shrimp

Feta cheese, black olives, fresh dill, and a sprinkling of fennel seeds give the savory warmth of the Greek flavors to this shrimp dish. If you have not peeled and deveined shrimp before, give yourself a little extra time to prepare this. It won't be long before you get the hang of it. The key to success is a very sharp paring knife.

PREPARATION TIME: 45 minutes

COOKING TIME: 12 to 15 minutes

YIELD: Serves 8

CAN BE MADE AHEAD? Yes. You can peel and devein the shrimp up to 4 hours ahead. Store in a covered container in the refrigerator. The remaining ingredients can be mixed up to 12 hours ahead. Store in a covered container in the refrigerator.

CAN BE FROZEN? No

CAN BE DOUBLED? Yes

CAN BE HALVED? Yes

4 garlic cloves, peeled and mashed with the side of a knife

½ cup olive oil

4 pounds uncooked jumbo shrimp

⅓ cup lemon juice

1 cup coarsely chopped fresh dill

2 teaspoons fennel seed

1 large Spanish onion, peeled and sliced into ¼-inch rings

1 cup oil-cured pitted black olives

2 cups crumbled feta cheese

Place the garlic together with the olive oil in a jar and allow to marinate for 1 hour before starting. Place the shrimp in a colander or large strainer and rinse well with cold water. Use your fingers to pull off the shells and tails. Under a gentle stream of cold water, use the tip of a sharp knife to make a ¼-inch slit down the length of the "spine" of the shrimp to expose the dark vein. Allow the water to wash the vein out. Shake off any excess water and refrigerate the shrimp while you proceed with the rest of the dish.

Discard the garlic and pour the oil into a mixing bowl. Add the remaining ingredients and mix to combine. Preheat the broiler to high with the rack in the upper third but not highest position. Place the shrimp in one layer over the bottom of a broiler-proof pan and distribute the feta mixture over it.

Broil for 12 to 15 minutes, stirring the mixture to turn the shrimp once during the cooking time. The shrimp are done when they are pink on both sides and the cheese has started to brown. If the dish begins to brown too quickly, move the rack to a lower position.

Grilled Scallops Primavera

This is a more elegant alternative to hot dogs and hamburgers. You can make this outdoors on the grill or under the oven broiler. Use the large sea scallops if you can find them, or you can substitute 1½-inch chunks of tuna or swordfish. The vegetables will remain firm and crisp while the fish will be tender and cooked through.

Wooden skewers can be found in gourmet shops or hardware stores. Soak them in water for a few minutes to prevent the food from sticking and the wood from burning.

PREPARATION TIME: 20 minutes

COOKING TIME: 12 to 15 minutes

YIELD: Serves 8

CAN BE MADE AHEAD? Yes. Must be assembled and marinated at least 45 minutes ahead.

CAN BE FROZEN? No

CAN BE DOUBLED AND TRIPLED? Yes

CAN BE HALVED? Yes

3½ pounds large sea scallops, rinsed and patted dry

1 pound yellow squash, cut crosswise into 1-inch pieces

2 red bell peppers, seeded and cut into 1-inch pieces

24 cherry tomatoes

16 whole mushrooms, wiped clean and stems trimmed

2 large sweet onions, such as Vidalia or Spanish, peeled and cut into 1½-inch chunks (do not separate the pieces from the root end)

½ cup olive oil

¼ cup soy sauce

Juice of 1 large lemon

1 cup basil leaves, torn into pieces

Thread the scallops and vegetables and mushrooms on the soaked skewers, alternating vegetable and scallop. Place the skewers in a shallow pan.

Combine the oil, soy sauce, lemon juice, and basil in a mixing bowl and pour over the prepared skewers. Cover with plastic wrap and marinate in the refrigerator for at least 45 minutes, or as long as 6 hours, turning once or twice to coat evenly.

To grill: Brush the grilling rack with vegetable oil and preheat the grill. Arrange the skewers in a single layer, leaving at least 1 inch between each. Grill for 3 to 4 minutes on each of four sides, basting with the marinade, until the scallops are no longer translucent in the center and the vegetables are crisp and browned.

To broil: Place the rack in the upper third of the oven and set the broiler on high. Place the skewers in a single layer on a slotted broiler pan set over a drain pan. Broil for 2 to 3 minutes on each of four sides, basting with the marinade, until the scallops are no longer translucent in the center and the vegetables are crisp and browned.

Side Dishes: Cold

Carrot Raisin Salad

A terrific (and colorful) alternative to coleslaw, this is a staple of every potluck supper buffet table.

PREPARATION TIME: 20 minutes

YIELD: Serves 8 as a side dish

CAN BE MADE AHEAD? Yes, up to 24 hours. Refrigerate in a covered container.

CAN BE FROZEN? No

CAN BE DOUBLED AND TRIPLED? Yes

CAN BE HALVED? Yes

2 tablespoons vegetable oil

2 tablespoons olive oil

1 tablespoon cider vinegar

3 tablespoons soy sauce

2 tablespoons honey

$\frac{1}{4}$ teaspoon ground cinnamon

$\frac{1}{4}$ cup chopped fresh parsley

1 pound carrots, peeled and coarsely grated

$\frac{1}{2}$ cup raisins

$\frac{3}{4}$ cup sunflower seeds

In a large bowl, combine the oils, vinegar, soy sauce, honey, cinnamon, and parsley. Add the grated carrots, raisins, and sunflower seeds and toss to coat.

Summer Salad

This salad is best made in midsummer when farm stands are overflowing with big juicy flavorful tomatoes and basil can be picked right from the garden. If the ingredients have been refrigerated, hold the salad at room temperature for 30 minutes; cold dulls the flavors.

Serve on individual plates or arrange it on a large platter for a buffet.

PREPARATION TIME: 20 minutes

YIELD: Serves 8

CAN BE MADE AHEAD? You can slice the cheese ahead of time (wrap it in plastic wrap and refrigerate) and wash and dry the basil, but the rest should be left until the last moment or the tomatoes will get soggy.

CAN BE FROZEN? No

CAN BE DOUBLED AND TRIPLED? Yes

CAN BE HALVED? Yes

1 pound fresh mozzarella cheese, cut into ½-inch slices (use a serrated knife to do this)

4 large ripe tomatoes, at room temperature, cut into ½-inch slices

1 large red onion, cut into ¼-inch slices

24 large fresh basil leaves, rinsed, patted dry, and torn into several large pieces

½ cup olive oil

¼ cup basalmic vinegar

Freshly ground black pepper

About 2 teaspoons salt

On eight salad plates, arrange overlapping slices of mozzarella, tomato, and onion. Scatter the torn basil leaves on top. Drizzle each plate with 1 tablespoon of olive oil and 2 teaspoons of vinegar. Grind some pepper on top and sprinkle with a scant ¼ teaspoon of salt. Serve immediately.

Sweet Corn and Tomato Salad

Here's a great alternative to coleslaw or potato salad. You can use either leftover corn on the cob or frozen corn. Do not use canned, it's too salty and mushy.

PREPARATION TIME: 20 minutes

COOKING TIME: 2 minutes for frozen corn; 10 minutes for corn from the cob

YIELD: Serves 10

CAN BE MADE AHEAD? Yes, up to 48 hours.

CAN BE FROZEN? No

CAN BE DOUBLED? Yes

CAN BE HALVED? Yes

Kernels stripped from 8 ears of cooked corn on the cob
    (see the Note) or 2 1-pound bags frozen corn, defrosted

1 large green bell pepper, cored, seeded, and diced

1 large red bell pepper, cored, seeded, and diced

1 red onion, thinly sliced

1 pint cherry tomatoes, halved

6 scallions, chopped (both white and green parts)

½ cup mayonnaise

½ cup sour cream

1 teaspoon salt

Freshly ground black pepper

Mix all the ingredients in a large bowl and refrigerate until serving time.

NOTE: To remove the kernels from the cob, set the cob on end in a shallow bowl or pan and slice downward with a sharp paring knife.

Easy Potato Salad

Another classic made easy, and made a bit more interesting with the addition of scallions. Using either a homemade vinaigrette or a good-quality bottled Italian salad dressing instead of mayonnaise cuts some of the fat and adds a zesty flavor. While this recipe suggests russet potatoes, you can use unpeeled small red-skinned potatoes. Scrub them well, then cut them in half and cook until tender.

PREPARATION TIME: 20 minutes

COOKING TIME: 20 minutes

YIELD: Serves 8

CAN BE MADE AHEAD? Yes, up to 24 hours. Store in a covered container in the refrigerator.

CAN BE FROZEN? No

CAN BE DOUBLED AND TRIPLED? Yes

CAN BE HALVED? Yes

4 4- to 5-inch russet potatoes

½ cup Vinaigrette Dressing (page 306) or bottled Italian dressing

¼ cup mayonnaise

¼ cup chopped scallions (reserve 1 tablespoon for garnish)

½ teaspoon paprika

Wash and peel the potatoes and cut them into quarters. Place them in a medium-sized saucepan and cover with water. Bring the water to a boil, cover the pan, and reduce the heat. Cook for approximately 20 minutes, or until the potatoes are tender when pierced with a fork. Drain and let cool until they can be handled easily.

Slice the potatoes into a plastic container with a tight-fitting lid. Add the dressing and cover. Gently shake the container to mix. Refrigerate the potatoes for at least 1 hour, or overnight.

Add the mayonnaise and scallions to the potatoes and toss with a fork until well mixed. Place on a bed of mixed greens, sprinkle with paprika, and garnish with the reserved scallions.

Vinaigrette Dressing

PREPARATION TIME: 10 minutes

YIELD: Serves 6 to 8

CAN BE MADE AHEAD? Yes, up to 3 days. Refrigerate in a small covered container.

CAN BE FROZEN? No

CAN BE DOUBLED? Yes

CAN BE HALVED? Yes

4 tablespoons red wine vinegar

⅓ cup olive oil

1 teaspoon salt

1 tablespoon Dijon mustard

½ teaspoon freshly ground black pepper

1 teaspoon dried basil

½ teaspoon dried oregano

Combine all the ingredients in a 1½-cup jar or container. Shake well, and shake again before using.

Texas Slaw

Here's a hot and spicy version of a classic. You can control the degree of heat by using either mild or hot jalapeño peppers.

If you have a food processor with a fine shredding blade, use it to shred the vegetables.

PREPARATION TIME: 20 minutes

YIELD: Serves 8 to 10

CAN BE MADE AHEAD? Yes, up to 24 hours. Store in a covered container in the refrigerator until ready to serve.

CAN BE FROZEN? No

CAN BE DOUBLED AND TRIPLED? Yes

CAN BE HALVED? Yes

1 medium head of green cabbage, outer leaves, core, and stem removed, shredded

1 large red onion, thinly sliced

1 cup corn kernels, either canned and drained of liquid or defrosted frozen

1 red bell pepper, cored, seeded, and thinly sliced

1 large carrot, peeled and shredded

2 to 3 canned jalapeño peppers (mild or hot, as you wish), chopped

¼ cup fresh coriander, chopped

⅓ cup red wine vinegar

⅓ cup soy sauce

2 tablespoons dark brown sugar or 2 tablespoons honey

1 teaspoon chili powder

1½ cups mayonnaise

Salt to taste

Place all the vegetables, peppers, and coriander in a large bowl or pot. In a small bowl, mix together the vinegar, soy sauce, sugar, chili powder, mayonnaise, and salt. Pour over the vegetable mixture and mix well to combine all the ingredients. Refrigerate in a covered container until ready to serve.

Side Dishes: Hot

Pesto Orzo

Orzo is a rice-shaped pasta I discovered when I was a new cook and having trouble getting rice to come out right. All you do to orzo is boil it in lots of water, drain it, and add the sauce.

This dish can be served hot as a main course, cold as a salad on a bed of greens, or added as a side dish with cold meat, fish, or chicken. Really good pesto is available in the supermarket, usually in the refrigerated fresh pasta section.

PREPARATION TIME: 5 minutes

COOKING TIME: 8 to 10 minutes

YIELD: Serves 6 as a main course; 10 as a side dish

CAN BE MADE AHEAD? Yes, up to 2 days, only if you plan to serve it cold. Refrigerate in a covered container.

CAN BE FROZEN? No

CAN BE DOUBLED? Yes. Use a very large pot (6 to 8 quarts) to cook the pasta.

CAN BE HALVED? Yes

1 tablespoon salt (for the cooking water)

1 pound orzo

1½ cups (12 ounces) pesto

Freshly grated Parmesan cheese

Place 3 quarts of water and the 1 tablespoon salt in a large pot set over high heat. When the water comes to a rapid boil, add the orzo and stir with a long spoon to separate the pieces. Cook it according to the package directions—I prefer to cook the minimum amount of time so the pieces of pasta remain firm but not crunchy.

If you are serving the pasta hot, heat the serving bowl by placing it in a warm (250°F) oven for 10 minutes or filling it with very hot water. Drain the orzo well, but do not rinse it. Add the pesto to the serving bowl and pour the pasta on top. Toss well to coat.

If you are serving the pasta hot, add the grated cheese, or pass it separately. If you are serving it cold, add the cheese after the pasta has been chilled for several hours, or just before serving.

Lemon Orzo

A little bit of lemon peel gives a special zing to this versatile accompaniment to roast chicken, fish, or "light" meat.

PREPARATION TIME: 5 minutes

COOKING TIME: 8 to 10 minutes

YIELD: Serves 8

CAN BE MADE AHEAD? No

CAN BE FROZEN? No

CAN BE DOUBLED? Yes. Use a very large pot.

CAN BE HALVED? Yes

1 tablespoon salt (for the cooking water)

1 pound orzo

1 stick (4 ounces) unsalted butter

Juice and finely grated rind of 1 large lemon

½ cup Italian parsley leaves, chopped

Place 3 quarts of water and the 1 tablespoon salt in a large pot set over high heat. When the water comes to a rapid boil, add the orzo and stir with a long spoon to separate the pieces. Cook according to the package directions—I prefer to cook the minimum amount of time so the pieces of pasta remain firm but not crunchy. Drain well.

Add the butter and lemon juice and rind to the cooking pot. Add the drained orzo and parsley and toss to coat. Serve hot.

Lemon Rice

This cold rice makes a lovely side dish for chicken or fish. It also makes a great stuffing for tomatoes. Use large vine-ripe tomatoes. Cut a 1-inch circle around the stem and scoop out some of the pulp, filling the cavity with the rice.

Make sure to use long grain white rice (or brown rice, if you wish). Do not use instant rice.

PREPARATION TIME: 15 minutes

COOKING TIME: According to the package directions

YIELD: Serves 8

CAN BE MADE AHEAD? Yes, up to 8 hours. Store in a covered container in the refrigerator.

CAN BE FROZEN? No

CAN BE DOUBLED? Yes

CAN BE HALVED? Yes

⅔ cup mayonnaise

Juice and grated rind of 1 lemon

½ cup chopped scallions

¼ teaspoon white pepper

½ teaspoon salt

4 cups cooked long grain white rice (about 1¼ cups uncooked rice; cook according to package directions)

Mix together the mayonnaise, lemon juice and rind, scallions, pepper, and salt in a large bowl. Add the cooked rice and stir until well mixed. Keep refrigerated until served.

Parmesan Rice Casserole

If the thought of making rice makes you nervous, this foolproof cook-in-the-oven version is just for you.

PREPARATION TIME: 20 minutes

BAKING TIME: 55 minutes

YIELD: Serves 8

CAN BE MADE AHEAD? Yes, up to 1 day. Refrigerate and then reheat in a microwave or conventional oven.

CAN BE FROZEN? Yes. Thaw completely before reheating.

CAN BE DOUBLED? It's easier to make it in 2 batches.

CAN BE HALVED? Yes. Use a 1-quart casserole dish and bake for 35 minutes.

½ stick (2 ounces) unsalted butter or margarine

2 medium onions, finely chopped

1 cup oil-packed sun-dried tomatoes, cut into ¾-inch pieces

2 cups uncooked long grain white rice

4 cups chicken or vegetable broth or 2 chicken or vegetable bouillon cubes dissolved in 4 cups boiling water

1¼ cups freshly grated Parmesan cheese

1 cup pine nuts

Preheat the oven to 400°F with the rack in the center position. Spray a 2-quart casserole dish with vegetable oil spray.

Melt the butter in a medium-sized sauté pan over medium-high heat. Add the onion and sauté for 3 to 5 minutes, stirring occasionally, until the onion is transparent. Transfer to the prepared casserole.

Add the sun-dried tomatoes, rice, broth, and Parmesan cheese. Stir to mix. Cover the dish tightly with foil and bake for 45 minutes.

Uncover the casserole and sprinkle with the pine nuts. Move the rack to the upper position and bake 10 minutes more, or until the top of the casserole is golden and the rice is tender. Serve hot.

Apricot Squash Casserole

Butternut squash is a colorful and tasty departure from potatoes or rice. Many supermarkets offer bags of peeled and cut squash—which makes this dish even easier to make. Dried apricots give a zing to the taste. Serve this in an oven-to-table casserole.

PREPARATION TIME: 20 minutes

COOKING TIME: Stove top 20 minutes; oven 20 minutes

YIELD: Serves 8

CAN BE MADE AHEAD? Yes. This can be reheated in an oven or microwave.

CAN BE FROZEN? Yes

CAN BE DOUBLED? Yes

CAN BE HALVED? Yes. Use a 1-quart baking dish and reduce the baking time to 20 minutes.

8 cups butternut squash, peeled, seeds removed, and cut into
   ¾-inch chunks

1 cup dried apricots, cut into quarters (use kitchen scissors)

½ stick (2 ounces) unsalted butter or margarine, melted

1 teaspoon salt

1 teaspoon ground cardamom or ½ teaspoon ground nutmeg

3 tablespoons light or dark brown sugar

½ cup walnuts

Preheat the oven to 375°F with the rack in the center position.

Place the squash and apricots in a 2-quart saucepan with 2 inches of water. Cover and bring to a boil. Reduce the heat to low and simmer, covered, for 20 minutes.

Drain and transfer the cooked squash and apricots to a 2-quart baking dish or casserole that has been sprayed with nonstick vegetable spray.

Mix together the butter, salt, cardamom, and brown sugar.

Sprinkle the walnuts on top of the cooked squash and apricots and drizzle the butter mixture over all. Bake for 30 minutes, until the top is slightly brown.

Roasted Red Potatoes

As good as these are hot from the oven, they make an equally tasty side dish or salad when served at room temperature, nestled in a bed of greens. Add a can of Italian tuna, a few string beans and a sliced hard-boiled egg, an anchovy or two, black olives, olive oil and vinegar, and you have a classic salad niçoise.

PREPARATION TIME: 10 minutes

BAKING TIME: 30 to 40 minutes

YIELD: Serves 8

CAN BE MADE AHEAD? Yes. Reheat in a microwave or serve at room temperature (see the headnote).

CAN BE FROZEN? No

CAN BE DOUBLED? Yes. Use a baking pan large enough to spread the potatoes in a single layer.

CAN BE HALVED? Yes

4 tablespoons olive oil

2½ pounds 1½-inch red-skinned potatoes, scrubbed and halved

3 tablespoons fresh thyme or rosemary or 1½ teaspoons dried thyme or rosemary

1 teaspoon salt

½ teaspoon freshly ground black pepper

Preheat the oven to 425°F with the rack in the center position.

Pour the olive oil into a shallow baking pan. Add the potatoes. Sprinkle with the thyme or rosemary and toss to coat.

Bake for 30 to 40 minutes, or until the potatoes are tender when pierced with a fork and appear brown and crisp. Sprinkle with the salt and pepper and serve warm or at room temperature.

Garlic Potatoes

~~~~~~

The mild sweet taste of elephant garlic gives this dish its unique flavor. Look for elephant garlic in your supermarket or in stores specializing in gourmet produce. If you can't locate elephant garlic, regular is fine. Use two heads of regular garlic in place of one head of elephant garlic.

PREPARATION TIME: 20 minutes

BAKING TIME: 45 to 50 minutes if cooked directly after assembly; 45 to 60 minutes if assembled ahead and cooked just before serving

YIELD: Serves 10

CAN BE MADE AHEAD? Yes. Use an ovenproof glass dish or other casserole dish that can withstand the change from cold to hot. Assemble the casserole, cover with plastic wrap, and refrigerate. One hour before serving, remove it from the refrigerator to bring it to room temperature. Bake 45 to 60 minutes, or until the potatoes are heated through and golden on the top.

CAN BE FROZEN? Yes. Cover the top of the dish with plastic wrap and then cover completely with foil.

CAN BE DOUBLED? Yes

CAN BE HALVED? Yes

5 pounds Idaho potatoes, peeled and quartered

1 head of elephant garlic, cloves separated, peeled, and cut in half

1 chicken or vegetable bouillon cube

1 stick (4 ounces) unsalted butter or margarine

½ cup freshly grated Parmesan cheese plus an additional ¼ cup, for topping

½ cup heavy cream

½ cup sour cream

½ teaspoon freshly ground black pepper

Place the potatoes, garlic, and bouillon cube in a 4-quart lidded pot. Add water to cover, set the pot over high heat, and bring to a boil. Reduce the heat to medium, cover, and cook for 30 minutes, or until the potatoes are tender. Drain and mash the potatoes and garlic.

Preheat the oven to 350°F with the rack in the upper position. Spray a 2-quart casserole dish with nonstick vegetable oil spray or coat it with butter.

Add the butter, the ½ cup of Parmesan cheese, heavy cream, sour cream, and pepper to the potatoes and mix well. Transfer the potato mixture to the prepared casserole and smooth the top. Sprinkle with the ¼ cup of Parmesan cheese.

Bake for 45 to 50 minutes, or until the potatoes are golden on top. Serve warm.

Stove-Top Cranberry Sweet Potatoes

Here's a way to make sweet potatoes, using either fresh or canned, when your oven is full to capacity with turkey. An electric frying pan is great for this or even a Slow Cooker (increase the cooking time to 1½ hours for canned potatoes and 3 hours for fresh).

PREPARATION TIME: 10 minutes with canned sweet potatoes; 25 minutes with fresh sweet potatoes

COOKING TIME: 30 minutes

YIELD: Serves 8

CAN BE MADE AHEAD? Yes, up to 2 days. Place the cooled potatoes in a microwavable container in the refrigerator and re-heat in a microwave just before serving. Remove the dish from the refrigerator 1 hour before heating.

CAN BE FROZEN? Yes. Defrost at room temperature or in a microwave.

CAN BE DOUBLED AND TRIPLED? Yes. You'll have to use several skillets.

CAN BE HALVED? Yes

3 tablespoons unsalted butter, cut into 6 pieces

2½ pounds sweet potatoes, peeled and cut into 1-inch slices, or 2 16-ounce cans sweet potatoes, cut into 1-inch slices

½ cup dark brown sugar, firmly packed

½ cup maple syrup

1 cup dried cranberries (available in gourmet food shops)

1 cup orange juice

1 teaspoon salt

½ teaspoon freshly ground black pepper

Using your largest skillet or two smaller skillets, melt the butter over medium heat. Lower the heat and add the ingredients in the order listed. When the liquid comes to a boil, lower the heat so that the mixture is just simmering. Cover the skillet (you can use foil if you don't have a large enough top) and cook for 20 minutes for canned potatoes, and 40 minutes for fresh potatoes.

Easy Potato Pancakes

Even if you don't have the time to peel and grate potatoes, you can still enjoy the taste of homemade potato pancakes. Served with applesauce or sour cream, they are great for brunch or Sunday night supper. Potato pancakes make a perfect cold-weather vegetarian entrée. Serve a hearty soup as a first course.

PREPARATION TIME: 20 minutes

COOKING TIME: About 30 to 40 minutes

YIELD: 2½ dozen pancakes, serves about 6 as a main course; 8 as a side dish

CAN BE MADE AHEAD? Yes. Although you can make them the day before, refrigerate, and reheat them in a 350°F oven, the results are better if you make them within 1 hour of serving time. You can keep the pancakes hot by placing them, uncovered, in a single layer on a cookie sheet in a 200°F oven.

CAN BE FROZEN? No

CAN BE DOUBLED? Yes. Make the mixture in 2 batches.

CAN BE HALVED? Yes

(continued)

3 cups frozen Southern-style hash brown potatoes

2 eggs, beaten

1 medium onion, cut into chunks

¼ cup unbleached all-purpose flour

½ teaspoon baking powder

½ teaspoon salt

Vegetable oil for frying

Applesauce or sour cream, for garnish

Place the potatoes in a wide-mesh strainer or colander and let them thaw completely. Use the back of a mixing spoon to gently press out as much liquid as possible.

Place the potatoes and the remaining ingredients except the oil in a food processor or blender and process, on and off, until the mixture is finely chopped but not mushy.

Preheat the oven to 200°F with the rack in the center position. Set a baking sheet on a nearby counter and cover it with a layer of paper towels. Place a second baking sheet in the oven.

Pour the oil to a depth of 1½ inches in a large skillet. Heat the oil until a drop of batter sizzles and almost immediately begins to turn golden brown.

Use a ¼-cup measure to place the batter in the skillet, cooking only 4 to 5 pancakes at a time. Fry them on each side until golden brown, 2 to 4 minutes.

Drain the cooked pancakes on the paper towels and then place them in the oven to keep warm. Serve with a generous dab of applesauce or sour cream.

Garlic Mashed Potatoes

The key to success in this stick-to-your-ribs side dish is to not allow the garlic to brown or it will become bitter. For even more spice in your life, consider adding 2 tablespoons of chopped canned jalapeño pepper and ¼ cup chopped fresh coriander. WOW!

PREPARATION TIME: 25 minutes

COOKING TIME: 20 minutes

YIELD: Serves 8

CAN BE MADE AHEAD? Yes, up to 24 hours. Spoon the cooked potatoes into a microwavable casserole, cover with plastic wrap, and refrigerate. Reheat in a microwave.

CAN BE FROZEN? No

CAN BE DOUBLED? Yes

CAN BE HALVED? Yes

1 stick (4 ounces) unsalted butter

3 large garlic cloves, minced

2 teaspoons salt, plus additional to taste

4 large Idaho potatoes, scrubbed, peeled, and cut into 1-inch slices

½ cup heavy cream

Freshly ground black pepper to taste

Heat the butter in a small skillet until melted and add the garlic. Cook over low heat for 5 minutes, stirring often. Do not let the garlic brown. Remove from the heat and reserve at room temperature.

Bring a large pot of water to a rolling boil. Add the 2 teaspoons of salt and potatoes and when the water returns to a boil, reduce to a simmer and cook for 20 minutes, or until the potatoes are soft. Drain off the water and add the garlic butter (with the chopped garlic) and cream. Use a potato masher or wooden spoon to mash the potatoes, adding salt and pepper to taste. Serve hot.

Baked Parmesan-Stuffed Zucchini

You can assemble these zucchini "boats" ahead of time, then pop them in the oven to bake just before serving. Served hot or at room temperature, they make an amusing and tasty vegetable dish.

PREPARATION TIME: 20 minutes

BAKING TIME: 40 minutes

YIELD: Serves 8

CAN BE MADE AHEAD? Yes, up to 4 hours. Serve at room temperature, or assemble up to 4 hours ahead, uncooked, store at room temperature, and then cook just before serving.

CAN BE FROZEN? No

CAN BE DOUBLED? Yes

CAN BE HALVED? Yes

8 small zucchini, all about the same size, cut in half lengthwise

¼ cup plus ½ to ⅔ cup olive oil

1 medium Spanish onion, finely chopped

2 garlic cloves, chopped

1 teaspoon dried oregano

1 cup Italian-flavored bread crumbs

1 cup freshly grated Parmesan cheese

Freshly ground black pepper

Preheat the oven to 350°F with the rack in the center position. Spray a 13 × 9-inch baking pan with nonstick vegetable spray.

Using a grapefruit spoon or a regular teaspoon, scoop out two thirds of the insides of the zucchini to form a trough down the center of each. Neaten the edges with a sharp knife if necessary. Save the pulp and chop finely.

Heat the ¼ cup olive oil in a frying pan and add the chopped onion. Sauté for 2 to 3 minutes, or until the onion is transparent. Add the chopped zucchini and garlic and sauté for another 3 minutes. Remove from the heat and add the oregano, bread crumbs, and Parmesan cheese. Stir to mix.

Fill the scooped-out zucchini with the mixture, pressing down gently with the back of a spoon. Mound the mixture on the tops. Place the zucchini in the prepared pan and drizzle each with the remaining olive oil and sprinkle them with the pepper. Cover the pan with foil and bake for 30 minutes. Remove the foil, move the rack to the top position, and continue baking for an additional 10 minutes, until golden brown.

Steamed Asparagus with Lemon Butter

The tiny asparagus that are available in the late winter and early spring are a godsend to busy cooks since the stems don't have to be peeled. Best of all, they require only a few minutes to cook. A microwave is a perfect way to cook them, and instructions for stove-top steaming are also given.

Asparagus are also great either as a vegetable side dish or as an appetizer or salad when served with Lemon Mustard Sauce (recipe follows) instead of butter.

PREPARATION TIME: 5 minutes to wash the asparagus and trim the ends

COOKING TIME: 2 to 4 minutes, depending on the method (see below)

YIELD: Serves 8 as a side dish or salad; 4 to 6 as an appetizer

CAN BE MADE AHEAD? Yes, if you want to serve them cold or at room temperature.

CAN BE FROZEN? No

CAN BE DOUBLED AND TRIPLED? Yes. Cook them in several batches.

CAN BE HALVED? Yes

2 pounds very thin asparagus

Salt

6 tablespoons (3 ounces) unsalted butter or margarine, melted

Grated rind and juice of 1 lemon

Microwave method: Place the asparagus in a microwavable dish large enough to hold them in several layers. Add ½ cup boiling water and ½ teaspoon salt. Cover with plastic wrap and microwave on high, 3 minutes for very thin stems, and 4 minutes for thicker stems. Take care not to get a steam burn when removing the plastic wrap. Test for doneness by inserting the point of a sharp knife into the bottom end of a stalk. If the asparagus are unappetizingly firm, microwave another minute or two. Drain immediately.

Stove-top method: Fill a large pot with water and 1 teaspoon salt and bring to a rapid boil. Add the asparagus and lower the heat to a simmer. Cook 2 minutes for thin stalks and 3 to 4 minutes for thicker ones, testing as above. Drain immediately.

Arrange the asparagus on one large platter or divide among eight salad plates. Stir the melted butter together with the lemon juice and serve separately.

If you choose to serve the thicker stalks which come later in the season, snap off the woody stem (up to where the green begins) and use a vegetable peeler to remove the outer skin to within 1½ inches of the tips. Increase the cooking time by 1 minute in a microwave and 2 minutes on a stove top, testing with the point of a sharp knife to make sure the asparagus are tender, but not mushy.

Lemon Mustard Sauce

In a small bowl, mix ¾ cup Dijon mustard with ¼ cup freshly squeezed lemon juice until well blended. Makes 1 cup, or enough for 8 people.

Pesto-Stuffed Tomatoes

I love to serve this in summer when big, juicy tomatoes are in season. Pesto is available in your supermarket and Italian specialty food stores. Served cold or at room temperature, this makes an unusually good first course. Served hot, it makes a great sidekick to poultry or fish dishes.

PREPARATION TIME: 15 minutes

BAKING TIME: 25 to 30 minutes

YIELD: Serves 8

CAN BE MADE AHEAD? Yes. The tomatoes can be stuffed 2 hours ahead and refrigerated until ready to bake just before serving. Or, they can be baked up to 3 hours ahead and served at room temperature.

CAN BE FROZEN? No

CAN BE DOUBLED? Yes

CAN BE HALVED? Yes

8 large flavorful tomatoes, all approximately the same size and shape

¾ cup (6 ounces) pesto

⅔ cup freshly grated Parmesan cheese

Preheat the oven to 375°F with the rack in the center position. Spray a baking dish large enough to hold all the tomatoes in one layer with nonstick vegetable spray.

Using a small sharp knife, cut a thin slice off the bottom of each tomato to help it stand upright, then cut a 2-inch circle in the top of each tomato and scoop out a 1-inch-deep section. Chop the scooped-out sections and place them in a small mixing bowl. Add the pesto to the chopped tomato and mix. Pile the pesto tomato mixture into the scooped-out tomatoes, mounding it slightly. Sprinkle the tomatoes with Parmesan cheese and bake for 25 to 30 minutes, or until the tops are golden brown. Use two large serving spoons to carefully transfer the hot tomatoes to dinner plates or a serving dish. Serve hot or at room temperature.

Marinated Green Beans

Use the freshest green beans you can find for this make-ahead vegetable dish. Don't overcook the beans or they will lose their vibrant green color. If you don't like anchovies, leave them out or substitute capers.

PREPARATION TIME: 15 minutes

COOKING TIME: About 4 minutes

YIELD: Serves 8

CAN BE MADE AHEAD? Yes, up to 2 days. Refrigerate in a tightly closed container.

CAN BE FROZEN? No

CAN BE DOUBLED AND TRIPLED? Yes

CAN BE HALVED? Yes

2 pounds fresh green beans, ends trimmed

5 tablespoons olive oil

2 tablespoons red wine vinegar

2 garlic cloves, chopped

½ teaspoon salt

4 anchovies, chopped (optional) or 1 tablespoon capers
  (if you use the anchovies or capers, omit the salt)

Fill a saucepan with 1 inch of cold water and bring it to a boil. Add the green beans. When the water returns to a boil, cook them for 3 minutes. Drain them immediately in a colander and rinse with cold water.

In a serving bowl, whisk together the olive oil, vinegar, garlic, and salt (or anchovies). Add the green beans and toss until coated.

Sesame Green Beans

When you see piles of freshly picked green beans in your market, then it's time to make this dish. It can be served hot, at room temperature, or even cold as part of a salad or cold plate. Be sure to use mild sesame oil—not the hot kind.

Take care not to overcook the beans. You want them crisp—not mushy.

PREPARATION TIME: 10 minutes

COOKING TIME: 5 minutes

YIELD: Serves 6 to 8

CAN BE MADE AHEAD? Yes. They can be served hot or cold.

CAN BE FROZEN? No

CAN BE DOUBLED? Yes

CAN BE HALVED? Yes

1½ pounds green beans, washed and ends trimmed

2 garlic cloves, finely chopped

¼ cup soy sauce

1 tablespoon mild sesame oil

2 teaspoons oyster sauce

2 teaspoons lemon juice

1 teaspoon sugar

¼ teaspoon freshly ground black pepper

¼ cup sesame seeds, toasted (see the Note)

Fill a saucepan with 1 inch of water and add the green beans. Cover and bring to a boil. Cook for 3 minutes, or until the beans are crisp-tender. Drain them into a strainer and rinse with cold water, draining well.

In a small saucepan, combine the garlic, soy sauce, sesame oil, oyster sauce, lemon juice, sugar, and pepper. Heat over medium-high heat until bubbles appear at the edge of the pan. Watch carefully; when the bubbles extend to the middle of the pan, remove from the heat immediately. Pour the sauce over the beans and toss to mix. Add the sesame seeds and toss again. Serve warm or cold.

NOTE: To toast sesame seeds, set a heavy skillet over high heat. Add the sesame seeds and stir continuously so they don't burn. As soon as the seeds start to turn brown, lower the heat and cook for 1 to 2 minutes more, until they are all toasted. Immediately scrape the sesame seeds into another container to cool. You can do this up to a week ahead. Store the completely cooled seeds in a plastic container or plastic bag in the freezer.

Couscous with Currants and Pine Nuts

Now that there is quick-cooking couscous even the newest cook can create mouth-watering dishes with this versatile semolina product.

Serve this either as a side dish instead of rice or as a vegetarian main course. You can also chill it and stir in 2 cups of smoked turkey for a delightful summertime entrée.

PREPARATION TIME: 20 minutes

COOKING TIME: 5 minutes

YIELD: Serves 8 to 10

CAN BE MADE AHEAD? Yes, up to 24 hours. Serve cold.

CAN BE FROZEN? No

CAN BE DOUBLED? It's easier to make this in 2 batches.

CAN BE HALVED? Yes

3½ cups (28 ounces) vegetable broth or 3½ cups water
  and 2 vegetable bouillon cubes

2 cups quick-cooking couscous

Juice and finely grated rind of 1 large orange

1 teaspoon cumin

1 teaspoon salt

1 cup chopped dried apricots

½ cup currants

¾ cup toasted pine nuts (see the Note)

Bring the broth to a simmer in a large pot placed over high heat. Add all the ingredients except the pine nuts. Stir vigorously, then cover the pot tightly and turn off the heat. After 10 minutes remove the lid and use a fork to fluff up the couscous while gently stirring in the pine nuts. Serve hot, at room temperature, or cold.

NOTE: To toast pine nuts, heat 1 tablespoon vegetable oil in a large skillet. Cook the pine nuts over medium heat, stirring constantly, until they turn golden brown. Drain them on paper towels.

Breakfast and Brunch Dishes

Tropical Papaya Boats

Papayas are available year-round. Choose the ones that yield when lightly pressed. When the dark seeds are scooped out, the fruit can hold a refreshing array of other exotic fruits.

PREPARATION TIME: 25 minutes

YIELD: Serves 8

CAN BE MADE AHEAD? Yes, up to 4 hours. Sprinkle with lemon or lime juice, cover with plastic wrap, and refrigerate until serving.

CAN BE FROZEN? No

CAN BE DOUBLED AND TRIPLED? Yes

CAN BE HALVED? Yes

4 ripe papayas, each about 6 inches long

Juice of 2 limes

4 kiwifruits, peeled and cut into ½-inch pieces

1 small ripe pineapple, cored and cut into 1-inch pieces

1 mango, peeled, seeded, and cut into 1-inch chunks

Fresh mint, for garnish

Cut the papayas in half lengthwise and use a pointed teaspoon to scoop out the seeds. Sprinkle the halves evenly with the lime juice. Place the "boats" on individual serving plates. Toss the remaining fruits just to combine, then fill the papayas. Garnish each with a sprig of fresh mint.

Grandola

No, that's not a typo. This is upscale granola studded with uncommonly luscious ingredients to please company (or for when you want to treat yourself). Use a pair of scissors to cut up the dried fruit.

PREPARATION TIME: 15 minutes

BAKING TIME: 30 minutes

YIELD: Serves about 20

CAN BE MADE AHEAD? Yes. Store in an airtight container in the refrigerator for 2 to 3 months.

CAN BE FROZEN? No

CAN BE DOUBLED? Yes

CAN BE HALVED? Yes

3 cups quick old-fashioned rolled oats

1 cup pecan halves

1 cup silvered almonds

$\frac{1}{2}$ cup wheat germ

$\frac{1}{2}$ cup shelled pistachios

1 cup Grape-Nuts cereal

$\frac{1}{2}$ cup sesame seeds

1 cup sunflower seeds

1 cup chopped pitted dates

$\frac{1}{2}$ cup dried figs, chopped

$\frac{1}{2}$ cup brown sugar

1 cup unsweetened shredded coconut

$\frac{1}{4}$ cup almond oil (available in health food stores)

$\frac{1}{2}$ cup polyunsaturated vegetable oil

$\frac{1}{4}$ cup molasses

$\frac{1}{2}$ cup honey

2 teaspoons almond extract

Preheat the oven to 350°F with the rack in the center position. Place everything except the oils, molasses, honey, and almond extract in a large bowl or soup pot. Mix well to combine. Add the oils, molasses, honey, and almond extract. Mix very well and spread half of the mixture on the bottom of a large roasting pan or rimmed baking sheet. Bake for 30 minutes, stirring occasionally. Repeat with the remaining mixture.

Cool completely before storing in a tightly covered container or heavy-duty plastic freezer bag in the refrigerator.

Baked Winter Fruit Salad

This recipe calls for both fresh and dried fruits. The dried fruits must be soaked overnight, so you'll need to plan ahead. If you don't wish to use the sherry, you can substitute all apple cider or orange juice. Serve this with a dollop of plain yogurt or, if you're feeling indulgent, some heavy cream poured over the top.

PREPARATION TIME: 30 minutes, plus 12 hours to soak the dried fruits

COOKING TIME: 45 minutes

YIELD: Serves 8

CAN BE MADE AHEAD? Yes. It can be assembled to the point to just before baking, up to 1 day ahead.

CAN BE FROZEN? No

CAN BE DOUBLED AND TRIPLED? Yes

CAN BE HALVED? Yes. Bake for 30 minutes.

3 cups mixed dried fruits, such as apricots, apples, peaches, pears, figs, raisins, and pitted prunes

3 navel oranges, peeled and cut into 1-inch wedges

1¼ cups medium-dry sherry

1½ cups apple cider or orange juice

1 cinnamon stick

Plain yogurt or heavy cream, for topping

Place all the fruits, the sherry, and cider in a large bowl. Toss to combine, then cover and let sit overnight at room temperature.

Place the rack in the center position and preheat the oven to 350°F. Pour and scrape the fruits and liquid into a 2-quart baking dish. Add the cinnamon stick and cover the dish with foil.

Bake until the liquid is bubbling and the fruits are very soft, about 45 minutes. Remove the dish from the oven and allow to cool slightly before spooning into individual serving dishes. Top with a dollop of plain yogurt or a few tablespoons of heavy cream.

Brandied Fruit Compote

I love this served hot over French toast in place of syrup. It's also great served warm on top of a scoop of vanilla or rum raisin ice cream, or served cold on top of yogurt or granola. If you don't want to use brandy, substitute additional orange juice.

PREPARATION TIME: 15 minutes

COOKING TIME: 6 to 9 minutes in a microwave; 20 to 30 minutes on the stove

YIELD: 8 to 10 servings.

CAN BE MADE AHEAD? Yes. It's actually much better if made at least 3 days ahead. The compote will keep for 4 weeks in a covered container in the refrigerator.

CAN BE FROZEN? No

CAN BE DOUBLED? Yes

CAN BE HALVED? Yes

4 ounces jumbo pitted prunes

4 ounces dried apricots

4 ounces dried apple rings

4 ounces dried peaches or pears

1 cup golden raisins

2 lemons, cut into quarters and seeds removed

3 cups orange juice

1 cup brandy or an additional 1 cup orange juice

Place all the ingredients in either a large microwavable container covered with plastic wrap or in a heavy-bottomed saucepan fitted with a cover. Microwave on high for 6 to 9 minutes, or until the mixture simmers and the fruit has softened, or cook over medium heat until the liquid simmers, then lower the heat and continue cooking for 20 minutes, stirring occasionally. Cool for a half hour at room temperature, then refrigerate for at least 24 hours before serving. Serve hot, warm, or cold.

Baked Pesto Frittata

Cream cheese is the secret ingredient that gives flavor and smoothness to this hot breakfast or brunch dish. You can even serve it for a simple supper entrée along with soup or a salad. You can buy pesto in the refrigerated section of your supermarket.

PREPARATION TIME: 15 minutes

COOKING TIME: 25 to 30 minutes

YIELD: Serves 8

CAN BE MADE AHEAD? Yes, up to 2 hours. Store and serve at room temperature.

CAN BE FROZEN? No

CAN BE DOUBLED? Yes. Use a 17 × 11-inch baking pan and increase the cooking time to 35 to 40 minutes.

CAN BE HALVED? Yes. Use a 5-cup soufflé dish or 8-inch square pan and reduce the baking time to 20 to 25 minutes.

2 tablespoons unsalted butter or margarine, softened

3 large baking potatoes, peeled and grated to make 3 cups

1 8-ounce container cream cheese with garlic and herbs, softened

¼ cup whole milk

1 medium Spanish onion, cut into ¼-inch slices

6 large eggs, lightly beaten

⅔ cup pesto

1 cup shredded Cheddar cheese or Monterey Jack cheese

Preheat the oven to 350°F with the rack in the center position. Use the butter to coat a 9-inch square baking pan or 8-cup shallow baking dish.

Place the grated potatoes in a wide-mesh strainer and rinse them with water to remove some of the starch. Squeeze out any excess liquid with your hands or the back of a large mixing spoon. Mix the cream cheese together with the milk in a 2-quart mixing bowl until well blended. Add the rest of the ingredients except the cheese, stirring well to combine.

Pour and scrape the mixture into the prepared pan and bake for 25 to 30 minutes, or until the frittata is just set. Remove it from the oven and immediately sprinkle the cheese on top. Let stand 5 minutes before serving.

Grilled Pound Cake with Raspberry Sauce and Mascarpone

You can make this better-than-waffles breakfast treat on the barbecue or under your oven broiler. The sweetness of the pound cake is cut by the tart raspberry sauce and mellowed by the lovely taste and texture of the creamy mascarpone cheese. You can buy mascarpone in most Italian specialty food shops and gourmet stores.

PREPARATION TIME: 15 minutes for the sauce; 15 minutes to assemble

COOKING TIME: 4 minutes to grill the pound cake

YIELD: Serves 8

CAN BE MADE AHEAD? Yes. The raspberry sauce can be made the day before. Store in a covered container in the refrigerator.

CAN BE FROZEN? No

CAN BE DOUBLED? Yes

CAN BE HALVED? No

½ cup red currant jelly

3 cups fresh or defrosted frozen raspberries

1 10- or 12-ounce plain pound cake

3 to 4 tablespoons unsalted butter, at room temperature

1 16-ounce container mascarpone

(continued)

335

Place the currant jelly in a small pan or microwavable container and heat it, stirring constantly, or microwave until melted. Place the raspberries in a mixing bowl, add the hot jelly, stir to combine, and allow to cool to room temperature.

Cut the pound cake into eight 1-inch slices. Spread each side with a thin layer of butter. Scrape and clean the rack on your grill and set it to high, or preheat the oven broiler to high with the rack in the highest position. If you are using the grill, place the slices of cake directly on the rack and grill for 2 minutes on each side, or until the grill marks begin to show and the cake has turned golden brown. If you are using the broiler, lay the pieces of cake on a heavy-duty baking sheet and broil for 90 seconds to 2 minutes, or until the cake turns golden brown.

Place one piece of cake on each of eight serving dishes. Top with the sauce and a generous dollop of mascarpone. Serve immediately.

Heart-Healthy Bran Muffins

If you are watching your fat intake but don't want to pass up your morning muffin, try these—you'll be amazed at the rich taste and moist texture. They're even great the next day. Warm them in a toaster oven or microwave.

PREPARATION TIME: 15 minutes

BAKING TIME: 20 minutes

YIELD: 12 muffins

CAN BE MADE AHEAD? Yes. Cool and store in plastic bags for up to 2 days.

CAN BE FROZEN? Yes. Use plastic freezer bags. Defrost still wrapped, then heat in a microwave or conventional oven set at 300°F for 10 minutes.

CAN BE DOUBLED? Yes

CAN BE HALVED? No

1¼ cups unbleached all-purpose flour, measured after sifting

⅓ cup dark brown sugar, firmly packed

¼ teaspoon salt

1 tablespoon baking powder

1½ cups bran cereal, such as All-Bran

1¼ cups milk (skim, 2%, or whole)

2 egg whites

½ cup applesauce

1 cup raisins

½ cup walnuts, coarsely chopped

Preheat the oven to 400°F with the rack in the center position. Spray a 12-cup muffin pan generously with vegetable spray. Do not use muffin papers.

Whisk together the flour, sugar, salt, and baking powder in a medium-sized bowl. Combine the cereal, milk, and egg whites in a large mixing bowl and let sit 2 to 3 minutes. Mix in the applesauce until well combined.

Add half of the flour mixture to the cereal mixture and stir gently with a fork until the flour disappears. Add the remaining flour mixture and stop mixing as soon as the flour disappears. Overmixing will cause tough, chewy muffins. Gently mix in the raisins and nuts.

Distribute the batter in the muffin cups, filling each cup about two thirds full. Bake the muffins for 20 minutes, until they spring back when pressed with a finger. Do not overbake. Cool 5 minutes in the pan, then run a knife around the edge of each muffin to loosen it. Turn the pan upside down to remove the muffins, tapping the pan gently on the edge of the counter if necessary.

Brandied Croissant Flan

~~~~~~

This fabulously rich and deliciously satisfying concoction has a crispy top layer, a creamy inside, and a buttery sweet brandied topping. It is perfect for brunch, for dessert after a light meal, or for any special occasion that calls for a memorable dish. It can be made and baked several days ahead of time, then refrigerated until time to add the topping and reheat. I have doubled and even tripled the recipe for a large crowd. Since it is so rich, count on one recipe feeding at least twelve people. Leftovers heat up beautifully in the oven or in a microwave. I make mine in an oval glass baking dish, although any dish with at least 2-inch-high sides is fine.

This recipe calls for stale croissants. Buy day-old croissants at half price from your local bakery. Or buy fresh croissants at least 3 days before you plan to make the flan, and stale them by leaving them uncovered on a counter or table on cake racks.

PREPARATION TIME: 30 minutes

COOKING TIME: 55 minutes

YIELD: Serves 12

CAN BE MADE AHEAD? Yes, the flan up to 2 days, the topping just before serving. Store, tightly wrapped in plastic wrap, in the refrigerator.

CAN BE FROZEN? Yes, up to 2 months. Assemble the flan (but not the topping), bake and cool, then freeze. Defrost, then add the topping and complete the cooking.

CAN BE DOUBLED? Yes. This is made in a very large baking dish, so you're better off simply making the recipe twice.

CAN BE HALVED? Yes. Reduce the baking time to 35 minutes.

THE FLAN

¼ stick (1 ounce) unsalted butter, softened (for greasing the pan)

Approximately 1 dozen stale plain croissants

5 cups heavy cream

1 stick (4 ounces) unsalted butter, melted and slightly cooled

½ cup brandy

6 extra-large eggs

1⅓ cups sugar

Pinch of salt

2 teaspoons vanilla extract

Use the softened butter to generously grease a 13 × 9-inch glass ovenproof baking dish or an oval dish approximately the same size that has at least 2-inch-high sides. Slice the croissants the short way so that you get about 7 to 8 ½-inch slices from each croissant. Layer the slices, slightly overlapping, in the buttered pan. You will have enough slices to make several layers, making the center slightly higher than the sides.

In a large mixing bowl, combine the heavy cream, the melted butter, and brandy. Add the eggs, sugar, and salt. Beat with an electric mixer, by hand, or with a wire whisk for 5 minutes. Stir in the vanilla.

Pour the mixture on top of the croissant slices. Cover the dish with plastic wrap and refrigerate for at least 3 hours, or as long as overnight. This allows the croissants to soak up the custard.

Preheat the oven to 350°F with the rack in the center position. Remove the plastic wrap and bake the flan for 45 to 50 minutes, until the top has turned golden brown. If you find that the top is browning too fast, cover the dish loosely with foil. While the flan is baking prepare the topping.

THE TOPPING

1 cup brown sugar

¼ cup molasses

3 tablespoons brandy

½ stick (2 ounces) unsalted butter

½ cup orange juice

Combine all the ingredients. Remove the flan from the oven and let it sit for 5 to 10 minutes. Then cook the topping, stirring constantly, until the sugar has melted and the mixture is smooth. Pour over the flan and serve hot or warm.

Sticky Bun Bread

The enticing fragrance of fresh-from-the-oven sticky buns will perfume your kitchen. Store-bought frozen bread dough makes this a snap to make. While the buns are magnificent hot from the oven, they also can be made ahead and rewarmed. Be sure to make plenty, because they will disappear fast.

PREPARATION TIME: Frozen dough must be thawed. It takes 20 minutes to assemble the bread and 1½ hours to rise.

BAKING TIME: 20 to 25 minutes

YIELD: Serves 10

CAN BE MADE AHEAD? Yes. Unbaked bread may be assembled and refrigerated overnight and risen in the morning. Baked bread may be warmed in a 300°F oven for 10 to 12 minutes.

CAN BE FROZEN? Yes, up to 6 months. After cooling, wrap in plastic, defrost covered.

CAN BE DOUBLED? Yes. You must use 2 pans. Be sure that you have room for both pans in your oven, or bake separately.

CAN BE HALVED? Yes. After defrosting the dough, reserve and refreeze half for another time.

¾ cup dark brown sugar, firmly packed

1 teaspoon ground cinnamon

¾ cup pecan halves

3 tablespoons unsalted butter, melted and slightly cooled

1 1-pound loaf frozen white bread dough, thawed according
   to package directions

Spray a tube pan or a 10-inch springform pan with nonstick vegetable spray.

Mix together the brown sugar and cinnamon in a large bowl, breaking up any large lumps. Sprinkle ¼ cup of the cinnamon sugar mixture evenly over the bottom of the prepared pan, reserving the rest. Distribute the pecans over the cinnamon sugar.

Roll bits of the thawed dough into 1½-inch balls. Drop the dough balls, one at a time, into the melted butter and turn with a fork until evenly coated. Transfer the balls to the reserved cinnamon sugar mixture and roll until evenly coated. Distribute the balls evenly in the bottom of the pan over the pecans. The balls will rise and spread to fill in any empty spaces.

Cover the pan with a clean towel, place it in a warm, draft-free place, and let the dough rise 1½ hours. If your room is not at least 72°F, place the pan on a rack over a large bowl of hot water. Cover the pan and the bowl with a towel and add more hot water as necessary (a turned-off oven is a good place to do this, especially if there is a gas pilot light). The dough should double in bulk and will leave an indentation when pushed gently with your finger.

Preheat the oven to 375°F with the rack in the center position. Bake for 20 to 25 minutes, until the bread is a deep golden brown.

Let the bread cool for 5 minutes in the pan. Loosen the bread from the sides of the pan by running a knife around the edge. Place a plate on top of the pan and flip the pan and plate together. Lift off the pan and serve the bread warm.

You can rewarm the bread by wrapping it in foil and placing it in a 300°F oven for 10 to 12 minutes.

Walnut Currant Scones

This breakfast treat is a cross between a muffin and a biscuit. Served hot from the oven, it deserves to be spread with really fine jam or preserves and sweet butter. You can make the scones the night before and refresh them in the toaster for a special start to the next day.

PREPARATION TIME: 25 minutes

BAKING TIME: 15 to 17 minutes

YIELD: 12 scones

CAN BE MADE AHEAD? Yes, the night before. Store, uncovered, at room temperature.

CAN BE FROZEN? Yes, up to 2 months. After cooling, store in a plastic bag. Defrost covered.

CAN BE DOUBLED? Yes. Make 2 disks of dough and cut each into 12 pieces.

CAN BE HALVED? No

2 cups unbleached all-purpose flour, sifted before measuring

1 tablespoon baking powder

¾ teaspoon salt

¼ cup plus 2 tablespoons sugar

¾ cup currants or raisins

⅔ cup walnuts, broken in pieces

1¼ cups heavy cream

3 tablespoons unsalted butter, melted

Preheat the oven to 425°F with the rack in the center position. These will bake on an ungreased heavy-duty baking sheet. Sift the flour, baking powder, salt, and the ¼ cup of sugar together into a 2-quart mixing bowl. Mix with a fork to combine all the ingredients thoroughly. Mix in the currants and walnuts, then add the cream, mixing with the fork until the mixture holds together. The dough will be sticky.

Lightly sprinkle a clean, smooth work surface with flour and place the dough on it. Sprinkle the dough lightly with flour and knead the dough 10 times by pushing it down and away from you with the heel of your hand, folding it back over itself, giving it a quarter turn each time. Pat the dough into a 9-inch round. Flatten the top so it becomes a disk shape. Brush the top with the melted butter and then sprinkle with the 2 tablespoons of sugar. Use a long knife to cut the dough into 12 pie-shaped wedges and transfer each wedge to the baking sheet, leaving about a 1-inch space between the edges.

Bake for 15 to 17 minutes, or until the tops are golden brown. Serve warm or at room temperature. To refresh the scones, split them in half and toast lightly.

Buttermilk Berry Pancakes

My family loves berries in their pancakes, but I hate getting up extra early on Sunday mornings to make the batter. When I discovered dried blueberries and cranberries, I realized I could make my batter the night before without having to worry about the berries falling apart and making a mess of the batter. Buttermilk lends a lightness and the sweet blue and red nuggets add a special zing to this ethereal breakfast treat.

This recipes makes a lot of pancakes. Feel free to make half a recipe or save the rest of the batter to use later on in the week.

PREPARATION TIME: 20 minutes

COOKING TIME: About 30 minutes, depending on how many pancakes you wish to make

YIELD: Serves 8, generously

CAN BE MADE AHEAD? Yes. The batter can be made up to 3 days ahead and stored in a covered container in the refrigerator.

CAN BE FROZEN? Yes. Leftover pancakes can be frozen after they are completely cool. Place a piece of waxed paper or plastic wrap between each pancake before stacking, then place them in a plastic freezer bag.

CAN BE DOUBLED? Yes. You'll need to make this in a huge bowl or soup pot.

CAN BE HALVED? Yes

4 large eggs, slightly beaten

4 cups buttermilk

1 stick (4 ounces) unsalted butter, melted

4 cups unbleached all-purpose flour, unsifted

4 tablespoons sugar

1 tablespoon baking powder

1 teaspoon salt

1 teaspoon baking soda

½ cup dried blueberries

½ cup dried cranberries

Place the eggs, buttermilk, and melted butter in a large bowl and beat for 30 seconds until well combined. Place the flour, sugar, baking powder, salt, and baking soda in a large sieve set over the mixing bowl. Sift the dry ingredients over the egg mixture and sprinkle on the dried berries. Very gently mix the dry ingredients together with the wet ingredients, taking care not to beat or overmix or the pancakes will be tough.

Preheat the oven to "warm" and place a baking sheet in the center position. Heat a nonstick griddle or skillet until a few drops of water sprinkled on top sizzle. Use a ⅓-cup measure to pour the batter onto the griddle, leaving room between each pancake. Cook until the top begins to bubble, about 1 minute. Turn the pancakes and cook until the underside is dry and slightly brown, about 30 seconds.

Keep the cooked pancakes in the warm oven, loosely covered with foil, until ready to serve. Serve with butter and pure maple syrup.

Desserts

Frozen Espresso Chocolate Mousse

Everyone loves chocolate, and here is the ultimate frozen chocolate mousse. You couldn't ask for a more dazzling, delicious, yet simple-to-whip-up dessert. Make it ahead and scoop it into wineglasses (or dessert dishes).

Buy the very best bittersweet chocolate you can find.

PREPARATION TIME: 25 minutes

YIELD: Serves 8

CAN BE MADE AHEAD? Yes. It must be made ahead, at least 4 hours and up to 24 hours. Cover tightly with plastic wrap and freeze until ready to serve.

CAN BE FROZEN? Yes. It must be frozen.

CAN BE DOUBLED? Yes, although if you don't have a large bowl to whip the cream, you should make it in 2 batches.

CAN BE HALVED? Yes

8 ounces bittersweet chocolate, chopped (1⅔ cups)

½ cup brewed double-strength espresso or 2 tablespoons instant (powdered) espresso dissolved in ½ cup boiling water

3 tablespoons crème de cacao (optional)

2 cups heavy cream, well chilled

½ cup sugar

1 cup heavy cream, whipped, for garnish

About 8 tablespoons crème de cacao, for garnish

In a microwave, a double boiler, or a small bowl set over (but not in) a pan of simmering water, melt together the chocolate and espresso. Stir gently with a rubber spatula until the mixture is melted and smooth. Remove from the heat and stir in the 3 tablespoons of crème de cacao, if desired. Let the chocolate cool to room temperature.

Using a chilled metal bowl and chilled beaters, whip the 2 cups of heavy cream with the sugar until it forms stiff peaks. Use a rubber spatula to fold the cream into the cooled chocolate mixture so that no traces of cream remain. Cover the bowl with plastic wrap or foil and freeze for at least 4 hours, or up to 24 hours.

To serve, scoop the mousse into wineglasses or dessert dishes and garnish with whipped cream, then drizzle each with about 1 tablespoon of crème de cacao, if desired.

Oreo Ice-Cream Cake

Get the kids in the family to help make this the first time and they can do it themselves the next time. You can also make this with vanilla cream sandwich cookies and strawberry ice cream. And you can substitute Raspberry Sauce (page 366) for the chocolate syrup.

PREPARATION TIME: 15 minutes, after slightly thawing the ice cream

FREEZING TIME: 6 hours or overnight

YIELD: Serves 9

CAN BE MADE AHEAD? Yes. It must be made ahead.

CAN BE FROZEN? Yes. It must be frozen.

CAN BE DOUBLED AND TRIPLED? Make 2 or 3.

CAN BE HALVED? No

1 rectangular-shaped half gallon chocolate chip ice cream

30 Oreo cookies

⅓ cup (2⅔ ounces) unsalted butter or margarine, melted

⅔ cup (about 5 ounces) chocolate syrup

Whipped cream, for garnish (optional)

Whole Oreos, for garnish (optional)

Additional chocolate syrup (optional)

Thaw the ice cream in the unopened container until it starts to feel soft when pressed on the sides. This takes about 15 minutes in a 70°F kitchen. Spray a 9-inch pie plate or 8-inch square pan with nonstick vegetable spray.

Place the cookies in a food processor fitted with the steel blade and process until they form fine crumbs, or place them in a heavy plastic bag and crush them with a rolling pin. Add the melted butter to the bowl or bag and mix to combine.

Press the crumb mixture into the bottom and up the sides of the prepared baking pan. Drizzle the chocolate syrup evenly over the crumb mixture.

Unfold the ice cream package until it lies flat. Cut the ice cream vertically in thirds (you will need only two thirds of the ice cream; rewrap and freeze the rest). Lift the slices with a wide spatula, one at a time, and place them side by side on top of the crumbs. Press down gently with the back of the spatula to even out. Cover with plastic wrap and freeze until firm.

Decorate the cake with whipped cream and whole Oreos, if desired, or drizzle each piece with additional chocolate syrup before serving.

White Chocolate Cheesecake

A chocolate crumb crust holds a heavenly smooth white chocolate cream cheese filling. Be sure to use real white chocolate made with cocoa butter. I prefer Lindt or Tobler. Three-ounce bars will be enough for this recipe. If you want to make chocolate shavings to decorate the top of the cake, buy one or two extra bars.

PREPARATION TIME: 15 minutes

COOKING TIME: 30 minutes

YIELD: Serves 8

CAN BE MADE AHEAD? Yes, up to 24 hours. Refrigerate until time to serve.

CAN BE FROZEN? Yes, up to 3 months. Chill completely, wrap in plastic wrap, and defrost at room temperature while still wrapped.

CAN BE DOUBLED? No. Make 2 separate cakes.

CAN BE HALVED? No

8 ounces white chocolate, broken into 1-inch pieces

2 8-ounce packages cream cheese, softened

⅓ cup sugar

2 teaspoons vanilla extract

2 large eggs

1 chocolate crumb pie crust (available in the baking aisle of the supermarket)

Raspberries or strawberries, for garnish

Chocolate shavings, for garnish (see the Note)

Preheat the oven to 350°F with the rack in the center position. In a microwave, a double boiler, or a small bowl set over (but not in) a pan of simmering water, melt the chocolate. Stir gently with a rubber spatula until it is smooth.

In a food processor or in a 1½-quart mixing bowl, using an electric mixer set on low, process or mix the cream cheese together with the sugar, vanilla, and eggs. When well mixed, add the chocolate and continue mixing or processing, until just blended.

Pour and scrape the mixture into the crumb crust and bake for 30 minutes, or until the outer edge is very light golden brown and slightly bubbled and a small damp spot remains in the center.

Cool at room temperature for 1 hour, then refrigerate for at least 4 hours, or overnight.

To garnish, place raspberries (or halved strawberries, cut side down) around the rim and sprinkle the center with chocolate shavings.

NOTE: To make chocolate shavings, run a vegetable peeler down the edges of a chocolate bar, collecting the little shavings on waxed paper. If you are able to find a thick bar of chocolate you can make thicker shavings. You can do this several days ahead and leave the chocolate, uncovered, at room temperature—away from heat.

Olga's Carrot Cake

This cake is especially moist and flavorful, and the cream cheese frosting (recipe follows) is a favorite with everyone. I've made it for celebrations ranging from birthdays to weddings and every occasion in between. It makes a great dessert for a party which includes multigenerations; kids as well as grown-ups love it. It can also be made as muffins (see the Note).

PREPARATION TIME: 20 to 30 minutes for the cake; 20 to 30 minutes for the frosting

BAKING TIME: 50 to 60 minutes

YIELD: Serves 8 to 10

CAN BE MADE AHEAD? Yes. The layers can be made up to 2 days ahead. Cool completely, wrap in plastic wrap, and refrigerate. Frost no more than 4 hours before serving.

CAN BE FROZEN? Yes, unfrosted. Wrap the cooled cake in plastic wrap and seal tightly with foil. Defrost while still wrapped at room temperature, then frost.

CAN BE DOUBLED? Make 2 separate cakes.

CAN BE HALVED? No

2 cups unbleached all-purpose flour, measured after sifting

2 teaspoons baking powder

1½ teaspoons baking soda

1 teaspoon salt

2 teaspoons ground cinnamon

1 teaspoon ground ginger

½ teaspoon ground nutmeg

1¾ cups sugar

1½ cups vegetable oil

4 large eggs, beaten

2 cups grated carrots

1 8-ounce can crushed pineapple, drained

½ cup pecans, coarsely chopped

Preheat the oven to 350°F with the rack in the center position. Spray a 10-inch tube pan with nonstick vegetable spray (or coat it with butter), sprinkle with enough flour to coat the bottom and sides, and tap out the excess.

Sift together the flour, baking powder, baking soda, salt, cinnamon, ginger, and nutmeg into a medium-sized mixing bowl and set aside.

In a 2-quart mixing bowl, beat together the sugar, oil, and eggs. Add half of the flour mixture and stir with a spoon until just blended. Stir in the remaining flour. Add the carrots, pineapple, and pecans and gently stir until well blended.

Pour and scrape the batter into the prepared pan. Bake for 50 to 60 minutes, or until a toothpick inserted in the center comes out clean and dry. If the top seems to be browning too quickly, cover it with a piece of foil, shiny side up.

Let the cake cool for 15 minutes in the pan, then place a flat plate or baking sheet on top of the pan, invert it, and unmold the cake. Cool completely before frosting.

Cream Cheese Frosting

1 stick (4 ounces) unsalted butter or margarine, softened

1 8-ounce package cream cheese, softened

1 pound confectioners' sugar, sifted

2 teaspoons vanilla extract

1 cup sweetened shredded coconut, for garnish (optional)

Using a food processor, electric mixer, or spoon, mix together the butter, cream cheese, confectioners' sugar, and vanilla until smooth. Frost the sides and top of the cake and garnish the top with coconut, if desired.

NOTE: To make as muffins, line a muffin pan with paper liners and fill each one two thirds full of batter. Bake for 25 minutes at 350°F, or until a toothpick or cake tester inserted in the center comes out clean.

Chocolate Cassata

This elegant layered chocolate cake from Sicily looks much more difficult to make than it really is. The layers of a store-bought pound cake are spread with a chocolate/ricotta mixture, then the cake is frosted with a chocolate/espresso icing. If you plan to freeze the cake, wrap it after it is frozen so you won't mess up the frosting.

PREPARATION TIME: 30 to 40 minutes

YIELD: Serves 8 to 10

CAN BE MADE AHEAD? Yes, up to 8 hours. Refrigerate, unwrapped.

CAN BE FROZEN? Yes, up to 2 months (see the headnote). Wrap securely in plastic and then in foil. Defrost while still wrapped.

CAN BE DOUBLED? Make 2.

CAN BE HALVED? No

4 ounces (¾ cup) semisweet chocolate, chopped

1½ sticks (6 ounces) unsalted butter, at room temperature

½ cup brewed espresso or 1 tablespoon instant espresso powder dissolved in ½ cup boiling water

1 pound whole milk ricotta cheese

¼ cup confectioners' sugar

Finely grated rind of 1 orange

⅓ cup mini chocolate chips

1 10- or 12-ounce store-bought chocolate or white pound cake (if frozen, defrost before using)

½ cup crème de cacao (optional)

In a small bowl set over a pan of gently simmering water, melt the chocolate with the butter and espresso. Stir to combine completely and then refrigerate, stirring every 15 minutes until firm.

In a food processor, or with an electric mixer or a whisk, blend together the ricotta, sugar, and orange rind. Fold in the chocolate chips. Use a serrated knife to cut the pound cake twice lengthwise, making three layers. Place one layer on a flat plate and sprinkle half the liqueur, if desired, over it. Spread half the ricotta mixture on top. Top with the second layer and repeat the process. Top with the third and final layer. Use a narrow cake spatula to frost the entire cake with the cooled chocolate frosting. Refrigerate until ready to serve. To serve, cut the cake in thin vertical slices.

Denver Chocolate Pudding

This lush concoction is a cross between a chocolate cake, a chocolate pudding, and heaven. It's simple to make—the sauce is created in the baking. Great for a birthday celebration, it makes a substantial dessert after a dinner party, especially when served warm with vanilla or coffee ice cream.

The recipe has a lot of ingredients, but the technique is very simple.

PREPARATION TIME: 20 to 30 minutes

BAKING TIME: 1 hour

YIELD: Serves 8

CAN BE MADE AHEAD? Yes, but it's best served warm from the oven.

CAN BE FROZEN? No

CAN BE DOUBLED? Yes. Bake in 2 pans.

CAN BE HALVED? No

1 stick (4 ounces) unsalted butter, at room temperature

1 ⅓ cups granulated sugar

1 cup unbleached all-purpose flour, sifted before measuring

1 ½ teaspoons baking powder

½ teaspoon salt

½ cup whole milk

2 ounces unsweetened baking chocolate (⅓ cup), melted and cooled slightly

2 teaspoons vanilla extract

½ cup dark brown sugar, firmly packed

3 rounded tablespoons unsweetened cocoa

1 ½ cups boiling water

Preheat the oven to 350°F with the rack in the center position. Butter or grease a 9-inch square baking pan.

Place the butter and ⅔ cup of the granulated sugar in a 2-quart bowl. Using an electric mixer set on high or a whisk, beat until the mixture is light and fluffy.

Place the flour, baking powder, and salt in a sifter or fine-mesh sieve and set it over the mixing bowl. Sift or shake the flour mixture onto the butter mixture. Add the milk and mix on low speed, or whisk, until the ingredients are combined. Do not overbeat. Use a rubber scraper to fold in the melted chocolate and 1 teaspoon of the vanilla. Pour and scrape the mixture into the prepared pan.

In the same bowl (no need to wash it), stir together the brown sugar, the remaining ⅔ cup of granulated sugar, and cocoa. Sprinkle this mixture over the batter in the pan. Add the remaining teaspoon of vanilla to the boiling water and slowly pour this over the cocoa mixture and batter in the pan, trying not to disturb it too much.

Bake for 1 hour or until the top of the pudding is firm. Cool slightly, then cut into squares, spooning some of the sauce from the bottom over the cake. Serve with a scoop of ice cream, if desired.

Raspberry Trifle

This classic English dessert combines cake, fruit, vanilla custard (pudding, in this case), and sherry (which can be optional). It's a perfect midsummer dessert, especially when made with beautifully ripe berries. A trifle is traditionally served in a clear glass straight-sided bowl that sits on a pedestal. Lacking one, feel free to use any clear glass bowl that will show off the pretty layers of the dessert.

COOKING TIME: According to package directions

YIELD: Serves 8 to 10

CAN BE MADE AHEAD? Yes, up to 6 hours, although the whipped cream will lose a little volume. Garnish just before serving.

CAN BE FROZEN? No

CAN BE DOUBLED AND TRIPLED? No. If you need more, make 2 separate trifles.

CAN BE HALVED? No

3 cups whole milk

1 4½-ounce package noninstant vanilla pudding mix (the kind you have to cook)

1 10½-ounce frozen pound cake, thawed, or a small homemade or bakery pound cake

½ cup cream sherry (optional) or ½ cup orange juice

½ cup seedless raspberry preserves

2 cups heavy cream

3 tablespoons sugar

2 10-ounce packages frozen raspberries, thawed and drained

½ pint fresh raspberries, for garnish

¼ cup sliced almonds, for garnish

In a 2-quart heavy-bottomed saucepan, heat the milk over medium-high heat until tiny bubbles begin to appear around the edge of the pan. Whisk in the pudding mix and keep whisking until the pudding has thickened and just begins to boil. Whisk constantly or the pudding will burn. Cool the pudding slightly, then put a piece of plastic wrap directly on the surface of the pudding to prevent a skin from forming. Refrigerate the pudding until it is completely cooled.

Slice the pound cake in half lengthwise. Sprinkle the sherry or orange juice on the cut surfaces of the cake. Spread the preserves on the bottom half of the cake and replace the top. Slice the cake, like a loaf of bread, into ½-inch slices, keeping the slices together. Slice the cake lengthwise, top to bottom, into thirds.

In a chilled 1-quart metal bowl with a rotary hand mixer, whisk, or electric mixer, whip the cream until it starts to thicken. Add the sugar gradually, continuing to beat. Beat only until the cream holds stiff peaks.

Reserve 1 cup of the whipped cream for garnish and gently fold together the remaining whipped cream and pudding by gently scraping a rubber spatula around the edge of the bowl, across the bottom, and up through the middle of the mixture. Continue only until evenly mixed.

Place one half of the cake slices in the bottom of a large (2-quart) trifle bowl, a large, footed glass bowl. If you don't have a trifle bowl, any large glass bowl will do. Add half the thawed raspberries, followed by half the pudding mixture. Repeat with the remaining cake slices, thawed raspberries, and pudding.

Just before serving, garnish with the remaining whipped cream topped by the fresh raspberries. Sprinkle the almonds around the edge.

Fruit Salad
in a Watermelon Bowl

The choice of serving this fruit salad in a watermelon or in a bowl is up to you (see the Notes); the watermelon bowl is a fancy touch. If you want to make this even fancier, try adding the champagne and candied ginger suggested in the recipe. For maximum flavor, use fresh, in-season fruits, such as those listed below. Try to avoid fruits that get squishy, such as pears.

PREPARATION TIME: 30 minutes

YIELD: Serves 20

CAN BE MADE AHEAD? Yes, earlier in the day. Add bananas, if using, at the last minute.

CAN BE FROZEN? No

CAN BE DOUBLED? Yes. You can make as much filling as you want (see the Notes) and keep refilling the watermelon when it gets low.

CAN BE HALVED? Yes. Make half the amount of fruit salad and serve it in a bowl or in individual melon halves.

1 large watermelon, cut in half the long way (see the Notes), seeded, pulp cut into chunks or balls, rind reserved

3 seedless navel oranges, peeled, cut into quarters, and sliced ¼ inch thick

1 large fresh Hawaiian pineapple, peeled, cored, and cut into bite-sized pieces, or 3 16-ounce cans of pineapple chunks in their own juice, undrained

1 pound seedless green, red, or purple grapes

1 pint strawberries, cut in half

3 melons of your choice, such as cantaloupe, honeydew, Persian, or Cranshaw, seeds removed and cut into chunks (or you can use a melon baller to form balls)

3 kiwifruits, peeled, cut in half, and sliced

2 star fruits, sliced crosswise so that the slices form star shapes

1 pint fresh blueberries

2 firm bananas

½ cup orange juice or the juice of 1 lemon (if using apples, peaches, or pears)

2 cups champagne (optional)

¼ cup candied ginger, chopped (optional)

The amounts and the kinds of fruits you choose depend on your preference and the fruit's availability. Do not choose fruits that are too soft, such as raspberries, because they don't hold up well. Frozen fruits also disintegrate and their colors run.

Whichever fruits you choose, think about color and a balance of sweet and sour. If you use bananas, apples, peaches, or pears, toss them with ½ cup orange juice or the juice of a lemon to keep them from turning brown.

Place the prepared fruit in a large mixing bowl and toss until well mixed. Fill the scooped-out watermelon or a serving bowl, storing the extra fruit in the refrigerator and refilling the watermelon or bowl as necessary. Sprinkle the champagne over the fruit. Garnish with the candied ginger.

NOTES: To serve the salad in a watermelon, buy a lengthwise half of a large watermelon or cut the top third off a whole watermelon. Using a melon baller or a metal measuring teaspoon, cut melon balls from the seeded pulp of the melon. Scoop out and discard any remaining pulp to form a smooth-sided serving bowl. The edge of a metal measuring tablespoon, or a grapefruit spoon, works well for this.

If you don't want to bother with the watermelon, the salad may be served in a bowl, on a platter, or in individual dessert or parfait dishes.

To increase the size of the salad, add 1 cup of champagne for each additional quart of fruit. Garnish with 2 additional tablespoons of chopped ginger.

Mega Apple Crisp

Need to feed a crowd? Here, as the name implies, is the dessert for you. Be sure to use large, firm, and very flavorful apples. I like the flavor and texture of Granny Smiths. Bake this homey dessert in an oven-to-table baking dish and serve it with a scoop of butter pecan ice cream or a dollop of whipped cream.

COOKING TIME: 40 minutes

YIELD: Serves 12 to 14

CAN BE MADE AHEAD? Yes, but it is especially good warm from the oven with ice cream.

CAN BE FROZEN? Yes. Store tightly wrapped. Defrost at room temperature and warm in a 350°F oven for 15 minutes.

CAN BE DOUBLED? Yes. Use a 15 × 11-inch pan.

CAN BE HALVED? Yes. Use a 6-cup baking dish and bake for 30 minutes.

3 pounds firm, tart apples, such as Granny Smith

½ cup sugar

½ cup dark brown sugar, firmly packed

½ cup unbleached all-purpose flour, measured after sifting

1 teaspoon ground cinnamon

½ stick (2 ounces) unsalted butter, melted and slightly cooled

1 quart butter pecan ice cream or 1 pint heavy cream,
   whipped, for topping

Preheat the oven to 375°F with the rack in the top position. Spray a 10-cup glass baking dish with nonstick vegetable spray.

Peel, quarter, and remove the cores from the apples. Cut the apples into ½-inch-thick slices and overlap the slices in rows in the prepared baking dish.

In a small bowl, mix together the sugars, flour, and cinnamon with a fork until well blended. Drizzle the butter over this mixture and mix with a fork until crumbly. Sprinkle the mixture evenly over the apples.

Bake for 40 minutes, or until the apples are tender when pierced with a fork and the topping looks golden and crisp. Serve warm or at room temperature, topped with ice cream or whipped cream.

Cider Baked Apples

This satisfyingly scrumptious dessert is low in fat and high in flavor. It's a fall favorite when big Cortland apples and fresh cider are plentiful. Use real apple cider, not apple juice, for the most flavor. You can serve this with vanilla ice cream or frozen yogurt.

PREPARATION TIME: 25 minutes

COOKING TIME: 30 minutes

YIELD: Serves 8

CAN BE MADE AHEAD? Yes, up to 6 hours to the point to just before baking. Cover with plastic wrap or foil and refrigerate until ready to bake. Or, bake up to 4 hours ahead and let rest at room temperature until ready to serve.

CAN BE FROZEN? No

CAN BE DOUBLED? Yes

CAN BE HALVED? Yes

8 very large Cortland or other firm baking apples
2 cups dark brown sugar, firmly packed
1 teaspoon ground cinnamon
1 cup raisins
1½ cups apple cider
1 quart vanilla ice cream or frozen yogurt, for garnish (optional)

(continued)

Preheat the oven to 350°F with the rack in the center position. Select either one large ovenproof baking dish to hold all the apples, or two smaller baking dishes.

Stick the tip of a sharp teaspoon or serrated grapefruit spoon deep into the top of each apple, making a circle around the stem. Lift out the stem and use a knife to core the apple. Use the spoon to scrape out any remaining core and seeds, trying not to pierce the bottom of the apple.

Combine the brown sugar and cinnamon. Divide the raisins among the apple cavities, then pack them with brown sugar, using all of the sugar/cinnamon mixture. Place the apples in the pan(s) and pour in the cider. Bake the apples for 20 to 30 minutes, or until tender. Overcooking will make the skins split (which will not affect the taste, only the appearance), so check them after 20 minutes. Serve hot, cold, or at room temperature with a scoop of ice cream or frozen yogurt, if desired.

Strawberries Romanoff

My favorite recipes often come from friends. This easy-to-make, yet very elegant dessert is a cross between a mousse and a strawberry ice-cream sundae. Served in wineglasses and garnished with a mint leaf, it makes a show-stopping finale to any dinner.

Prepare the strawberries at least 2 hours (or up to 8 hours) before you plan to serve them and the cream topping at the very last minute.

PREPARATION TIME: 15 to 20 minutes for the strawberries; 10 minutes for the topping

YIELD: Eight ½-cup servings

CAN BE MADE AHEAD? The strawberries can be prepared up to 8 hours ahead, placed in a covered bowl, and refrigerated until serving. The cream topping should be made just before serving.

CAN BE FROZEN? No

CAN BE DOUBLED AND TRIPLED? Yes. Use a very large bowl to whip the cream or make it in 2 batches.

CAN BE HALVED? No

1 quart fresh strawberries

¼ cup orange juice, freshly squeezed if possible

2 tablespoons sugar

2 tablespoons orange liqueur such as Grand Marnier or curaçao

½ pint (1 cup) best-quality vanilla ice cream

1 pint (2 cups) heavy cream

Rinse the strawberries under cold water, remove the hulls, and cut the strawberries in half. Place them in a bowl and sprinkle them with the orange juice, sugar, and liqueur. Cover and refrigerate for at least 2 hours, or up to 8 hours.

Just before serving, soften the ice cream in a microwave (or let it sit at room temperature for ½ hour). Whip the heavy cream in a chilled bowl using chilled beaters. Beat in the softened ice cream.

Divide the strawberries and their juice among eight dessert dishes or wineglasses. Top each serving with a generous amount of the cream.

Strawberries
with Raspberry Sauce

This is a perfect low-calorie, low-fat dessert masquerading as a sinfully indulgent one. Make this when you can get the lovely sun-sweet strawberries of summertime. Even if fresh raspberries are available, however, it's better to use frozen for this sauce, since you get a much more intense flavor and the other ingredients would mask the delicate flavor of fresh raspberries.

You can spoon the strawberries and sauce over a scoop of low-fat strawberry or vanilla yogurt to make a luscious parfait.

PREPARATION TIME: 20 minutes for the strawberries; 10 minutes for the sauce

YIELD: Serves 8

CAN BE MADE AHEAD? Yes. The strawberries can be rinsed and coated with sugar up to 4 hours before serving. They should not be served ice-cold, so if you do them ahead, refrigerate them in a covered dish, then remove ½ hour before serving. The sauce can be made up to 2 days ahead, then refrigerated until ready to serve.

CAN BE FROZEN? The sauce can be frozen up to 6 months.

CAN BE DOUBLED AND TRIPLED? Yes

CAN BE HALVED? Yes

1 quart fresh strawberries, rinsed but not patted dry, stems and white tops removed, sliced (if they are the very small native variety, leave them unsliced)

¼ cup sugar

2 10-ounce packages frozen raspberries, slightly defrosted and liquid reserved

1 8-ounce container best-quality seedless raspberry jam

¼ cup raspberry liqueur (optional)

Place the sliced strawberries in a bowl, sprinkle them with the sugar and stir gently to mix. Cover and set aside for at least 1 hour at room temperature, or cover and refrigerate for up to 4 hours, removing the berries a half hour before serving time.

Place the raspberries, jam, and liqueur, if desired, in a food processor or blender. Purée until smooth. Set a wide-mesh strainer over a mixing bowl and pour the purée into the strainer. Use a rubber scraper or large metal spoon to work the sauce through the strainer, leaving the seeds behind. You will have to rub and scrape to force as much purée through the strainer as possible.

To serve, divide the strawberries and their juice among 8 wineglasses or dessert dishes. Pour about ½ cup of sauce over each.

VARIATION: Place a scoop of low-fat frozen strawberry, raspberry, or vanilla yogurt in the dish before adding the strawberries and sauce.

Pecan Squares

Once you discover what a crowd pleaser these are, you'll want to make extra and keep some in the freezer for unexpected company (or to indulge yourself). These are quite rich, so you can cut them into small squares and still satisfy anyone's craving for a buttery, nut-filled sweet.

PREPARATION TIME: 20 minutes

COOKING TIME: 40 minutes

YIELD: 24 squares

CAN BE MADE AHEAD? Yes, up to 1 week. Cool completely, cover with plastic wrap, and store at room temperature.

CAN BE FROZEN? Yes, up to 3 months.

CAN BE DOUBLED? Yes. Use 2 pans.

CAN BE HALVED? No

(continued)

2 sticks (8 ounces) unsalted butter or margarine, at room temperature

2 cups unbleached all-purpose flour

¼ cup confectioners' sugar

½ cup dark corn syrup

¾ cup dark brown sugar, firmly packed

2 large eggs, slightly beaten

1 stick (4 ounces) unsalted butter or margarine, melted

2 cups (10-ounce package) coarsely chopped pecans

Preheat the oven to 350°F with the rack in the center position. Spray a 13 × 9-inch baking pan with nonstick vegetable spray.

Using a food processor, pastry blender, or fork, process or mix the butter, flour and confectioners' sugar until the dough forms a ball. Press the dough into the bottom of the prepared pan, forming a ½-inch-high rim along the edges of the pan to make a crust. Bake the crust for 15 minutes and remove from the oven, leaving the oven on.

While the crust is baking, mix together the corn syrup, brown sugar, eggs, and melted butter. Add the pecans and stir until well mixed.

Pour the pecan mixture into the baked crust and return to the oven for 25 minutes, or until the edges are golden and the center is no longer liquid. Cool completely and cut into squares.

Linzer Bars

There is nothing as special as homemade pastry. Raspberries and almonds combine to give these rich, tender bars a Continental flavor. They will dress up any dessert table.

PREPARATION TIME: 25 minutes

BAKING TIME: 20 minutes

YIELD: 24 bars

CAN BE MADE AHEAD? Yes. Store, tightly wrapped, at room temperature for up to 3 days.

CAN BE FROZEN? Yes. Tightly wrap with plastic and store in heavy-duty plastic freezer bags. Defrost while still wrapped.

CAN BE DOUBLED? Yes. Use 2 pans.

CAN BE HALVED? No

1½ sticks (6 ounces) unsalted butter

1 cup granulated sugar

2 large eggs, beaten

1½ cups unbleached all-purpose flour, sifted before measuring

¼ teaspoon salt

½ teaspoon baking soda

¼ teaspoon ground cloves

½ teaspoon ground cinnamon

Finely grated rind of 1 lemon

1 cup almonds, finely ground

1 12-ounce jar seedless red raspberry preserves

1 tablespoon confectioners' sugar

Preheat the oven to 400°F with the rack in the center position. Spray a 13 × 9-inch baking pan with nonstick vegetable spray or coat it with butter. Place the pan in the freezer while you prepare the dough.

(continued)

Place the butter, sugar, and eggs in a food processor and process until well mixed, or mix with a spoon until well combined.

Sift the flour, salt, baking soda, cloves, and cinnamon together into a food processor or mixing bowl and process or mix until a dough forms. Add the lemon rind and ground almonds and process or stir until well mixed.

Press the dough into the bottom of the prepared pan, forming a ¼- to ½-inch rim around the edge. Drop the preserves by tablespoonfuls on top of the dough, then use a rubber scraper to spread them to the edges of the crust.

Bake 20 minutes, or until the edges are golden and the preserves are bubbly. Cool completely, then sprinkle with the confectioners' sugar and cut into bars.

Lemon Bars

The light, refreshing taste of these delicate bars goes wonderfully well with fresh strawberries. Don't let the lightness fool you; they are plenty rich!

PREPARATION TIME: 20 minutes

BAKING TIME: 45 minutes

YIELD: 24 bars

CAN BE MADE AHEAD? Yes. Cool and cover with plastic wrap. Store at room temperature for 1 day, or refrigerate for up to 3 days.

CAN BE FROZEN? Yes. Wrap several bars at a time in waxed paper or plastic wrap and put the bars in a heavy-duty plastic freezer bag. Defrost while still wrapped.

CAN BE DOUBLED? Yes. Use 2 pans.

CAN BE HALVED? No

2 sticks (8 ounces) unsalted butter, softened

2¼ cups unbleached all-purpose flour, measured after sifting

¼ cup plus ⅓ cup confectioners' sugar

4 large eggs

2 cups granulated sugar

6 tablespoons freshly squeezed lemon juice

½ teaspoon baking powder

Grated rind of 1 lemon

Preheat the oven to 350°F with the rack in the center position. Spray a 13 × 9-inch pan with vegetable spray or coat it with butter.

Place the butter, 2 cups of the flour, and ¼ cup of the confectioners' sugar in a food processor or the bowl of an electric mixer and process or mix until the dough forms a ball. (Or mix by hand with a pastry blender or fork.) Press the dough into the bottom of the prepared pan, forming a ½-inch rim around the edges. Bake for 15 minutes.

Using a food processor, mixer, or whisk, mix together the eggs, granulated sugar, lemon juice, the remaining ¼ cup flour, the baking powder, and lemon rind until smooth. Pour the mixture over the center of the cooked dough, and spread it to the edges.

Return the pan to the oven and bake for another 30 minutes, or until the filling has set and the edges are golden. Cool completely at room temperature. Sift the ⅓ cup of confectioners' sugar over the top and cut into bars.

Germaine's Fudgy Brownies

My very special friend, Germaine Gaudet, shared this recipe for quick-as-a-wink fudgy brownies. She says they are the best she's ever eaten. When I saw how fast they disappeared, I knew she'd found a winner. If you wish, you can omit the pecans or use another kind of nut.

PREPARATION TIME: 15 minutes

COOKING TIME: 30 minutes

YIELD: Serves 8 to 10

CAN BE MADE AHEAD? Yes, up to 3 days. Store at room temperature in an airtight container.

CAN BE FROZEN? Yes. Wrap airtight and freeze up to 2 months.

CAN BE DOUBLED? Yes. Make 2 batches.

CAN BE HALVED? No

1 stick (4 ounces) unsalted butter, at room temperature

1 cup sugar

4 extra-large eggs

1 16-ounce can Hershey's chocolate syrup or 2 cups chocolate syrup

1¼ cups unbleached all-purpose flour, measured after sifting

1 cup pecans, chopped (optional)

Preheat the oven to 350°F with the rack in the center position. Generously butter or grease a 13 × 9 × 2-inch baking pan.

In a medium-sized mixing bowl, using either a spoon or an electric mixer, cream together the butter and sugar until light and fluffy. Beat in the eggs, one at a time, mixing until completely blended. Stir in the chocolate syrup and flour, mixing until just blended; don't overbeat, as it will make the brownies tough. Stir in the pecans, if desired.

Bake for 30 minutes, then cool the pan on a rack for 30 minutes. Make the glaze.

Quick Glaze

²⁄₃ cup sugar

3 tablespoons whole milk

3 tablespoons unsalted butter, cut into small pieces

½ cup semisweet chocolate chips

While the brownies are cooling, place the sugar, milk, and butter in a small saucepan. Cook over medium heat, stirring constantly, until the mixture starts to boil. Boil for 30 seconds without stirring, then remove from the heat and add the chocolate chips. Stir until the chocolate chips melt; the mixture will be very thin. Pour the glaze over the brownies, spreading it evenly. Cool for at least 1 hour, then cut them into 2-inch squares.

Brownie Sundae

You can use completely store-bought components or make the brownies yourself from a mix or from scratch, using the recipe on page 372. Ditto with the hot fudge sauce (page 375). The added indulgence of whipped cream (page 376) is up to you.

Be sure to buy premium ice cream—it really does make a difference.

PREPARATION TIME: 10 minutes

YIELD: Serves 8

CAN BE MADE AHEAD? Yes. You can buy or make the brownies ahead. The sauce can be made up to 1 week ahead. Don't store the ice cream for more than a week since it will take on an unpleasant freezer smell.

CAN BE DOUBLED? Yes

CAN BE HALVED? Yes

8 3 × 3-inch brownies

1 quart premium ice cream, flavor of your choice

16 ounces (2 cups) hot fudge sauce

1 pint heavy cream, whipped (optional)

Just before serving, place a brownie on each of eight medium-sized plates or in shallow bowls. Top with a generous scoop of ice cream, then hot fudge, then whipped cream if desired. Serve immediately.

Lora's Quick
Hot Fudge Sauce

The taste of this sauce will depend on the quality of chocolate you use. My favorites are Lindt Elegance or Côte d'Or bittersweet.

PREPARATION TIME: 10 minutes

COOKING TIME: 10 minutes

YIELD: 3¼ cups

CAN BE MADE AHEAD? Yes, up to 1 week. Store in an airtight container in the refrigerator and reheat in a microwave or double boiler before serving.

CAN BE FROZEN? Yes, up to 6 months. Defrost at room temperature and reheat as above.

CAN BE DOUBLED? Yes

CAN BE HALVED? Yes

1 pint (2 cups) heavy cream

10 ounces best-quality bittersweet or semisweet chocolate, cut into small pieces

Pour the cream into a 1½-quart saucepan set over medium heat. When the mixture begins to simmer (small bubbles form around the edges), lower the heat and add the chocolate. Whisk for 1 minute over low heat, then turn off the heat. Continue whisking until the mixture is smooth. Cool slightly before using.

The sauce will remain liquid at room temperature for about 2 hours, then will thicken. You can soften it by microwaving it on high for 40 to 50 seconds or whisking it on the stove top over very low heat until it just begins to get soft. Take care not to burn it.

Sweetened Whipped Cream

This is the perfect garnish for almost any dessert. Either place a dollop on each plated dessert or serve it separately.

The key to success with whipped cream is having the cream, the bowl (metal is best), and the beaters very cold. Place the bowl and beaters in the freezer for 1 hour before making the whipped cream.

> **PREPARATION TIME:** 5 minutes with an electric mixer; 15 minutes with a hand beater or whisk
>
> **YIELD:** Serves 12
>
> **CAN BE MADE AHEAD?** Yes, up to 4 hours. Prepare the whipped cream and place it in a fine-mesh strainer set over a mixing bowl. Cover both with plastic wrap and refrigerate.
>
> **CAN BE FROZEN?** No. It becomes too watery.
>
> **CAN BE DOUBLED?** Only if you have a very deep 4-quart bowl. Otherwise the cream splatters all over.
>
> **CAN BE HALVED?** No

2 cups (1 pint) heavy cream, very cold

3 tablespoons superfine sugar (granulated sugar is acceptable if you don't have superfine)

1 tablespoon vanilla extract

If you are using an electric mixer, place the cream in a chilled 2-quart metal bowl. Run the mixer on medium-high until the cream starts to thicken. Sprinkle in the sugar and add the vanilla. Set the mixer on high and continue beating until the cream holds soft peaks. Don't overbeat, or you'll end up with butter!

If you are making whipped cream by hand, using a hand beater or whisk, place the cream in a chilled 2-quart metal bowl and set this bowl into another bowl (or a large pot) filled with ice water. Whisk or beat until the cream starts to thicken. Add the sugar and vanilla and continue whisking or beating until the mixture holds soft peaks. Use immediately or store as directed above.

Chocolate Truffles

Three simple ingredients make up one of the best-tasting chocolate morsels in the world. Make sure to use the finest-quality bittersweet chocolate you can find. My favorite for this is Côte d'Or or Tobler bittersweet.

PREPARATION TIME: 20 to 30 minutes, plus several hours to cool the mixture

YIELD: 2½ dozen, serves 12 to 16

CAN BE MADE AHEAD? Yes, up to 1 week. Store in a single layer in a covered container in the refrigerator. Return to room temperature covered.

CAN BE FROZEN? Yes, as above. Defrost covered.

CAN BE DOUBLED AND TRIPLED? Yes

CAN BE HALVED? Yes

1 cup heavy cream

12 ounces best-quality bittersweet chocolate, coarsely chopped

⅓ cup cocoa

Heat the cream in a small saucepan until tiny bubbles form around the rim. Place the chocolate in a food processor or blender. Add the hot cream. Allow to sit 15 seconds before processing or blending until the mixture is smooth. Pour the mixture into a shallow pan, cover with plastic wrap, and chill until very firm.

Place the cocoa in a small bowl. Using a teaspoon, scoop out the chocolate mixture and use your fingertips to form it into a small irregularly shaped ball about 1 inch in diameter. Roll it in the cocoa to coat completely. Place the finished truffles in one layer on a tray or in a shallow container, cover, and refrigerate until serving.

Beverages

Irish Coffee

I like the mellow taste of Bailey's Original Irish Cream, which is more subtle than the traditional Irish whiskey usually used to make Irish coffee. You can make this either with regular or decaf coffee. If you want to forgo the alcohol, you can use one of your favorite "flavored" coffees or add ½ ounce (1 tablespoon) of one of the specially flavored syrups sold in coffee emporiums. The other two secrets of success are to use top-quality, fresh-brewed coffee (decaf is fine) and to use real whipped cream. Homemade is best; the kind in the can is acceptable, but nondairy whipped topping should not even be considered.

It's nice to serve Irish coffee in mugs that have been heated by filling them with boiling water while you are brewing the coffee.

PREPARATION TIME: 10 minutes, plus 10 minutes to whip the cream

YIELD: Serves 4

CAN BE MADE AHEAD? The cream can be whipped ahead (see page 376).

CAN BE FROZEN? No

CAN BE DOUBLED? Yes

CAN BE HALVED? Yes

4 8-ounce cups freshly brewed coffee, regular or decaf

4 ounces (8 tablespoons) Bailey's Original Irish Cream

1 cup Sweetened Whipped Cream (page 376)

Fill 4 heated mugs two thirds full with coffee. Add 2 tablespoons of Bailey's to each cup and top with whipped cream. Serve immediately.

Hot Chocolate

I promise this will be the richest, creamiest, most chocolaty hot chocolate you've ever had. Since the quality depends directly on the quality of the chocolate you use, don't skimp; buy a couple of bars of premium dark sweet, semisweet, or bittersweet chocolate. Don't use chocolate chips; they're not right for this recipe.

PREPARATION TIME: 10 minutes

COOKING TIME: About 15 minutes total

YIELD: Serves 6

CAN BE MADE AHEAD? Yes, up to 1 hour. Leave at room temperature, then gently reheat over very low heat, stirring constantly, so it doesn't burn.

CAN BE FROZEN? No

CAN BE DOUBLED? Yes

CAN BE HALVED? Yes

8 ounces (1 cup) heavy cream

3 ounces dark sweet, semisweet, or bittersweet chocolate, broken into small pieces

3⅓ cups whole milk

Marshmallows or whipped cream, for garnish (optional)

In a 1- or 1½-quart saucepan, heat the cream over medium heat until tiny bubbles form around the edges; this is called scalding. Lower the heat, add the chocolate, and stir or whisk constantly until the mixture is smooth, scraping the bottom of the pan so the mixture doesn't burn. Divide this mixture among 6 cups or mugs, using a rubber spatula to scrape out all the chocolate.

Pour the milk into the same pan and set it over medium heat, cooking until the milk comes to a simmer and a skin starts to form on top. Do not let the milk boil (it will make a horrendous mess all over your stove top). Use a slotted spoon or small strainer to remove the skin, then pour the hot milk over the chocolate mixture. Stir and serve with marshmallows or whipped cream, if desired.

Hot Mulled Cider

This fragrant brew makes an inviting offering on a cold winter afternoon or evening. It's best served hot (though not scalding), but it's even delicious at room temperature. Serve it from a heat-proof pitcher or punch bowl, or ladle it from the pot into mugs in the kitchen. For a nonalcoholic punch, leave out the brandy and use one gallon plus one quart apple cider.

PREPARATION TIME: 10 minutes

COOKING TIME: 10 minutes

YIELD: 20 cups, serves about 15 to 20

CAN BE MADE AHEAD? Yes, up to 4 hours. Strain, but do not add the brandy until the mixture has been reheated. Let sit at room temperature after cooling. Reheat at serving time, then add the brandy.

CAN BE FROZEN? No

CAN BE DOUBLED? Yes, although to double it you will need either a huge pot or to make it in several batches.

CAN BE HALVED? Yes

1 gallon apple cider

1½ cups sugar

48 whole cloves

4 teaspoons whole allspice or 1½ teaspoons ground allspice

12 cinnamon sticks

⅓ cup freshly squeezed lemon juice

1 cup orange juice

4 cups apple brandy (optional, see the headnote)

Place all the ingredients except the brandy in a large pot set over medium heat. Bring to a low simmer and cook for 10 minutes. Cool for 10 minutes, then strain into another pot or other large container. Stir in the brandy and serve.

Fruit Punch

This nonalcoholic, refreshing punch can be put together several hours before you plan to serve it. Serve it out of a pitcher or punch bowl or, for a very informal occasion, out of a large pot.

PREPARATION TIME: 10 minutes

YIELD: Serves 12

CAN BE MADE AHEAD? Yes, up to 4 hours. Refrigerate until ready to serve, then add the ginger ale and ice.

CAN BE FROZEN? No

CAN BE DOUBLED AND TRIPLED? Yes, although you'll probably have to make it in batches.

CAN BE HALVED? Yes

2 6-ounce cans frozen orange juice concentrate

1 6-ounce can frozen lemonade concentrate

6 cups cold water

1 10-ounce package frozen sliced strawberries, thawed

2 large ripe bananas

3 cups ginger ale

Ice cubes

Dissolve the orange juice and lemonade concentrates in the water in a large punch bowl or pot. Place the strawberries and bananas in a blender and blend until smooth. Stir the fruit into the liquid. Just before serving, stir and add the ginger ale and ice.

Hot Cider Rum Punch

Use real apple cider to make this. To make this nonalcoholic, substitute an additional one cup each cranberry and orange juice for the rum.

PREPARATION TIME: 15 minutes

COOKING TIME: 20 minutes

YIELD: 8½ cups, serves 6 to 8

CAN BE MADE AHEAD? Yes, up to 4 hours. Leave at room temperature and reheat when ready to serve.

CAN BE FROZEN? No

CAN BE DOUBLED AND TRIPLED? Yes

CAN BE HALVED? Yes

2 cups (16 ounces) light rum

4 cups apple cider

1¼ cups cranberry juice

1¼ cups orange juice

2 cinnamon sticks

6 whole cloves

Place all the ingredients in a 3-quart saucepan set over medium heat. Stir to combine, then lower the heat and bring the mixture to a very low simmer. Cook 5 minutes, remove the cinnamon sticks and cloves, and serve hot or warm.

Bloody Mary

This classic brunch drink is also great for barbecues.

PREPARATION TIME: 3 minutes

YIELD: Serves 1

CAN BE MADE AHEAD? No

CAN BE FROZEN? No

CAN BE DOUBLED AND TRIPLED? Yes. Make them in a pitcher.

8 ounces (1 cup) tomato juice or V-8 juice, chilled

Juice of ½ lemon

1 teaspoon Worcestershire sauce

Dash of Tabasco Pepper Sauce

1 ounce vodka

Ice

Celery stick, for garnish (optional)

Fill a tall glass half full with tomato juice. Stir in the lemon juice, Worcestershire sauce, Tabasco Pepper Sauce, and vodka. Add ice cubes and serve with celery stick, if desired.

Orange-Spiked Ice Tea

With or without the addition of alcohol, this is a perfect summer refresher.

PREPARATION TIME: 10 minutes

YIELD: 16 cups

CAN BE MADE AHEAD? Yes, up to 12 hours. Refrigerate until ready to serve.

CAN BE FROZEN? No

CAN BE DOUBLED AND TRIPLED? Yes

CAN BE HALVED? Yes

6 teaspoons loose orange spice tea, in a strainer, or 6
   Constant Comment tea bags

2 cups boiling water

1 6-ounce can frozen lemonade concentrate

1 6-ounce can frozen orange juice concentrate

1½ cups superfine sugar

7 cups cold water

1 cup orange liqueur, such as Grand Marnier (optional)

½ cup vodka (optional)

Orange slices, for garnish

Place the tea in a nonmetal heat-proof container (such as a teapot) and add the boiling water. Steep until the water is cool and the tea is very strong. Remove the tea strainer or tea bags.

Pour the tea into a large pitcher. Add the remaining ingredients and stir until the frozen concentrates dissolve. Chill until very cold. Serve over ice in glasses, garnished with orange slices.

Mimosas

Another brunch classic. You don't have to buy premium champagne—you can use a dry Spanish sparkling wine instead. Freshly squeezed orange juice, though, is a must.

PREPARATION TIME: 5 minutes

YIELD: Serves 8 to 10

CAN BE MADE AHEAD? No. The bubbles will disappear.

CAN BE FROZEN? No

CAN BE DOUBLED? It's better to make one batch at a time (it only takes a few minutes).

CAN BE HALVED? Yes

2 quarts freshly squeezed orange juice, chilled

1 bottle champagne or sparkling wine, chilled

Just before serving, mix the two ingredients together in a pitcher. Serve in wineglasses or champagne flutes.

White Wine Sangria

Make this when fresh peaches, nectarines, or apricots are in season for the best of summer flavors. This drink is as beautiful to look at as it is wonderful to taste. You can serve it from a tall pitcher or from a punch bowl.

PREPARATION TIME: 20 minutes

YIELD: Serves 8

CAN BE MADE AHEAD? Yes, up to 6 hours. Refrigerate until ready to serve.

CAN BE FROZEN? No

CAN BE DOUBLED AND TRIPLED? Yes

CAN BE HALVED? Yes

3 cups total of any combination of the following fresh fruit: peaches, apricots, nectarines, sweet plums, cut into ½-inch slices

4 cups Riesling or other semisweet white wine

½ cup brandy

Place the sliced fruit in a tall glass pitcher, a punch bowl, or a large pot. Add the remaining ingredients and refrigerate until cold. Serve in tall glasses, spooning some of the fruit into the glass before you pour in the sangria.

Champagne Cocktails

If you are making these for a crowd, set up the glasses and sugar cubes, soaked with the bitters, ahead of time up to 1 hour. Then pour the champagne as you serve the cocktails. You don't have to spend a fortune on champagne, but it's important to select one that is dry; dry champagne is far more sophisticated than the sweet variety.

There are many very nice, affordable, nonvintage domestic and imported sparkling wines (only wine from grapes grown in the Champagne region in France can be labeled champagne). Ask for guidance from the expert in your wine shop. You should expect to pay between nine and fifteen dollars a bottle. There is usually a discount when you buy a case—ask if you can return any unopened bottles. You can buy Angostura or other bitters in the wine shop as well.

PREPARATION TIME: 2 minutes

YIELD: Count on 5 to 6 servings per bottle of champagne

CAN BE MADE AHEAD? See the headnote.

CAN BE FROZEN? No

Sugar cubes

Angostura bitters

Chilled champagne

Place one sugar cube in the bottom of each champagne flute. Soak the cube with 2 to 3 drops of bitters. Just before serving, fill the glass with chilled champagne.

Etc.

Cheddar Biscuits

This dough can be made ahead and the biscuits cut out so that all you have to do is bake them just before serving. They are great with cocktails (make them small) or as an unusual complement at dinner. I even serve them with Tomato Cheddar Soup (page 207) at lunchtime.

PREPARATION TIME: 20 minutes

BAKING TIME: 10 to 12 minutes

YIELD: 14 to 15 two-inch biscuits

CAN BE MADE AHEAD? Yes, up to 12 hours. Prepare the dough, roll and cut out the biscuits, and place them on a baking sheet. Cover with plastic wrap and refrigerate until ready to bake.

CAN BE FROZEN? Yes. The biscuits will keep for 1 or 2 weeks. Store tightly wrapped in a heavy-duty plastic freezer bag. The biscuits will have dried out a bit; heat them in a microwave in a plastic bag.

CAN BE DOUBLED? Yes

CAN BE HALVED? No

2 cups unbleached all-purpose flour, measured after sifting

2½ teaspoons baking powder

1 teaspoon salt

⅓ cup solid vegetable shortening

⅔ cup light cream

1 cup (4 ounces) grated sharp Cheddar cheese

Preheat the oven to 450°F with the rack in the center position. Sift the flour with the baking powder and salt into a medium-sized mixing bowl. Add the shortening and use two forks in a crisscross motion to cut the shortening into the dry ingredients until the mixture resembles coarse meal. Use the fork to blend in the cream and then the cheese, mixing only until the dough holds together. Don't overmix or the biscuits will be chewy and not tender.

Flour a smooth surface and use your hands to pat the dough into a rough circle about ½-inch thick. Flour a 2-inch round cookie or biscuit cutter and use it to cut out the biscuits. For cocktail biscuits, use a 1½-inch cutter. Place the biscuits on an ungreased baking sheet and bake for 10 to 12 minutes (8 to 10 minutes for the small version), until puffed and golden brown. Serve hot, warm, or at room temperature.

Garlic Cheese Bread

I make this so often that I've started buying garlic oil in half-gallon jugs. An innovation that became available in the past several years, garlic oil can be found in the specialty food section of many supermarkets.

PREPARATION TIME: 20 minutes

COOKING TIME: Approximately 10 to 15 minutes

YIELD: Serves 8

CAN BE MADE AHEAD? Yes. Wrap in foil and refrigerate for up to 12 hours.

CAN BE FROZEN? Yes, up to 3 weeks before cooking. Wrap in foil and freeze. Heat right from the freezer, following the baking instructions below.

CAN BE DOUBLED AND TRIPLED? Yes

CAN BE HALVED? Use a small loaf.

1 large, long loaf soft, unsliced Italian bread

⅓ cup garlic oil (see the Note)

1 stick (4 ounces) unsalted butter, cut into pieces

3 large garlic cloves, finely chopped

½ cup fresh parsley, finely chopped

½ cup fresh basil, finely chopped

½ cup grated Parmesan cheese

Preheat the oven to 400°F with the rack in the center position.

Use a serrated knife to cut the bread into 1-inch slices, about ¾ of the way down. Don't cut completely through to the bottom crust. Place the bread on a large sheet of extra-large, heavy-duty foil, shiny side up.

Place the garlic oil, butter, and garlic in a small saucepan set over low heat. Stir until the butter melts. Cook over low heat for another minute or so, taking care not to let the garlic brown. Remove from the heat and add the parsley and basil. Use a tablespoon or pastry brush to coat each side of each slice of bread with the garlic and herb butter. Sprinkle some of the cheese between the slices.

Spread any remaining garlic butter and cheese on top of the bread and wrap it in the foil, twisting the ends to close securely. Bake for 10 minutes. If you are preparing frozen bread, bake it for 15 minutes.

To brown the crust, open up the foil and bake 5 minutes more.

NOTE: If you can't find garlic oil, substitute ⅓ cup olive oil in which 3 large peeled garlic cloves have soaked overnight.

Spicy Corn Bread

Cool this off with a smear of sweet butter—or a dab of honey. Actually, the degree of heat is up to you. Add mild or hot chiles depending on your taste.

PREPARATION TIME: 10 minutes

BAKING TIME: 20 to 25 minutes

YIELD: Serves 9

CAN BE MADE AHEAD? Yes, up to 6 hours. Reheat in a microwave, toaster oven, or conventional oven.

CAN BE FROZEN? Yes. Wrap with plastic wrap and store in a plastic freezer bag.

CAN BE DOUBLED? Yes. Use two 9-inch square pans.

CAN BE HALVED? No

1 tablespoon unsalted butter, softened (for greasing the pan)

1 cup (4 ounces) unbleached all-purpose flour, measured after sifting

3/4 cup cornmeal

2 teaspoons baking powder

3/4 teaspoon salt

1 cup whole milk

2 eggs, beaten

6 to 8 drops Tabasco Pepper Sauce

2 to 4 tablespoons finely chopped, canned jalapeño peppers, hot or mild, depending on your taste

1 cup (4 ounces) grated Monterey Jack cheese

Preheat the oven to 400°F with the rack in the center position. Generously butter a 9-inch square pan.

Sift together the flour, cornmeal, baking powder, and salt into a 2-quart mixing bowl. Add the milk, eggs, and Tabasco Pepper Sauce and stir gently just until the flour disappears (overmixing will make the bread tough). Sprinkle the jalapeños and cheese over the batter and gently stir just until evenly mixed.

Spread the batter in the prepared pan and bake at 400°F for 20 to 25 minutes, or until the top is golden and a toothpick inserted in the center comes out clean and dry. Serve hot or at room temperature.

Index